# NEW RELIGIOUS
# MOVEMENTS AND
# THE CHURCHES

Edited by Allan R. Brockway
and J. Paul Rajashekar

# NEW RELIGIOUS MOVEMENTS AND THE CHURCHES

Report and papers of a consultation
sponsored by the Lutheran World Federation
and the World Council of Churches

Free University, Amsterdam, September 1986

WCC PUBLICATIONS, GENEVA

Cover design: Rob Lucas

ISBN 2-8254-0890-5

© 1987 WCC Publications, World Council of Churches,
150 route de Ferney, 1211 Geneva 20, Switzerland

Printed in Switzerland

# Contents

# Preface

The essays that constitute this volume represent a beginning effort on the part of the World Council of Churches and the Lutheran World Federation to comply with a request from their member churches for guidelines concerning appropriate response to the new religious movements (NRMs) that are active in their various societies. Since the advisory groups of both the WCC's Dialogue with People of Living Faiths and the LWF's Department of Studies had mandated a study of this issue, it seemed best for the organizations to combine their efforts. The result was a consultation, involving Christians who are knowledgeable about and/or involved with NRMs, held at the Free University in Amsterdam, the Netherlands, 7-13 September 1986.

The organization of the consultation took many months and involved many people. But certainly it was made possible by the dedicated efforts of Margaret Noetzlin of the LWF, with the help of Audrey Smith of the WCC, who handled transportation and other arrangements. To Margaret Noetzlin, in particular, are due heartfelt thanks for her editorial efforts in "cleaning up" the English translations of some of the papers.

We owe a tremendous debt of gratitude to Wim Hahn of the Free University for his untiring effort at making everything work in Amsterdam, and to Dirk Mulder, professor emeritus at the Free University, for chairing the sessions and in general smoothing the way.

We make no claim that this single consultation provides all the answers to the questions posed by members of the various churches. But we do claim that a beginning has been made that will facilitate further deliberation.

Allan R. Brockway
J. Paul Rajashekar

# Introduction

## J. PAUL RAJASHEKAR

During the past few decades societies around the world have experienced a tremendous spiritual ferment which has had a far-reaching impact upon the social, cultural and religious life of the people. This spiritual ferment has manifested itself in the form of innumerable "new religious movements" (NRMs). Many observers of this phenomenon consider that the explosive proliferation of such religious movements in recent years is historically unprecedented.

This does not mean, however, that the appearance of new movements is something totally new. Even a cursory reading of the history of religions will show that a wide variety of new movements have appeared in various periods, in virtually every cultural milieu and in relation to every major religious tradition in the world. What appears to be unprecedented is that contemporary NRMs have collectively made a significant impact upon various societies in a relatively short span of time and have become highly visible and prominent.

While there has been a great deal of publicity about new religious groups in Western countries, the phenomenon is not confined to the West. We have ample evidence of new movements proliferating in the continents of Africa ("Prophetic" or "Zionist" churches), South America (various kinds of Amerindian, Afro-Brazilian groups, folk Catholicism, Western-based or -influenced fundamentalist or neo-pentecostal movements), Asia (most notably in Japan, India, Korea), and in such regions as Melanesia (from cargo cults to recent Holy Spirit movements) and the Caribbean ("Spiritual Baptists", Rastafarians, etc.). The nature and extent of such religious upsurge in many non-Western societies have not been systematically studied.

The question of the significance, impact and implications of this phenomenon of NRMs has been the subject of much debate in recent years. It has not only been a matter of considerable academic interest to sociologists and others but has also caused serious concern among Christians and churches. This has been particularly the case in societies where Christianity has been traditionally the dominant faith. Churches in many Western countries have felt threatened or challenged by the sudden appearance of new religious groups in their midst and have often found themselves at a loss, not knowing what to make of this phenomenon or how to interpret it, let alone how to respond to it. The situation is much the same for churches in South America and the Caribbean where there has been increased activity of new movements in recent years.

The collection of papers and reports in this volume represents an initial ecumenical attempt on the part of the sponsoring organizations — the Lutheran World Federation and the World Council of Churches — to understand, interpret and enable the churches to respond meaningfully to the "challenge" of NRMs. Because NRMs are a global and multifaceted phenomenon, the subject is approached here in the most general way and, since the challenge of NRMs is felt more acutely in the Western countries, the focus of this volume is primarily on the situation existing there. However, some attention is paid to perspectives from other contexts as well.

## The phenomenon of NRMs in the West

The term "NRMs", in its newly developed usage, refers to a plurality of new kinds of religion or religiosity which in earlier terminologies were identified as "sects", "cults", "heresies" or "deviations". These earlier terms were found to be problematic and inadequate to describe the contemporary expressions of the phenomenon; not only were they judgmental and carried pejorative connotations; they were also very much tied to the framework of Christian heritage and therefore could not adequately accommodate the new religious groups originating from non-Christian and non-Western sources. The term NRMs has thus emerged as a convenient expression to designate a collective phenomenon, a pattern of religiosity that has become highly visible and popular in the West.

There has been considerable discussion among researchers regarding the "newness" of this phenomenon and the appropriateness of the designation "movements". Not all Western NRMs claim to be new or display a measure of religious innovation; indeed, some have a line of continuity with older religious traditions.

A large number of NRMs in the West are often perceived to be "new" because their ideas and beliefs come from non-Western and non-Christian cultures. Seen in isolation a particular new religious group may not appear "new", but viewed together with a number of other such groups, they are seen to have certain shared features or characteristics. One of the characteristics of contemporary NRMs is their unusual capacity to attract young, educated people into intense and committed involvement. It is this feature of today's NRMs in the West that makes them significantly different from "new" movements in previous periods of history.

Furthermore, the more or less simultaneous appearance of a vast number of ostensibly similar movements in the second half of the twentieth century and their collective impact on society have often given the impression that they represent a "movement". Such a view has gained credence in many Western societies in view of the fact that some of the most visible NRMs have aggressively sought new converts in a variety of ways and have often projected an ambitious programme for spiritual and individual transformation. While thus the manner and circumstances in which these new groups have come to prominence may suggest a sense of "movement", in reality there is an enormous diversity among them.

Because of this diversity some researchers doubt the usefulness of such an all-inclusive category. On the other hand the term "NRM" is neutral and value-free, unlike earlier terms such as "sects" and "cults". But it lumps together everything without discriminating between the authentic and the spurious, the benign and the malefic, the redemptive and the diabolic. The term can also mislead us into treating all NRMs as if they were a monolithic entity, or monochrome in character. Part of the difficulty is that there is no clear-cut classification or typology of these movements that can be readily used to understand them. NRMs are too numerous to be studied individually (except the most visible ones) and their basic characteristics vary from society to society. In addition, local conditions affect the form of religious movements and produce a variety of effects. There are also a vast number of ways in which we can view them. The diversity and complexity of NRMs force us to deal with the subject in the most general way but we should nevertheless be cautious of facile generalizations.

In the past few years there has been a growing body of sociological literature attempting to explicate the social significance of NRMs. It makes clear that there are a number of variable factors (social, political, economic, cultural and religious) that facilitate the emergence of new movements in society and offers a variety of plausible explanations and interpretations from diverse theoretical perspectives. Some sociologists believe that NRMs in non-Western cultures represent transformative religions of modernization and change, and that in Western contexts they are symptoms of the further extension of a secularization process, leading to privatization of religion. Others view Western NRMs as symptoms of a "crisis in meaning" affecting Western societies and of the failure of traditional cultural and religious values to provide a meaningful pattern for personal and social existence. In other words, Western NRMs would appear to represent a major cultural transformation of Western sensibilities and spiritualities.

These somewhat overlapping interpretations make the point that NRMs do not emerge in a social vacuum. Unlike most of the "new" movements in earlier periods of history which catered to the needs of the "have-nots", contemporary NRMs seem to appeal to the "haves". They offer the possibility of immediate religious experience, group intimacy and a sense of identity, belonging and wholeness. All these factors need to be taken into account in the churches' attempts to respond to the NRMs.

## The churches and NRMs

The mainline churches in many Western countries, already preoccupied with concerns of combating the growing "secular" outlook in their societies, were literally caught unawares by the sudden mushrooming of alternative forms of religion in the 1960s. The phenomenon was indeed baffling at first sight and was thought to be a by-product of the youth counter-culture. But the persistence of many of these movements into the eighties has forced the churches to pay attention to the spiritual change occurring in their midst.

In many respects NRMs are still a mystery to the Western churches. They have given rise to a sense of fear and threat. Frequently the beliefs and patterns of behaviour of many NRMs have appeared to be deviant from the norms and values of Western societies which have been traditionally influenced by Christianity. This fact has lent credence to allegations that NRMs subvert personal values, tear apart families and endanger the social fabric. The relative success of some NRMs in gaining new converts has provoked widespread suspicion of their recruitment practices. The allegiance of new converts to some unknown master, teacher or guru, their practice of strange rites, their use of unfamiliar languages with new terms and concepts, and their adoption of certain rituals conducted often in secret, have all contributed to allegations of conspiracy, manipulation, destructive mind-control, etc., supposedly employed by founders and leaders of NRMs. Such disturbing stories about the forced involvement of young people in many new movements has attracted much publicity, leading to considerable public hostility on the one hand and concern and pastoral challenge on the other for Western churches.

However, what has been more unsettling to Western Christians, especially in Western Europe, is the fact that the emergence of NRMs during the last two decades has coincided with the gradual decline of church attendance and membership, drastically in the case of youth. In terms of numbers, of course, the major churches still command the allegiance of millions in every Western country and the membership of new movements, even when put together, amounts only to a tiny portion of the religiously committed public. But the quality and intensity of commitment which NRMs have elicited are impressive and seldom matched by established churches. This has become a matter of utmost concern, and has indeed provoked a critical reflection on the shortcomings of the church in fulfilling the religious expectations of younger generations. Some have even interpreted the NRMs as a judgment on the church.

Faced with this situation the mainline churches in the West have found it difficult to provide a comprehensive analysis of and response to the NRMs. In the United States, it has been mainly certain Christian groups of a fundamentalist orientation which have attempted to counter the influence of NRMs by adopting a basically polemical approach. A few denominations have produced some informative literature on NRMs to help their congregations. The situation is slightly better in Western Europe where churches have appointed full-time pastors or supported institutions or centres to study NRMs. The Vatican has recently initiated a comprehensive study on the phenomenon and a progress report was released in 1986 and is included as an appendix to this volume.

Although the churches have begun to take seriously the challenge of NRMs, it will not be easy to forge a coherent response. In the face of widespread "spiritual illiteracy" in many Western countries, the churches are faced with the enormous task of educating their members in the Christian faith. There is no point in being simply alarmed about young people joining the NRMs when the churches have been unable to meet their spiritual needs. The solution to this lies not in naively emulating certain "surface characteristics" of NRMs, like introducing meditation or some Christianized forms of yoga in churches. Rather, the churches need to recover lost elements of their experiential tradition that may once again become relevant in today's context. But there is no guarantee that this will counter the influence of NRMs.

Far more urgent is the need to make people more aware of and acquainted with other faiths and cultural traditions. This does not mean the production of more polemical literature on other faiths and NRMs; rather, it will entail making a genuine attempt to help Christians understand other faiths so that they are better prepared to discriminate among the various forms of religion and religious traditions they encounter. The emergence of NRMs in the West has now created a new situation for the churches and signals a transition from Christian hegemony to a radical pluralism.

Researchers have pointed out that a substantial number of Western NRMs come from non-Western cultures and have roots in other religious traditions. Some of them, for example those of Asian provenance, are products of revival and revitalization of older religions, such as Hinduism and Buddhism, which are seeking to expand their base beyond their original cultural setting through new modes of public outreach. In the process of their transplantation to the West they have undergone a "sea change" and consequently appear "strange" and "exotic" and as diverging significantly from the religion of origin. As transplants they are neither more exotic nor more "impure" than transplants of Christianity in non-Western cultures. Some observers are of the opinion that what Western societies are experiencing today parallels the encounter of other cultures with Christianity at the turn of this century. Thus today's NRMs signal the appearance of a *new* religious pluralism in Western societies and imply an encounter of Christianity with ideas, beliefs and traditions of other cultures and social traditions. This encounter is certain to create tensions and conflicts, which churches must learn to understand and deal with responsibly.

This is not to claim that all NRMs in the West are legitimate expressions of religion and must therefore be defended *en masse*. Some of the movements are demonstrably fraudulent. In such cases churches should certainly confront them and minister to the victims and families affected. In evaluating NRMs, their religious significance and implications for society and the church, we must be cautious, but also sensitive to the changes occurring in society. It will not help to adopt a self-righteous and condemnatory attitude. There may be some things that the church might want to learn from NRMs, and its attitude towards NRMs should therefore shift from fear to an attempt to understand, from anathema to dialogue.

## Papers from the Amsterdam consultation

The papers included in this volume were presented at a consultation held in Amsterdam. As an ecumenical event, this consultation brought together individuals who have been involved in interpreting and respond-

ing to NRMs in divergent contexts. Admittedly, the focus of the consultation was on NRMs in Western societies but, even so, it was felt that some
measure of input from non-Western cultures should be included in order
to understand the phenomenon in a larger context.

Thus *Harold Turner's* paper, the first in this collection, attempts to
explore the new religions as a global phenomenon. Acknowledging that it
is extremely difficult to develop any satisfactory classification of new
religions and movements around the world, Turner makes an important
distinction between two kinds of new religious movements, those related
to primal religions (PRINERMs), especially in their interaction with one
or more universal religions, and those arising amid the universal faiths or
in the post-religious world (NRMs). The sheer number and variety of new
religious groups in both those categories and the hostility and persecution
meted out to them (especially to PRINERMs) leads Turner to offer two
generalizations: "The world has never seen more religious innovation and
creativity than in the second half of the present century," and "The
twentieth century is the great age of religious persecution." Given this
paradoxical situation, Turner states that the tension between new movements and older established religions ought not to lead to a blanket
condemnation of new movements but move in the direction of critical
interaction and dialogue.

*Reinhart Hummel's* contribution deals primarily with NRMs in the
West, particularly those that have come from non-Western backgrounds.
In spite of their diversity, Hummel claims that the majority of NRMs in
the West have come from Hindu or Buddhist backgrounds, and should be
looked upon as a "new stage of the encounter of Christianity" with these
traditions. The presence of these new groups owes a great deal to the
newly awakened sense of mission in Eastern religions and Hummel feels
that one should not therefore over-rate the significance of Christian
shortcomings and Western demand for Eastern spirituality. His paper
contains also an analysis of the causes of tension and conflict between
NRMs and society in general, the movements' organizational structures
and commitments, and draws attention to the attitudes of NRMs towards
Christianity and religious pluralism.

*Shinji Kanai's* paper on the new religious situation in Japan is primarily
a case study of two "neo-new" religions: Shin-nyo En and God Light
Association. Following a brief survey of the emergence of new religions
in the cultural context of Japan, the case studies illustrate how new
movements have succeeded in presenting the contents of older faiths
(Buddhism and Christianity) in new ways, sometimes involving a good

measure of syncretism. In Kanai's opinion the quest for a new spirituality in a "post-modern society" such as Japan calls for a flexible attitude on the part of churches whose understanding of faith is almost invariably defined in dogmatic terms and seldom in "experiential" terms.

If the first three papers thus deal with the phenomenon generally, the next set of papers in this volume address specific issues that NRMs have raised in society, from the perspective of the church.

The presentation made by *Johannes Aagaard* deals with the ideas, concepts and worldviews underlying many of the NRMs in Western societies. He provides a detailed analysis of traditions as represented in the Hindu- and Buddhist-based NRMs and in relation to theosophical and anthroposophical movements in the West that share the same presuppositions of occultism.

The imaginative cosmologies and the "transformative" (as opposed to informative) and esoteric language employed by some of the NRMs have not only a profound impact upon people but also pose a significant challenge to Christian theological reflection. Aagaard suggests that the challenge of NRMs to churches comes not so much from this or that religious group but rather from new worldviews they introduce into society (especially in the context of traditionally Christian societies), which are bound to have an impact upon people, although they may not necessarily be drawn to any particular NRM.

This is a conclusion that *Jean-François Mayer* confirms in his response to Aagaard. Referring to a wide range of contemporary NRMs, Mayer indicates subtle transformations of our spiritual environment brought about by NRMs through a redefinition of religiosity and through attempts to evolve a new religious synthesis that is certain to undermine traditional Christian perspectives.

One of the persistent issues of major controversy surrounding NRMs has to do with their recruitment tactics, especially mind-controlling techniques, alleged coercion, deception, fraud, etc. In the wake of the destruction of the People's Temple Community in Jonestown, Guyana, in 1978, there have been public campaigns to expose some of the so-called "destructive cults" and attempts made to use legal means to obtain release of members of NRMs, sometimes for the purpose of "deprogramming". *Eileen Barker's* paper addresses this question of recruitment. Looking at the issue from a sociological perspective, Barker emphasizes that the NRMs recruit people in widely different ways and the mode and methods used depend on the social environment and openness to proselytizing endeavours and the goals and objects of such recruitment. The paper points out some of the methodological and epistemological difficulties involved in assessing the recruitment methods of NRMs. Concepts such as brainwashing, coercion, mind-control and free-will can be used in a variety of ways and are not readily amenable to empirical verification. Thus the kind of meaning attributable to successful recruitment methods is subject to a number of variables that are illustrated with reference to some of the recruitment practices of the Moonies.

*Rüdiger Hauth's* response to Barker is based on his personal experience with certain controversial groups, especially in the context of ministering to families affected by those groups, and therefore adopts a point of view that is critical of NRMs. Hauth finds it difficult to adopt a neutral stance in judging the NRMs and argues that, given one's experience of various NRMs, and against the background of Christian faith, it is reasonably possible to make judgments on NRMs.

But much of the controversy over the recruitment practices of NRMs in Western societies has arisen because of certain legal decisions. There have been a number of court verdicts against NRMs and attempts to control NRMs through legislative and administrative measures. On the other hand, some NRMs have used legal means to counter public opposition. Such stances inevitably raise issues of civil rights, freedom of religion, and the nature of church-state relations in many Western countries. The paper by *Dean Kelley* focuses on the issue of legal threats to conversion in the United States. Kelley's paper illustrates some of the tactics often used against NRMs. In his view these endanger religious liberty and will also have considerable implications for all other established religious bodies.

A useful addition to this volume would have been a study comparing the situations in North America and Western Europe on questions such as civil and religious liberty. In a sociological study entitled *Cult Controversies*,[1] James A. Beckford indicates that issues of civil rights and questions about the separation of church and state have not been the central concerns of controversy in Europe. Because of significant cross-national differences, the nature of perceived threats from NRMs varies from country to country in Western Europe.

In Britain, according to Beckford's analysis, there is no public policy regarding matters of religion and hence opposition to NRMs has occurred mainly outside the courts of law (except in cases of libel). The government has been reluctant to take a visibly active role in either protecting or criticizing NRMs. The opposition to NRMs in Britain has by and large come from voluntary groups (seldom related to established religions or political organizations) whose attacks are against the allegedly dishonest and unscrupulous practices of NRMs. In contrast, in the Federal Republic of Germany, where anti-NRM sentiments are expressed in terms of the baneful influence of the so-called "youth religions" on the young, the allegedly harmful practices rather than the beliefs of NRMs are stressed. Similarly in France, according to Beckford, anxiety is expressed over their effects on the minds of new recruits.

Compared to the United States, the practice of deprogramming is rare in Western Europe, and Beckford explains how the French and German legal systems do not encourage or facilitate the individual's defence of personal rights through courts of law. Consequently the level of litigation in this area is much lower in Europe than in the USA.

The only significant step towards some form of quasi-judicial control of NRMs in Europe was the European Parliament's approval of a special motion in 1984. This motion (submitted by Mr Richard Cottrell, MEP from Britain), while affirming the freedom of religious beliefs, was concerned to ensure the lawfulness of the practices used by NRMs to recruit new members and their treatment. The resolution also set certain guidelines to be followed by NRMs in these matters. There has been some modest amount of protest over this motion in Britain but by and large the popular sentiment in Europe seems to favour social control of NRMs.

The next set of papers focus on the responses of the churches to the emergence of NRMs. *Reender Kranenborg's* paper surveys the Dutch reaction to some "old" new religious movements (Jehovah's Witnesses, Christian Science, the Theosophical Society, the Sufi Order and the Lou Movement) between 1860 and 1960. In the Netherlands, these new movements were evaluated from the perspective of Christianity as deviations and were rejected *a priori*. Kranenborg indicates that such negative reaction is somewhat representative of many Western countries and that historically the church has failed to grasp the sociological and spiritual implications of NRMs; its theological response is therefore rather arbitrary, if not superficial. In his response to Kranenborg, *Friday Mbon* confirms similar attitudes in the context of Nigeria where the so-called established Mission Churches have reacted negatively to Christian new religious movements (often referred to as African Independent Churches). The mushrooming of such Christian-based new movements, says Mbon, raises serious questions about the "parameters and perimeters of Christian faith itself" in Africa.

In most Western situations changes in immigration patterns, as well as the emergence of NRMs, have created a situation of new religious pluralism to which the churches must respond sensitively. Reporting on the North American situation, *Diana Eck* finds that very few churches have devoted any sustained attention to NRMs. In her survey of 36 national denominational offices of the Catholic, Orthodox and Protestant churches in the USA and Canada, Eck found only two conservative American denominations (Southern Baptist Convention and Lutheran Church-Missouri Synod) with extensive programmes and publications on NRMs. Generally, it is the conservative evangelical or the fundamentalist churches that have been most vocal on this subject; the mainline churches have been by and large silent.

The situation may be different in Europe where some of the mainline churches (e.g. Roman Catholic Church in France, Lutheran churches in the Federal Republic of Germany and Scandinavia, British Council of Churches) have been actively involved in responding to NRMs.

One of the most sensitive issues of the churches' response to NRMs is the question of dialogue. Many Western churches have been extremely cautious and reluctant to initiate dialogues with NRMs because of the fear that they would only lend credibility to questionable groups. *Kenneth Cracknell's* paper explores this question on the basis of "four principles" derived from the WCC *Guidelines on Dialogue with People of Living Faiths and Ideologies*. Cracknell argues that followers of NRMs are every bit as much entitled to be listened to, and sympathized with, as those who belong within the older religious framework. There are no limits to be set to dialogue and therefore drawing boundaries or establishing frontiers over which Christians cannot pass is morally and theologically wrong. Without such dialogues there will be little opportunity to understand the alien and, without understanding, little opportunity to influence the beliefs, values and practices that trouble Christians.

It should be noted that the "Summary Statement and Recommendations" included in this volume represents the views of the participants at the Amsterdam consultation. It is not an official document of the sponsoring bodies but it is intended as an aid to stimulate further study and reflection in churches.

Another appendix to this volume is the progress report released by the Vatican and entitled *Sects or New Religious Movements: Pastoral Challenge*.

NOTE

[1] London, Tavistock Publications, 1985.

# Part I:

# Understanding
# New Religious Movements

# A Global Phenomenon

## HAROLD TURNER

The brief given to me refers to new religious movements as a "global phenomenon" and asks for some account of the response of the older religions to them. I shall interpret this as involving some history and a little geography, and I shall try to concentrate on the concerns of the Christian churches in this subject. I shall not therefore be embarking on a wider, more general, theoretical and academic exercise. It is evident both from the minutes of the WCC Dialogue Working Group's meeting in 1985, and from the report submitted to them, that there is considerable uncertainty, great divergence of viewpoint and some inhibitions when it comes to Christian relationships with these phenomena. I hope I may contribute towards a more confident Christian stance.

We may start by changing the language for a moment and thinking of the existence of religious innovation in the history of all religions. Change and innovation are features of all human societies, and the religious dimension is not excluded from these processes. The particular forms taken are multitudinous — new kinds of places of worship, new rites and festivals, new specialists, developing myths, individuals with a new charisma, new teachers and reformers leading to renewal, revivals, heresies, schisms, even religious wars. Sometimes what began as a "movement" settles down and becomes recognized as a new religion. Changes may represent decay or degeneration into magical or even immoral forms, and both aspects may appear within a single new religious movement or its successor new religion. But these forms are only the more obvious developments. Behind them lie the usually uncharted range of legal and regional variations within a major tradition, and behind all these lie the personal, individual deviations and variants that we ourselves would represent within a single tradition. Dissatisfactions, larger visions, further searches are always simmering somewhere in our midst — as they ought to be. There is probably a potential new religious movement in every village in Europe in the sense of restless individuals silently developing their own beliefs and life-style, their own spirituality, and this is likely to increase.

Religious pluralism, therefore, of various kinds and degrees, is a fact of religious life. Whether this pluralism emerges as a new religious form in history depends on many other factors, such as the emergence of adequate leadership, the shedding of immoral practices, sufficient communal response, and the absence of effective repression. What becomes historically visible are only the tips of many submerged icebergs. And no religious system or tradition is as monochrome, as uniform, as consistent as it would like to believe.

We should also remember that most of the major faiths of today emerged as new religious movements during some period of history. While in New Testament and in theological terms Jesus did not start a new religious movement but represented the decisive event that placed all religions under judgment and in crisis, from secular historical, phenomenological and sociological points of view the Christian church was another religious movement, born in the midst of a jungle of fairly new religious systems in the ancient Greco-Roman world. And in the same fashion most of the later varieties of Christian denominations and other faiths began as new religious movements. There is nothing new in the mere fact of many new religious movements. And in most cases they met a hostile response, with no perception that anything significant or permanent was under way. This provides an important historical perspective, with something to be learned from the past, especially that most contemporary judgments on the movements have been seriously astray.

### Identifying our area of new religious movements

Keeping this general perspective, let me try to identify our own area of concern. I shall do so by first offering a working division of religious traditions into two main families, the group that is increasingly referred to as the *primal religions*, and those I call the *universal religions*. The former are usually, but not always, associated with what are commonly called tribal societies. The latter are usually associated with the larger, more sophisticated societies, and if not universal in any historical or geographical sense they are conceivably so, either by their own intentions or their potentiality. The simplest distinction between the two kinds of religion is that the primals are not missionary and cannot be thought of in this way, whereas the universals can at least conceivably be seen as missionary.

For some thirty years I have been involved with new religious movements arising in the *interactions* between a primal religion and one or more of the universal traditions, usually the Christian faith. These movements stretch back to the time of Columbus and the great expansion of the European peoples and the Christian faith into the tribal peoples of all other continents. They form a massive phenomenon of global dimensions and considerable historical depth and they cohere together as one main class of new religious movements, which we at the Centre in the Selly Oak Colleges refer to by the acronym PRINERMs. They are distinguished by the special interaction within which they arose, and the special dynamics of the relations between primal and universal religions. I cannot set this out here, but suffice it to say that we are not discussing such movements as African Independent churches, Melanesian cargo cults or spirit movements, Afro-Brazilian candombles, Rastafarians, or prophets and messiahs among the tribal peoples of the Americas, Indonesia, India, Oceania and many other areas.

This narrows our subject to new religious movements that have arisen either *within one of the universal traditions* (and I think the term "sect" best applies here), or else by *interaction between two or more of the universal faiths* (the term "cult" might apply here, but I am not too happy with it). This gives us an initial classification of what I shall now refer to as NRMs into two classes, commonly called "the sects and cults". The Jesus People, the Children of God, The Way International would belong to the first group; Divine Light, other guru movements, and Hare Krishna might also belong there; movements revealed upon examination to be more eclectic or syncretist would belong to the second group. This group could also embrace a further range of movements referred to as the "human potential" or "cult of man" type, insofar as we might decide these were to some extent religious. They could then be regarded as arising in the interaction between one of the universal religions and an ideology such as that of the Enlightenment, treating the latter therefore as a pseudo-religion or alternative to religion.

This discussion also shows how difficult it is to develop any simple classification system. In another more elaborate attempt I ended with ten different classes, and when the number reaches that size any classification becomes less and less helpful. The task is further complicated by the development of *new forms of irreligion* attempting to provide a working view of life, new nihilistic philosophies, secular ideologies, alternative life-styles and anarchisms within Western societies.

Then again there is a still further remarkable late twentieth-century development of alternatives to religion, or what become in effect pseudo-religions — the vast range of new "moral causes" for every conceivable issue. Each such movement arises in protest on issues of varying consequence, from nuclear disarmament to the protection of cats in Korea (against their cruel killing and use as human food). Many of us have causes to which we are deeply committed and some of our causes are included in this category. We may identify perhaps five main groups: the women's movement, the peace movement including concern about nuclear arms, the animal rights movement, the health and ecology movement, and human rights movements concerned with social justice, use of torture, and race discrimination; human rights movements then shade off into political movements and finally into terrorist groups.

Many of these moral causes have their activist members who *absolutize the cause*, adopt a totally uncompromising confrontational stance, regard their opponents as the incarnation of evil and themselves as the agents of righteousness, and therefore regard the end as justifying almost any means. The range and scale of these movements present a new and terrifying phenomenon in recent decades. These causes have become *para- or pseudo-religions*, alternative faiths that are demonic and dangerous whenever they lack the internal critiques and sense of finitude and humility that mark authentic religious traditions. At this point they are akin to the new fundamentalist fanaticisms that have arisen within some of the major religious faiths, or in some NRMs.

And it is all complicated by the fact that there are usually some genuine moral issues involved in their concerns, issues that no one else is doing enough about. Think of how much Arab terrorism traces back to the unsolved problem of the Palestinians displaced by the creation of the state of Israel. These new moral causes have also to be seen as *akin to new religious movements* and the question of dialogue with them arises for Christian bodies. Indeed it is already before us insofar as some of the NRMs we are thinking of themselves share in certain of the features and moral concerns of these other new causes.

The only clear gain from the above discussion is the distinction between the two kinds of new religious movements — those related to primal religions, PRINERMs, and those arising amid the universal faiths or in the post-religious world, NRMs. Even this distinction is qualified when some of the former migrate into Western societies. The Aladura-type churches from West Africa appear in Britain and in a number of Continental cities, the Rastafari from Jamaica appear in various parts of the English-speaking world and as far afield as New Zealand, and the Unification Church (arising amid Korean folk "shamanism") appears almost all over the world. On the other hand, most movements in this category do not migrate far from their own cultural backgrounds, and so those that do remain a small minority in relation to the plethora of NRMs in many Western and other nations. The distinction, therefore, remains as an important guide to the nature of the individual movement, and as to how we should relate to it.

In contrast, some of the NRMs in this second major category are quite striking in their international migrations. Hare Krishna has been in trouble in Siberia and in Moscow, Baha'i ranges from Canadian Indians to Papua New Guinea, the Children of God were recently expelled from China, the Unification Church (which belongs to both my categories!) is almost inescapable. Conservative South Africa has its colonies of NRMs, and a recent report from the Cameroon identifies some dozen NRMs which have entered this black African country from overseas in recent years, thus complementing any movement from Africa to the West.

The only Christian body to have attempted some global survey of all kinds of new religious movements is the Catholic Church. Four Vatican secretariats or agencies combined in 1984 to send out a questionnaire on the subject to all national and regional Bishops' Conferences and Eastern Patriarchates. After analysis of some 75 answers from all continents the Vatican published a "progress report" in May 1986 entitled "Sects or New Religious Movements: Pastoral Challenge". This is a notable document in the fairness and depth of its analysis (e.g.: "Very few people seem to join a sect for evil reasons"), and in the humility of its response; pastoral concern, and not polemics or doctrinal condemnation, predominates. My criticisms are two: firstly, its agenda is so wide and loosely defined that it makes no distinction between movements with a background in primal religions and all the rest — the one analysis of causes cannot cover both kinds of movement. Secondly, and surprisingly, it shows no knowledge of the great amount of important study of PRINERMs that has come from Catholic scholars — from people like Carl Starkloff, Paul Steinmetz, Joseph Owens, Laennec Hurbon, Eric de Rosny, Clive Dillon-Malone, Joseph Chakanza, James Kiernan, Stephen Fuchs, Hermann Janssen and others associated with the remarkable Catholic-founded Melanesian Institute. There would appear to be a gap between Bishops' Conferences and Catholic scholars. The report rightly suggests that further study of all these movements must be conducted ecumenically; it would appear that this ecumenicity might well begin at home!

One value of this document is the emphasis it gives to the global extent and the great variety of these faiths. Indeed, when we consider the NRMs found mainly in the West and the thousands of PRINERMs found mainly in the third world, I am prepared to offer the following generalization: that the world *has never seen more religious innovation and creativity than in the second half of the present century*. Religious pluralism has peaked in our time. And this may seem all the more remarkable when the world is becoming more monochrome and standardized in so many other directions — in its hotels and airports, its international life-styles, games and leisure pursuits, and in its communications media and technology, and indeed in its social problems. This is certainly not so for religion, and least of all for the particular kind of NRMs with which we are concerned, where this section's own diversity eludes any of our classification schemes.

## Responses of the established or older religions

The uncertainties evident in the reports from the WCC's Dialogue Working Group as to how to relate to NRMs are not surprising. I have already in passing noted that most religious innovation in history has met with a hostile response and with no allowance for any permanent significance of the new movement. It is important for us to explore this fact further.

Even the most casual catalogue is sufficient to remind us of this dimension of our own Christian history, starting with the crucifixion of Christ, the martyrdom of Stephen and the attacks on Paul, and then the persecutions of the next three centuries. The story continues through the treatment of the mediaeval sectaries, of John Hus and all heretics, of Luther and Calvin, of the Radical Reformation groups and other dissenters by all parties. We remember who the Pilgrim Fathers were, the imprisonment of the Quaker George Fox, the physical attacks on the early Methodists, and the lynching of the Mormon founder, Joseph Smith. Even that most widely respected body, the Salvation Army, was subject to abuse and violence when it was a new religious movement. Dr J.-F. Mayer has uncovered the story of the hysterical public reaction of Christian Switzerland to the coming of the Salvation Army a century ago. The charges against it were almost verbally identical with those made so widely in our own day against the Unification Church and similar NRMs. Who knows what some of these movements will be like, and how our reactions to them today will appear, in a hundred years' time?

Most of my catalogue of past mistakes is obvious enough. But there are two most striking examples of what we can call the "great might-have-beens" in Christian history, if Christian responses had been different. The first concerns the appearance of Muhammad as the founder of what became a new religious movement and then graduated to the firmer status of a new religion. Islam might be regarded as the first major PRINERM, born in the interaction between the religions of the tribal peoples of Arabia and the two Semitic faiths of the time. How different would world history have been if the Jewish communities of Medina and elsewhere had been less hostile and the Christians Muhammad met had been more positive in their attitudes to this new prophet! The second concerns the less known possibility that China might have become a nominally Christian country by the 1860s. The *Taiping Revolution* and military campaign, based on a version of Christianity derived from missionaries, came near to toppling the foreign Manchu dynasty and setting up a new indigenous and ostensibly Christian regime. This massive new religious movement was supported at first by Christian missionaries, but the military revolt was suppressed after the loss of some 30 million lives with the aid of the Western Christian powers. In this aid, that famous late nineteenth-century Christian military hero and martyr, General Charles Gordon, played a critical part as the young commander of a key local army raised to defend Shanghai. What would have happened in subsequent world history if China as a nation had entered the Christian orbit over a century ago? The answers to both the Arab and the Chinese possibilities remain of course highly speculative, but the fact remains that new religious movements lay at the heart of these developments, and how they were treated by Christians was a factor in their future. In the case of Islam it has taken over thirteen centuries for us to develop a generally more positive attitude; we now have to start all over again from the beginning, as is being done in the Centre for the Study of Islam and Christian-Muslim Relations at the Selly Oak Colleges, and elsewhere.

We may feel that these incursions into history have little to teach us now that we have entered upon a more enlightened age of religious tolerance and pluralism. As evidence we may claim that we would never dream of attacking any of the large range of NRMs that appeared in the nineteenth century and have settled down in our midst — the Mormons, the Spiritualist Churches, the various Plymouth Brethren, Jehovah's Witnesses, Christadelphians, Theosophy, Christian Science and Anthroposophy (to name only the most obvious ones). They may have had a rough ride to start with, but things are different now, and for any other such NRMs in the future. In a permissive and pluralistic society, known for its concern for human rights, this might seem to be true, but what actually happens seems to be just the reverse. Indeed I will make another surprising and paradoxical generalization: *that the twentieth century is the great age of religious persecution.*

## The twentieth century as the age of persecution

Once again a catalogue must suffice for our purposes. We recall·the persecutions by governments: of Armenians in Turkey, of all religion in Albania, of at least the smaller faiths in Marxist states and later in Togo, Zaire and other African nations, of the Catholic Church in Mexico in the twenties, of the Jews in Russia, Poland and later under Nazi rule, of the Christians in Nepal and Uganda, and in some African Islamic states, of Protestants in Colombia a generation ago, and of Catholics in Northern Ireland, Zoroastrians in Aden and Iran, and there especially Baha'i. Malawi would like to see itself as a country governed by Christians, but nowhere else in recent times has seen more vicious persecution of Jehovah's Witnesses, who still face trouble in many parts of the world.

My own country of origin, New Zealand, prides itself on being tolerant and fair-minded, but I could show you the documented story, "The God Squad", of a quite shameful and physically violent government attack in the 1970s on a peaceful if somewhat unusual NRM, the Full Gospel Mission community. I am still more ashamed that the churches showed no interest in defending this community, or in exposing the story, and that the documentation had to be assembled by — of all people! — a Scientologist, i.e. someone who knew what harassment was like. Likewise, in Australia, even more tolerant in its image of itself, a recent scandalous example of violent persecution of an NRM had to be documented as "The Jerangle Affair" (a small town in NSW) by the same member of a non-Christian movement. I know that the WCC monitors religious persecutions, and that Amnesty International has its own files on "prisoners of conscience" where the issue is sometimes a religious one. But I doubt if either has these two cases on record, and I rather fear that one of them might not want to include them, nor any other example of harassment of a current NRM. I have some personal reason to believe this might be so of Amnesty International, of which, as a "moral cause", I am myself a member. Another form of religious persecution is to refuse to recognize the persecuted! And yet the twentieth century can think of itself as a new era of religious toleration, especially in Western countries, and because religion doesn't matter much anyway.

I understand that one of the more gruesome of Dr David Barrett's fascinating statistics is that we can expect some 3,700 Christians to be martyred somewhere in the world each year! I would not expect many of these to be members of the NRMs with which we are concerned. But it helps to make my point. And the fact of our persecuting century comes home to us still further if we stop to look at the record of ostensibly Christian governments in relation to PRINERMs. Over twenty years ago I had occasion to write an account of the persecution of the first Nigerian prophet movement in 1916; I introduced that case study by a survey of similar persecutions of PRINERMS or their leaders across African history, and even those I knew of then numbered thirty — from the burning at the stake of prophetess Beatrice in 1706 in the Bakongo, through the death sentence upon Simon Kimbangu in 1921, to the then recent suppression of Alice Lenshina's Lumpa Church in Zambia. Most examples occurred in the twentieth century and right up to the time when I was writing.

One can find similar history among the PRINERMs of New Zealand Maoris, in the Philippines, among the tribal peoples of India, for the Rastafari across the Caribbean, and especially among the North American Indians where the persecution of the Peyote religion by all parties, white and Indian, for about a century is a classic example of everybody being wrong. Their efforts to stamp out this so-called drug cult were quite misinformed and counter-productive. The new religion survived and spread and only in the 1970s was it gradually achieving the religious liberty to which it was entitled from the beginning. Some anthropologists have played a notable part in this victory: again I am ashamed to say that the churches have been on the wrong side — with the notable exception of a group of Jesuit missionaries in the Western states who have developed a positive relation with some of the Peyotists; and there is a future in that.

The Centre to which I am attached has, I believe, the most extensive documentation that exists anywhere for the ways in which governments, the law, the media, Christian missionaries and churches have responded to the rise of PRINERMs since the oldest we have on record, about 1530, but especially in our century. The evidence includes some enlightened approaches with interesting positive results. Some 21 of those who are currently in the front line of these approaches in Africa met in the Ivory Coast for the first time in consultation in July 1986. But by and large the evidence reveals the same mistakes being made time and again all over the world. I am well aware that the issues were sometimes far from simple, that some PRINERMs were politically provocative or morally offensive, that the Xhosa cattle-killing and certain cargo cults could not be tolerated, and that in some situations no party could win. And yet I think few today would want to defend many of the responses made in the past by either public or religious bodies to the PRINERMs in their midst.

All of which goes to underwrite the statement that no previous century has seen more extensive or bitter religious persecution, ranging from petty harassment through deportation or imprisonment to torture and murder. As we in the Centre began to be more involved with the issues raised by NRMs in the West we felt we had seen it all before in our original main field of the third-world movements, and that while the dynamics of origins might be very different from the two groups of new religious movements, the issues raised for society and the nature of the responses made by society (including the churches) were very similar in each case. Except for what seems to be a wholly new form of persecution of NRMs that has arisen in the USA — the method of attack by "anti-cult" groups wherein a former member of an NRM is persuaded to bring a multi-million dollar civil claim for damages due to non-fulfilment of alleged promises of mental or spiritual benefits that would accrue to those who joined the movement. Several such suits have been initially success-ful in the lower courts, to the tune of $30 million or more, so that the method of destroying movements by bankrupting them may prove work-able. To have intangible spiritual benefits packaged and priced and used in this way is monstrous, and the churches should be the first to say so, if for no more altruistic reason than their own vulnerability to destruction by similar manipulation of the law, in a new kind of twentieth-century persecution.

### The lesson from ecumenism and dialogue in the twentieth century

Having attended to the witness of history about the still continuing failure to manage religious diversity and innovation in peaceful and positive ways, and having indicated the value of PRINERMs for an examination of the issues raised by NRMs and the mistakes that may be made in dealing with them, we could now turn to some analysis of the sources of the tensions between new and older religious forms, and how both parties may contribute to the problem. But I must move instead to the very important and relevant experience the Christian churches have accumulated as this century has proceeded in the areas of ecumenism among themselves and dialogue with other faiths.

Here I may be allowed to draw upon two papers I prepared for the British Council of Churches consultation on NRMs held in April 1986. In one of these I recalled the stages through which first ecumenical discussions and then interfaith dialogue had proceeded since the Protestants met in the Edinburgh Conference of 1910. Without being too concerned about starting points and exact order of events, we can identify the following further ever-outreaching developments: the inclusion of Eastern Orthodoxy and then of the Roman Catholic Church in ecumenical affairs, the new relations with the Jewish faith and since then with Islam, the opening of dialogue with the great Asian religions, the first positive outreach to PRINERMs in the form of the African Independent churches at the WCC consultation at Mindolo in 1962, and the commencement of structured dialogue with a major ideology in the shape of Marxism. And must it stop here? If with PRINERMs, what about NRMs? One Christian denomination, the United Reformed Church in the UK, through its appropriate committee, has said yes to this and made a small start on conversations with one of the NRMs, and I believe Catholic Bishops in the USA have made a similar move. And further, there are even signs of dialogue beginning between some of the NRMs themselves!

At the start of the century none of these stages could easily have been envisaged. At each stage of this remarkable process there were many ready to criticize that particular step, or to say "thus far, and no further". By now we should have learned from this twentieth-century movement of the Spirit and be open to the most unexpected relationships with people of other faiths. If a permanent exception is to be made in relation to some whole category of faiths, such as NRMs, it will have to be supported by overwhelming theological or other good reasons. I can imagine good reasons for not seeking dialogue with a particular movement or at a particular time; I cannot see justification for any blanket prohibition. This is not what the Spirit has been saying in the twentieth century.

Let me now make the same point from the other paper referred to, in terms of my own ecumenical journey. I was brought up as a Presbyterian who tended to regard Catholics as ignorant, dirty, dishonest and often drunken! I could not have imagined later rejoicing in having a Catholic priest as academic colleague in Nigeria, much less of asking the Society of Jesus to support a staff member for my Centre at Selly Oak and being so grateful for the man they sent, or of being deeply moved when the staff of the Catholic Centre in London, Housetops, said over the phone that they would pray for me when they met in fifteen minutes time, over a sticky problem I had with an NRM. As a Presbyterian student who found his permanent theological roots during the neo-orthodox revival of the 1930s I had a poor regard for some other traditions, especially those regarding episcopacy as basic, but in the ecumenical movement one learned to respect bishops and even like some of them!

When I was a Student Christian Movement chaplain in the days of mutual antipathy between SCM and the Evangelical or Christian Union in New Zealand, as elsewhere, I could never have envisaged finding close fellowship with people who had come up by the other student route. But in the 1950s in West Africa I did just this and have done so ever since. Much less that I should be proud of close association with so-called "sects" like the Seventh Day Adventists, and recently appreciated lecturing on PRINERMs at their college in England. Again, as one in the high Reformed tradition of sound doctrine and decency and order in worship it would have been nonsense to suggest that I might actually enjoy dancing in African Independent churches with a very uncertain Christology. And now the church where I did most of my dancing is a member of the WCC!

I am sure that many of you could tell your own stories of being personally stretched and stretched again in the course of ecumenical encounter and of dialogue. In each successive step of my own pilgrimage it was impossible even to envisage the next step that most astonishingly did occur. Each time one felt one was at the limits. One by one the barriers that we imagined protected us and the Christian faith itself have been broken down by the Holy Spirit.

Now we are together to consider yet another range of religious forms that are problematic to us. Dare we halt this process? Or repudiate the lessons and the perspective given us in this amazing century — by starting once again with limits and barriers? There certainly will be limits. We cannot prevent some NRMs from refusing to have anything to do with us, although we may well ask how far we have contributed to such an impasse. Or God may set limits for some of us or for some movements. God may not call us to this task, where God is more aware than we are of the limits set by our own time, or opportunity or competence, or by the readiness of a certain NRM for conversation with us. But *we ourselves must not set limits in advance*, in general, or from some prejudged or theoretical position.

I am well aware of the thorny problems of religious liberty, religion and the law, the activities of politicians in the religious sphere, the influence of the media, the problems of families and of educational institutions. I know that new religious developments may be constructive or destructive, can lead to a new freedom or new enslavement, can depersonalize individuals or reveal their fuller human potential, can depend on religious faith or on new rituals equivalent to magic and the occult, can reclaim the drug addict and encourage virtuous lives or exhibit immoral and demonic features. And above all there is the over-riding question of the truth as it is in Jesus Christ, which is not answered by moral and spiritual score-sheets for individual movements.

As we discuss such questions we are sure to find that the answers are not easy. But I hope that some of Kenneth Cracknell's words in the report on the British Council of Churches consultation on NRMs in April 1986 will guide us: "...dialogue does not exclude criticism, and therefore need not entail any kind of endorsement of the beliefs or practices of new religions... the teaching and example of Jesus Christ clearly indicates that no-one is beyond the pale when considering association." When Jesus associated with publicans, tax-gatherers and prostitutes he was neither condoning nor legitimating their ways of life; rather, he was endorsing the common humanity he shared with them and the love of God for them all.

Albrecht Hauser put it another way in a letter to me some years ago: "How often are attitudes of fear mixed up with what we call faith, so that instead of crossing frontiers in mission, we reinforce the frontiers... rather than let the crucified and risen Lord break down the barriers where they need to be broken down." Barrier-breaking and not barrier-building would seem to be the way of Jesus, and even though so much of history in the intervening centuries has denied his way there would seem to be little doubt that in the twentieth century the Holy Spirit has again opened up for us the way of Jesus, the way of ecumenism and of mission through dialogue, yes, even with the modern tax-gatherers and prostitutes who seem to figure in some of the NRMs of our time.

# Contemporary New Religions in the West

## REINHART HUMMEL

I shall start with some general considerations about terminology and typology with respect to NRMs. I shall argue that NRMs in the West are quite different from those of other continents in that most of them do not represent an indigenous reaction against some kind of impact from outside, but rather that the movements themselves come predominantly from outside.

I will then look at the NRMs against the background from which they come. I shall argue that the encounter of Christianity with them is — to a larger extent than is usually realized — one mode of encountering Hinduism and Buddhism.

The third part will deal with tension and conflict between the NRMs and society. I shall plead for a clear distinction between the sympathizing milieu surrounding the NRMs, the organized movements themselves and the small group of conflict-creating religious movements.

In the fourth part different types of NRMs will be analyzed in terms of organizational structure and degree of commitment. I shall argue that the monastic orders and/or religio-political movements among them demand the highest degree of commitment.

Finally I will analyze the attitude of NRMs towards Christianity and religious pluralism. I want to draw attention to the growing number of NRMs which maintain an ecumenical set-up of their own, based on the conviction that the new Messiah, Sadguru or Avatara has superseded Christ and will usher in a new age of religious unity.

### Diverse phenomena — unsatisfactory terminologies

The NRMs in the West originated or emerged in the wake of the unrest of the 60s and 70s. Most of them found their first large following in the counter-culture among hippies, young people experimenting with psychedelic drugs or involved in political activities of the New Left.

These events have already become part of history. Most of the NRMs reached their climax in the second half of the 70s when the unrest and attraction of the counter-culture subsided. Bhagwan Rajneesh was already a late-comer on the scene. Most NRMs have now entered upon a period of consolidation or have come into a crisis. Nevertheless, they are symptoms or surviving institutional remnants of the 60s and at the same time ways out of it — ways of "getting saved from the 60s", as S.M. Tipton, has put it. [1]

There is general agreement that many of the NRMs are new only in terms of their new appearance in the West, and that they are not full-fledged religions. In fact there is hardly any new religion among the "new religions" in the West. There are smaller offshoots of some of the new Japanese religions. The Unification Church is a new religion according to recognized standards, although for obvious reasons it would prefer to be classed among the Christian denominations. Scientology is new but hardly meets the requirements of a religion as far as cultic and ritual life is concerned, although it does claim the status of a religion. Bhagwan's Neo-Sannyas Movement was a religion for some years, until Bhagwan declared that the "Religion of Rajneeshism" was nothing but the invention of his secretary Sheela, and the small violet book about the fundamentals of Rajneeshism was solemnly burnt. Nevertheless the Bhagwan movement, in spite of its syncretistic and eclectic character, seems to meet the requirements of a religion. It has a complex but distinct identity of its own and contains all three dimensions of doctrine, practice (cult, ritual) and community life (according to Joachim Wach). Most of the NRMs in the West are offshoots of some religious tradition dominated by one of the great traditions, either Hinduism or Buddhism. The Radhasoami tradition, some of whose offshoots are very active in the West, may claim a certain independence from Hinduism as it rejects caste and idol worship; however, it can be, and indeed has been, interpreted as a Hindu reform movement. This is why the term NRMs seems preferable and more adequate when discussing the religious movements in the West.

As far as Europe is concerned, no indigenous religion or religious movement has originated there for a long time. Nearly all NRMs appearing in Europe have come from or via the United States. The typical NRM turns up in Europe dressed, metaphorically speaking, in an Indian *dhoti* and an American jacket, frequently infected by the virus of commercialism and free religious enterprise. As English has become the second (or even first) language of Neo-Hinduism and many NRMs, there is a language barrier as well. German Bhagwan-Sannyasins prefer to express some of their basic notions in English (love, awareness, etc.), English being to some extent their sacred language.

The NRMs in different continents may have many common traits. However, most of those in Africa and Latin America, apart from being much more numerous, are indigenous; some even attempt to complete what they feel to be half-hearted efforts by the traditional churches to inculturate and indigenize Christianity in their specific cultural context. But the majority of NRMs in the West are children of the third world and find it difficult to adapt to the Western situation. A substantial part of the problems created by them are problems of cultural alienation and unsuccessful indigenization: rigorous adoption of an Indian life-style, arranged marriages in accordance with traditional Korean customs, Japanese recruitment techniques, etc. — all these perhaps prompted and reinforced by the search of young people of the 60s and 70s, already alienated from society, for a new life-style and new cultural values.

It has turned out to be extremely difficult to fit NRMs coming from Asia into classifications and typologies developed in connection with Christian forms of organization. Although many of these NRMs have embodied mystical elements, their organizational structure does not fit into the famous Troeltschian typology of church-sect-mysticism. Frequently they are structured according to the pattern of a Sampradaya, a tradition based on guru-succession, guru-disciple-relationship and containing many doctrinal, cultic and ritual elements. If at all, they should be located somewhere between sect and mysticism. Furthermore, modern religious movements tend to combine, sometimes rather artificially, different and diverse motifs: they offer a mystical path, promise salvation from the coming cosmic catastrophe, proclaim the dawn of a Golden Age and engage in aggressive proselytizing; they are thus mystical, apocalyptic, millenial and conversionist at the same time, as though they wanted to thumb their nose at the sociologist of religion.

A similar difficulty arises when it comes to the problem of terminology. All-encompassing terms like NRMs are helpful in avoiding negative connotations, but they also help to elude definitional problems. They prompt demands for clarification: What do you have in mind, the Family of Love or Catholic Charismatics, Jim Jones or the Dalai Lama? Disputes about NRMs can become tedious and abortive when participants do not state clearly what they are talking about. The term "cult" was used before the NRMs of the 60s appeared on the scene. It carries negative connotations and has been applied, also by scholars, to ephemeral and bizarre movements without legitimating tradition. When the NRMs appeared, those among them which had become the subject of controversy were labelled "destructive cults". The terms "cult" and "destructive cult" can be and indeed often are used to deny the religious character of those movements.

In scientific language "cult" is often used together with "sect" without negative connotations. [2] Here sects are seen, roughly speaking, as deviant movements derived from mainstream (in the West: Christian) religion, whereas cults are deviant movements outside mainstream religion, either imported from outside or originated outside mainstream religion. This use of the term sect comes close to the traditional theological definition of a sect, and the term cult comes close to what is meant by NRMs, but in both cases the terms are not identical. I would like to add that I found Mircea Eliade's term "para-religious movements" helpful with respect to movements like modern Spiritualism and Theosophy, because it indicates that they rely on one or several host religions whom they claim to complement or interpret in terms of their deeper esoteric meaning.

Evidently the terminological efforts, however necessary, cannot reduce or overcome the vast diversity of phenomena and experiences in regard to origin, effect and other characteristics. We shall come back to this problem later.

## New religious movements and the world religions

A frequently used typology classifies NRMs according to background and origin: (1) movements originating from within Christianity; (2) movements bearing the imprint of Western psychology and therapeutic subculture; and (3) movements derived from Asiatic religions. Most of the movements from a Christian background move along traditional lines representing one type or another of pietistic-evangelical, pentecostal-charismatic or chiliastic-apocalyptic tradition, frequently with a strong fundamentalist touch. The Family of Love, previously Children of God, has become the most controversial among them. The Unification Church does not fit into this classification since it has also incorporated elements of Eastern traditions.

Among those movements drawing on values and techniques of Western psychology and therapy some (e.g. Scientology) are geared to the pursuit of traditional Western values like individual success, superiority, domination of circumstances and "how to win friends and influence people". Their ideal is self-improvement rather than self-realization. Others are committed to the "expressive" values of humanist psychology and the "human potential movement", focusing on human growth and the exploration and realization of the self. Erhard Seminars Training (EST) seems to cover both aspects. Both, Scientology and EST, have incorporated elements of Eastern religions (reincarnation, Zen, etc.) whereas some Indian guru movements like Transcendental Meditation and the Bhagwan Movement have gone through the reverse process and now represent a blend of Eastern religion and Western psychology, either of the self-improvement (TM) or the self-realization type (Bhagwan), TM being more of a "power-trip", Bhagwan an "ego-trip". Even comparatively authentic NRMs like those coming from Tibetan Buddhism (Tschögyam Trungpa's Naropa Institutes, the Kagyüdpa groups, etc.) have succeeded in interpreting themselves and in being understood in psychological terms in the West. Obviously it is difficult to draw a clear dividing line between religious movements from Asia and "psycho-movements". Many of the NRMs have established themselves on the borderline either between religion and psychology or between religion and politics.

The majority of the NRMs in the West have come from Hindu or Buddhist backgrounds: guru movements from India, either offshoots of different Hindu traditions or founded and led by eclectic, syncretistic gurus like Rajneesh; lamaistic groups from different schools of Tibetan Buddhism. The Zen movement in the West lacks coherence and organizational structure and has to some extent lost its Buddhist identity, especially where Zen is adapted to enrich Christian spirituality. Viewed from a Western cultural perspective, it may be justified to call all these NRMs, but from a religious viewpoint these movements, with the exception of the eclectic gurus, should rather be looked upon as a new stage of the encounter of Christianity with Hindu and Buddhist traditions or, metaphorically speaking, as new annual rings contributing to the growth of the trees of Hindu and Buddhist presence in Western cultures which were planted in 1893. In that year the World Parliament of Religions met in Chicago and the first emissaries of Hindu and Buddhist traditions stayed on, won their first Western disciples and started to set up their first organizations (Vedanta Societies, Western branches of Maha Bodhi Society, etc.). Hindu and Buddhist presence in the West has grown intermittently, the last being the emergence of NRMs in the 60s and 70s of this century. [3]

German Buddhists are quite aware of this continuity. The Buddhist Religious Community of Germany encompasses the older Buddhist congregations of the Theravada type, different offshoots of Japanese Buddhism, Tibetan groups and Buddhist retreat centres which welcome representatives from all these traditions. It is the Dharma that has gone West.

The Indian guru movements in the West have not been able to develop a sense of unity to the same extent. The traditions they come from are too different or even at odds with one another, and the degree of Westernization varies quite strongly. The Hare Krishna Movement (ISKCON) is still firmly rooted in the Chaitanya tradition, although its idea of creating a class of Brahmins out of the Western "Shudra Society" is far from orthodox. The ISKCON, more than others, enjoys the support of Hindu national organizations willing to accept even foreigners in the Hindu fold if they undergo the required purification ceremony (Shuddhikarana). Other guru movements have rather come from the fringe of Hinduism (e.g. the Sadgurus of the Radhasoami tradition), from different strands of Neo-Hinduism originated during the nineteenth or twentieth century (e.g. Ramakrishna Mission, Yogananda's Self-Realization Fellowship, groups related to Aurobindo and Auroville) or from tantric traditions (e.g. Muktananda and Narayanananda). Nevertheless, most of them are still closely tied to the Indian mother organizations which as a rule are more numerous. Some movements founded in the West like ISKCON and TM have, after some success there, started activities in India and are strengthening rather than severing their Indian umbilical cord.

All this makes clear that the majority of Indian guru movements in the West are new only in terms of their appearance here, that they are not full-fledged religions but rather represent different traditions belonging either to traditional Hinduism or Neo-Hinduism, and that they can be understood best as part of Hindu missions and presence in the West. It is interesting to note that in Accra, the capital of Ghana, a number of Hindu and Buddhist organizations are active among black Africans. The Hare Krishna movement has a temple and a training centre for black Krishna missionaries there, Svami Sivananda's "Divine Life Society" is running a "Hindu Monastery of Africa", a Sri Sathya Sai Baba Centre proclaims the "Sai Religion", a Guru Nanak Society the Sikh Dharma. The "Maha Bodhi Society of Ghana" has established a Buddhist temple, a library, a training centre for Ghanaian Buddhist missionaries and a printing press, and the Nichiren Shoshu is trying to spread its own Japanese version of Buddhism there. Add to this the Ahmadiyya Mission and some Sufi orders and you have the vision of a worldwide missionary outreach of all these traditions. This should alert us against over-rating the significance of Western shortcomings and Western demand for Eastern spirituality, and against underestimating the significance of the sense of mission newly awakened within the religions of the East as a result of the revival of the last century. The impact of these religious traditions on the West is

of course also an outcome of the worldwide cross-cultural communication. A lot of stranded goods are washed ashore and picked up at random,
but there are also complete shiploads brought to the Western shore by
single-minded captains like Svami Prabhupada. When Prabhupada
arrived in New York in 1965 he had no intention of founding an NRM, at
least no more than Carey, Ward and Marshman had wanted to found a
cult when they started their mission work in Serampore, near Calcutta,
India.

If this is true, the NRMs in the West with Hindu or Buddhist
backgrounds are part and parcel of Christian-Hindu and Christian-Buddhist relations and will sooner or later have to come on the agenda of
dialogue with these religions, although it seems more comfortable for
both sides to put them on a separate shelf and label them NRMs. It would
also indicate an awareness that the period of mission has not just given
way to a period of dialogue but that both mission and dialogue are at
present simultaneous processes. Phenomenologically speaking, mission
is the result of an interaction between a sense of mission on the one hand
and a sense of crisis or stagnation on the other. This interaction has not
yet ceased and may perhaps never do so; it has only changed its direction
since the great religions of the East have developed a sense of mission
whereas the West is gripped by a sense of crisis.

A word should be added about the new Japanese religions. Some of
these have started activities in Western countries, first among Japanese
minorities, but reaching out more and more to the "natives" (Nichiren
Shoshu, Soka Gakkai, Mahikari, etc.). So far they play only a minor role
in the West.

## Tension and conflict between NRMs and society

The popular typology assesses NRMs in terms of their effect on
members in separating them from family and society, endangering their
future prospects, etc. It ranges from harmless to harmful: charismatic
renewal is harmless, TM is bad, Unification Church worse, Family of
Love worst. Within this frame of reference NRMs are measured in terms
of conflict and tension. A widely accepted theory holds that NRMs
always start at a point of high tension within the surrounding society and
then mellow. When tension becomes too low, NRMs with high tension
come into being and the same cycle starts all over again. [4]

High tension seems therefore to be a mark of the incipient state of a
movement, of commitment to a newly discovered holy cause. At present
Moonies are in fact saying: "As we have families now, we will have

problems similar to yours in the churches." They are beginning to face the typical problems of the second generation. On the other hand the Watch Tower Society is still in a position to maintain a high degree of personal commitment, proselytizing with energy and separating members from the surrounding society in matters like celebrating Christmas, etc. Mormons had to give up polygamy in order to come to terms with society. It would seem that conflict and tension are in some way related to contents and structure as well, not only to newness.

It is difficult to foresee how the NRMs in the West will be able to come to terms with society and society with them. It seems that commitment to an alternative life-style and to a spirituality drawn from sources outside Christianity is not the main cause for creating conflicts and tension. A considerable number of people in the West have taken to different forms of meditation of Hindu and Buddhist origin, to a vegetarian life-style, etc., and are tolerated or even found fascinating by society. Conflict and tension arise when meditation is focused on a guru or when values upheld in the human potential movement are institutionalized, "sectarianized" and legitimized by a tantric Master from India like Bhagwan Shree Rajneesh, or when conservative and puritan values like family and anti-communism are "sectarianized" and legitimated by a Messiah from Korea. Even those who share such values will be shocked when a friend or relative of theirs joins these movements. The NRMs are not isolated phenomena. They operate in a milieu and environment of sympathizers or potential recruits.

On the other hand people practising meditation may feel attracted to the higher degree of commitment and intensity in a guru movement, hoping to experience the "real thing" there. People whose worldview is determined by psychology and who have read Wilhelm Reich and Gurdjieff would tend to expect the final peak experience from joining a Rajneesh commune. The surrounding milieu assumes a divided "Yes, but..." attitude towards organized movements: basic values are shared by the organizational and sectarian structure, the authoritarian leadership and the dependency of the individual member are rejected or even found disgusting.

In order to visualize the whole spectrum I use three concentric circles. Within the wider circle of new, or at least alternative, religiousness we find the circle of organized religious (or psycho-religious) movements and at the centre the smallest circle of what I prefer to call conflict-creating religious movements. This term does not necessarily imply that they are to be blamed exclusively for whatever conflicts may arise around them. It is only meant to indicate an inherent conflict potential of varying degree. It does not add a new category to that of NRMs, only a qualification expressing tension and conflict with society or parts of it.

## Organizational structure and commitment

The distinction between audience cult, client cult and cult movement is also helpful in explaining the varying degrees of commitment. In an audience cult the media of communication are magazines, books, tapes, radio and television. A client cult is a congregation that does not gather together but reads the same books and is fascinated by the same subject, as for instance UFOs. A client cult requires a personal relationship, not between individual members but between the person offering magical or similar services and the clients, without necessarily conveying a religious worldview and having formal membership. A client cult may develop into a full-fledged cult movement (in the sense of an NRM) with membership, a doctrine, etc. The development of L.R. Hubbard's early Dianetic Organization into the Church of Scientology can be understood as a transformation of a client cult into a cult movement. Rajneesh started, after leaving his college job, by gathering an all-India audience cult, then transformed it gradually into a movement and even temporarily into a religion.

Actually these two movements have never ceased to maintain a client relationship with many of those who have come into contact with them. Many persons practising Transcendental Meditation or taking Sannyas from Rajneesh are clients rather than disciples or devotees, although the borderline between them may be very difficult to determine in individual cases. In spite of being initiated they may not feel committed to the movement, its tenets and organization as a whole. (High figures regarding membership in NRMs are misleading because they tend to include all those who attended an introductory course, often without deep and lasting commitment.) At the same time, the movements could not function without a band of committed full-time workers bound to the Master by the bonds of discipleship and venerating him as the Enlightened One and the embodiment of the highest consciousness. This two-tier structure is a characteristic of movements which have established themselves on the borderline between religion (or magic) and psychology.

The Bhagwan Movement[5] can even be understood as a three-tier movement. Newcomers will first find a psycho-religious movement offering therapeutic and similar services. Quite soon they will discover that the Bhagwan Movement is a syncretistic guru-cult as well, Rajneesh being venerated as the Enlightened One who expounds the esoteric meaning of all religious traditions of humankind. Advanced members will find out that the movement is also a school of mysteries, an "incubator" meant to hatch new enlightened masters. The role of the Sannyasins may change accordingly from client to devotee and further on to adept or even master (although not without recognition by Rajneesh) with many possible combinations and nuances.

The structure of movements on the borderline between religion and politics seems to be more close-knit. The Unification Church with its political para-organization CAUSA and Ananda Marga with PROUT are religio-political movements. The genesis of both took place in areas of extreme tension between communism and its adversaries. Ananda Marga was founded in West Bengal, probably with a dominant political (anti-communist) motivation, for the purpose of creating a kind of combat unit based on spiritual motivation, guru-disciple relationship and a religio-political doctrine. Ananda Marga is said to have been involved in terrorist and criminal activities but also in social work. From this perspective, the Unification Church can be understood as a political theology of the 38th parallel, but the religious motivation seems to be dominant, with the political aspect remaining only one among several strands. Nevertheless Moonies have been used for "We love Nixon" demonstrations and CAUSA is at present very active under Korean leadership in Latin America. Here the problem of NRMs coincides with that of militant fundamentalist forms of religion.

A strong dualism underlies the Unification doctrine and evil is identified in political terms. Such a concept seems to appeal to people who want to devote themselves to a holy cause and feel the need for a clear-cut black/white contrast of good and evil. An interesting classification[6] distinguishes between "integrative" religion, appealing to the conservative personality type that feels threatened by (Durkheim's) anomie, and "transformative" religion, appealing to the liberal personality type that suffers from a feeling of (Marx's) alienation. This classification coincides to some extent with the distinction between dualistic and monistic religions and between NRMs on the borderline between religion and politics and between religion and psychology. It can also serve to obtain a more specific picture of predisposition and susceptibility to NRMs.

It is interesting to note that the Hare Krishna movement too has a political, or at least a societal, doctrine. It aims at transforming Western society into a caste or, to be more precise, a varna society based on merit and spiritual qualification. The ISKCON, as well as Ananda Marga, is organized as a monastic order with lay members and requires a high degree of commitment, like the Unification Church. These movements have no clients. Such a blend of monastic discipline and religio-political commitment may account at least partially for the potential of conflict inherent in them. In conclusion one can say that the term NRM covers a far greater variety of organizational structures and individual commitments than is usually realized.

## Attitude towards Christianity and religious pluralism

A number of NRMs are assuming a competitive attitude towards Christianity and other religions, and aim at conversion, which usually results in the convert leaving the church. Other movements are claiming a complementary function. TM, for instance, presents its meditation technique as a means to deepen the realization of God within the churches, although its attitude towards Christianity is in fact quite negative. On the whole NRMs demonstrate a high awareness of religious pluralism and at the same time present themselves as a unique way of overcoming it by harmonizing and unifying denominational and religious divisions and diversities. Indian movements would of course rely to some extent on the well-known neo-vedantic concept of religious unity as expounded by Swami Vivekananda. This concept is still prevalent in the Ramakrishna movement and the Sivananda tradition. In modern guru movements this inclusive attitude is often combined with exclusive claims on behalf of the guru and/or a specific meditation technique. Where a guru is supposed to embody in some way the highest state of consciousness encompassing the whole range of the religious experience of humankind, the neo-vedantic conception of religious unity, even when emphatically confessed, takes on a different shape. The Sadgurus of the Radhasoami tradition will concede that Jesus was also a master, but only during his life-time, so that Christians would need to be initiated by the present master if they wanted to attain the highest level of god-realization. More important is the inflationary use of the Avatara concept. Many gurus lay claim to an avataric function, and Sathya Sai Baba[7] is even conceived of as an Avatarin on the same level as Krishna, i.e. as sending Avataras into "incarnation". In this sense John 3:16 is applied to him: "Sathya Sai Baba so loved the world that he sent a son, Jesus Christ, into the world..." All these different notions are meant to deny the finality of Christ and make him appear a religious figure of the past, superseded by the new Guru-Avatara or Living Master. Modern guru movements with such a Guru-Avatara at the centre represent a post-Christian type of Hinduism.

Among conservative Hindu nationalists two differing conceptions of Hinduism's world mission are prevalent.[8] The concept of "Vedantization of religions" relies on Vivekananda and aims at the "co-existence of all religions side by side... This brotherhood is promoted by the acceptance of Vedanta by the intelligent and forward members of all religious communities." According to this notion the primary function of guru movements in the West seems not to be conversion as such, but rather acceptance of Vedanta as unifying philosophy *within* the existing religious communities. The concept of "aryanization of the world" implies that Hinduism should become a universal, proselytizing faith but the goal of its "mission", as it is called, would be "to evolve such a social set-up wherein each and every human being can reach this Summum Bonum of human life". What is meant is the introduction of the varna system throughout the world, the Sannyasin being the supreme ideal on the top of the pyramid of society. Obviously the Hare Krishna movement is committed to the concept of aryanization whereas the concept of Vedantization may be the guiding principle of Neo-Hindu movements like Vedanta societies and the Sivananda tradition. There is a considerable gap between such goals and the small size and strength of Hindu movements in the West. Nevertheless, it should not be overlooked that the final goals go far beyond winning some converts for individual gurus.

It should be noted in passing that the image of Jesus in most Hindu movements in the West is becoming more and more influenced by the apocryphal gospels of the twentieth century such as G.J.R. Ouseley's "Gospel of the Holy Twelve", also known as the "Gospel of Perfect Life", Levi H. Dowling's "Aquarian Gospel", E.B. Szekely's "Gospel of Peace" and Nikolaus Notovitch's "Unknown Life of Jesus Christ". These "gospels" depict Jesus as a vegetarian who brought his message from India where he travelled before taking up his public ministry, and that he did not die on the cross but of old age in Srinagar/Kashmir. This picture represents a blend of theosophical and Ahmadiyya notions.

In spite of its quite different doctrine, the Unification Church and its attitude towards Christianity and religious pluralism come close to those of the guru movements led by a guru-avatara. For reasons which need not be explained here Jesus is said to have been superseded by the Lord of the Second Advent from Korea. The original name "Holy Spirit Association for the Unification of World Christianity" indicates even more clearly the significance attached to overcoming religious dissension within Christianity. That even the great world religions outside Christianity are encompassed in this task has become more evident since the publication of a new version of the Divine Principle for Muslims, with Qur'anic quotations and a special chapter on the role of Islam.

Both the inclusive attitude and the exclusive claims have led the Unification Church and some Hindu movements to maintain a "WCC" of their own. The Unification Church has established a "Council for the World's Religions" willing to "assist believers who wish to examine the roots of the diversities and divisions within their own communities" and "to facilitate 'ecumenical movements' within all the world's religions"(!). A number of "intra-religious" conferences and "interfaith assemblies" in different continents are planned, culminating in the "celebration of the Centenary of the World Parliament of Religions held in Chicago in 1893" (where the whole process started). It is difficult to ascertain how closely these activities are related to the task of CAUSA to bring about an anti-communist front based on the concept of "Godism". Godism plays an important part in the quasi-ecumenical activities of New Era as well as in the political involvement of CAUSA.

On a smaller scale different Radhasoami groups and the "Brahma Kumaris World Spiritual University" are sponsoring similar international conferences in India and in the West. All these movements propagate what may be termed a "monocentric ecumenism", putting themselves into the centre and as satellites inviting others to gather around them and to share what they claim to be the inner secret of all religions. The Indian movements claim that in the beginning of all religions was the Vedantic experience of oneness or the Yoga of Sound and Light or Transcendental Meditation..., whereas in the Unification doctrine the unification of all religious traditions is rather a part of the final consummation of God's plan to restore humankind. Many participants of inter-religious conferences sponsored by NRMs seem to be quite unaware of the problems involved in this type of monocentric ecumenism.

It seems that the quest for religious unity is more than just an appendix on the agenda of NRMs. It is of course also part of their strategy to buy respectability and legitimation (and it costs them a great deal of money). But the present religious situation is highlighted by the fact that NRMs centred around a new messiah or avatara are expected to bring about religious unity and thus succeed where others have seemed to fail.

NOTES

[1] *Getting Saved from the Sixties*, University of California Press, 1982.
[2] See e.g. R. Stark & W.S. Bainbridge, *The Future of Religion*, University of California Press, 1985, esp. pp.19-37.

[3] For a detailed analysis of the origin, history and surrounding Western milieu of Hindu movements in the West, see R. Hummel, *Indische Mission und neue Froemmigkeit im Westen*, Kohlhammer, 1980.

[4] R. Stark & W.S. Bainbridge, *op. cit.*, *passim*.

[5] For a detailed analysis of the Bhagwan Movement, see R. Hummel & B. Hardin, "Asiatic Religions in Europe", in *Concilium*, No. 1, 1983, pp.23-28.

[6] B. Hargrove in J. Needleman & G. Baker, *Understanding the New Religions*, Seabury Press, 1978, pp.257-266.

[7] R. Hummel, "Guru, Miracle Worker, Religious Founder: Sathya Sai Baba", in *Update*, a quarterly journal on new religious movements, Vol. 9, No. 3, 1985, pp.8-19.

[8] The quotations are from different articles in *Hindu Vishva*, the magazine of the Vishva Hindu Parishad. See R. Hummel, *Gurus in Ost und West*, Quell Verlag, 1984, pp.98-103.

# The New Religious Situation in Japan

## SHINJI KANAI

Recently there has been increasing discussion about the "neo-new religions" in Japan, expressive of a remarkable new religious situation in contemporary Japanese society. Although the term "neo-new religion" has not yet found general acceptance, the existence of the new situation as such is widely acknowledged among scholars. This essay will only sketch the trend, giving two examples characteristic of a rising new spiritualism. Some considerations concerning the possible impact of this new spiritualism on Japanese Christianity will also be developed.

I

To gain a more accurate understanding of this trend, it would be helpful to have an overview of the recent history of new religions in post-war Japan. This may be seen as part of a historical process consisting of three stages: the birth of new religions (1945-50), their growth (1951-72), and their institutionalization (1973-).

The stage of the birth of new religions was described by an American scholar, MacFarland, in the famous catch-phrase "rush hour of the gods". The reference is to the time in the morning when people rush to get to work and create congestion in the heart of the city. It symbolized the national post-war endeavour to overcome the many hardships following the war and defeat. Numerous gods mushroomed after the rain of bombs. But why "new" gods? Were not the many traditional religions adequate to console and encourage the people in their suffering? A keen observer answered this question by pointing to the spiritual vacuum in Japan caused by the fact that Shinto, with its connection to the Emperor, had lost credibility with the defeat; Buddhism had not been a vital religion for a long time and Christianity was still a religion that many people were unable to turn to, particularly since defeat had been at the hands of so-called Christian countries.

The second stage is the period of "rapid growth" of the new religions. During the two decades between 1951 and 1972 Japanese economy had expanded enormously because of the rapid industrialization of the country. There is a striking correspondence between the growth of the economy and the new religions. Another factor for the unexpected success of the new religions was the intensive urbanization caused by industrialization. Shinto and Buddhism suffered enormous losses. Rural community ties (on which Shinto rested) and rural family ties (on which Buddhist ancestral veneration rested) were seriously damaged. In the urban areas there were great floating masses of city workers, part of a "lonely crowd" (Riesman) who sought to quench their spiritual thirst by turning to the new religions.

Thus, many new religions propagated themselves very aggressively and with considerable success during this period, despite occasional critical campaigns in the media. Their main sales pitch centred round the practical benefits which would release humanity from the three evils of daily life, namely: poverty, illness and conflict.

The third stage saw a broad change in the character of what became the mainline new religious groups. Their numerical growth had stopped. They now seemed established, with relative stability in their organization, finance and membership. Aggressive campaigns were no longer the order, and the fundamentalist orientation, including a strong magical worldview, became much weaker. These were symptoms of a period of institutionalization, though seen clearly only among the largest groups.

This was a process of "rationalization", or of *Entzauberung* in Weberian terms, and clearly a very natural and rather inevitable development of the new religions towards acceptance in a modernized society. It is where the so-called neo-new religions with forbidden "irrational" traits make their appearance and where we can see a parallel process.

Notable changes occurred in the period from about 1973 to the present. This period has been characterized by catch-words such as "post-modern society" and in regard to the new religious elements by terms such as "religious boom", "resurgent occultism". In any case, a certain fundamental tendency appeared which is more or less antithetical to the thrusts of modernizing rationalism. And just in this situation, some religions began to expand rapidly. We call these newer religions neo-new religions.

Scholarly research into this newer religious situation is only just beginning. At present there is a hypothetical classification of neo-new religions into two categories: the sectarian type with strong eschatological and fundamentalist assertions, and the cultic type of mysticism based on magic. However, this classification is incomplete, since the largest of these neo-new religions, Shin-nyo En, does not fit into either; it includes characteristics of both categories. Scholars are also uncertain as to the number of these neo-new religions and have only identified about eight to ten of them so far.

II

Let us now examine one of the most remarkable of these neo-new religions, Shin-nyo En, because it is typical of a new spiritualism. Shin-nyo En (literally, the garden of the truth of Buddha) claims to be a development of esoteric Buddhism in Japan. Throughout this group's history, it has stressed a fervent loyalty to esoteric Buddhist traditions. According to Shin-nyo En's self-definition it has six main distinctive features:

1. Shin-nyo En is a lay Buddhist group, but it does not disregard the traditional ascetic practices of priestly Buddhism.
2. The group relies mainly on the Nirvana-Sutra. This Buddhist Sutra contains the last sermon of the Buddha, as well as the stress on the miraculous power of the Buddha.
3. The principal Buddha image sacred to the group is that of the reclining Buddha about to enter his eternal nirvana. This Buddha image was carved by the founder of Shin-nyo En, Shinjo Ito, himself.
4. The sufferings of group members caused by karma and fate will be borne substitutionally by the founder's two sons who are dead and now live in the spiritual world.
5. The group is encouraged to accept and to lead all people in the world, and this unrestricted Buddhist love is guided by the founder's dead wife, Shoju-In. This love is now directed especially towards all other religions. Shin-nyo En seeks peaceful relations with all religions.
6. The members practise daily spiritual training called "heart to heart training" through which they seek to acquire a perfect and peaceful state of mind, identified with nirvana.

The basic thought of Shin-nyo En is rather orthodox, seen in the context of Japanese traditions, and its strong devotion to the founder and his family is not unique. There are many similarities between this and other new religions. Shin-nyo En's uniqueness and novelty lie in its well organized spiritual training, and it is undoubtedly this spiritual practice which is so attractive to many. Through it anyone can attain the power not only to contact spirits and their world but also, at least in principle, to reach the level of Buddha himself. What deserves further attention is the fact that members are said to receive reasonable and safe advice from the spiritual world.

Extreme actions and procedures are reproved. Reasonableness and security are said to be guaranteed as long as the ideal of Rita (caring for the welfare of others) is firmly upheld, while the extreme search for something miraculous is considered to be egocentric.

The crucial factor in the explosive growth of Shin-nyo En (it has a membership of 2,100,000 with about 500 spiritual practitioners) is the successful combination of the old (tenet) and the new (form). This explosion is not only due to general social circumstances of the post-modern society but also to the religious-historical fact that Shin-nyo En has found a new way to express the traditional Buddhist faith.

Let us now turn from Shin-nyo En to GLA (God Light Association), and examine an even more unabashedly occultic religiosity. GLA has about 14,000 members and represents a recent cultic tendency especially among younger people. It is difficult to characterize this in a few words because it is a combination of many elements and includes the esoteric Buddhist ideal of obtaining super-human power, various forms of divination of Chinese origin, prophecies from medieval Europe, methods of mental and physical training and healing associated with Yoga, Jungian psychoanalysis, UFO phenomena, transcendental meditation, and so on. GLA could be described as "a new spiritualism". It is a typical example of this trend, but its appropriation of these diverse elements is not arbitrary. GLA seems to have two main poles, derived respectively from Buddhism and Christianity. It is a unique combination of the Buddhist teaching of the transmigration of the human soul and the Christian concept of the apocalyptic new age and the heavenly mission of angels. The founder of this group, Shinji Takahashi, once had inner contact with a powerful spirit named "One-Two-Three" (called "Moses" in 1300 BC Egypt). He was then visited by another much more powerful spirit named "Phuan-Shin-Phuai-Shinpho" (called "Jesus" in the first century in Palestine). These two great spirits seemed to have been critical of present-day Christianity and that was why they used new names rather than their historical ones. But the more decisive experience was the encounter with

Bosatsu, who is one of the messianic forms of Buddha. Since this experience, Shinji Takahashi's religious thoughts have been expressed chiefly in Buddhist terminology.

The tenets of the group are not complicated and can be summarized as follows: to awaken to the true self which is living now in this body, and which in its essence has a Body of Light. This Body of Light is a symbolic expression of a state of mind which feels itself in ultimate accord with universal truth. To accomplish this, angels have constant contact with human individuals. The chief angel, Michael, is said to have descended upon the founder's daughter Nobuko, to entrust her with a new dispensation and to authorize her as the genuine successor of the founder.

From this brief summary we can see that GLA tends towards syncretism. This is also a basic characteristic of many new Japanese religions.

### III

Let me briefly comment on the problems facing Christianity in view of this new spiritualism. Christians should not simply adopt or imitate the spiritual training or thinking of these neo-new religions. But it may be beneficial and indeed necessary to be stimulated by them in order to cope with the emotional and spiritual needs of our time. If there is a general search or need for spirituality Christians should attempt to meet this. In fact, this newer spiritualism seems to be urging Christians to think anew about Christian spirituality as such.

Firstly, let us observe some of the basic characteristics of this new spiritualism more closely, and see it as a new challenge to contemporary Christianity. We could say that it is a response to the "spiritual" needs of the age. This becomes clear when we contrast this spiritualism with the "former" new religions which were oriented very strongly towards more physical needs such as relief from poverty and illness. The new spiritualism, on the other hand, is a phenomenon occurring in the relatively affluent post-modern society and reflects the need for the freedom of the human spirit from a technologically and rationally controlled society. It is a quest for human possibilities. It must be pointed out that there may be a tendency to manipulate or utilize spirits for this worldly happiness and success at the mass level and this has led some observers to point to a kind of "magicalization" of religion.

The reactions of Japanese Christianity to this new spiritualism appear to be generally negative. Japanese Christianity as a whole seems to be ill-prepared to accept the challenge, although not without reason. The historical churches have recognized the crucial importance of inner spirituality as a matter of course, and have devoted great care towards cultivating it. But attempts at direct contact with spirits have generally been avoided, even prohibited, not only as improper but as dangerous. There are two main criteria for this. One criterion can be called confessional-dogmatic. On the basis of this criterion Christians tend to see the new spiritualism simply as a renewal of old heretical ways. All so-called spiritualism in Christian history, from Gnosticism in the New Testament period, through the diverse trends of spiritualists of medieval and modern times up to the new spiritualism of today, are seen as more or less false insofar as they seek more than what is permitted and authorized in the confessions and dogmas of the historical churches. More simply, they are false because they are the attempts of an arbitrary and human-centred spirit. The other criterion is historical-rational. Here we have such well-known dichotomies as pre-modern vs. modern and rational vs. irrational. From this point of view the various types of this new spiritualism seem to appeal to the pre-modern or irrational in people's minds. For the modernists, on the contrary, religions, if they are acknowledged at all, are better to be moralized and thus rationalized. Other religious forms such as this new spiritualism are only passing anachronistic phenomena which will surely be overcome in the course of history.

These two views are held so strongly that they may be said to be representative, at least to some degree, of almost all Christian groups and churches. Japanese Christianity is no exception.

In my view, Christians should maintain a flexible attitude to the new spiritualism of today. They can and must accept it as a challenge of postmodern human existence. This challenge raises two questions: in regard to the confessional-dogmatic criterion, is it enough merely to adhere to the historically formed confessions and dogmas, without renewing them through the living experience of faith? Or, more forcefully, does dogma save humanity? And in regard to the historical-rational criterion, is it enough to think of religiosity only in a historical-rational framework? Or can human religiosity be meaningfully categorized by the dichotomies such as premodern-modern and rational-irrational?

We think that the insights of historical churches are right insofar as they insist upon a kind of "certainty" of the historical churches against the "uncertainty" of numerous adventures of faith by historical spiritualisms. But this certainty can also become stereotyped and fossilized. It is possible that the certainty of the churches guarantees only their traditions and conventions but it should be a "mellow certainty" (P. Berger), enabling Christians to think and behave more flexibly in a changing world. Turning to the Bible with this renewed flexibility, one finds there, as it were, a biblical spiritualism. It was assuredly in this framework that Jesus drove out the evil spirits and Paul was caught up into the third heaven. This spiritualism has much in common with the historical spiritualism of the past and also with many contemporary spiritualisms, to the extent that they share the same religious mould, i.e. contact with spirits and their world.

The crucial question thus arises as to why the historical churches could not/did not retain or develop this fundamental element in Christian faith. The new spiritualism in contemporary Japan seems to demand that Christians in the modern world look afresh at this historical issue and that they reflect both on the legitimacy and the limitations of the two criteria.

# Part II:

# Some Aspects of
# New Religious Movements

# The World-view / Cosmology of the New Religious Movements

## JOHANNES AAGAARD

### Introduction

The theme implies that responsible generalizations are possible within this field to such an extent that common denominators are found for the whole field of new religious movements (NRMs). This is, however, hardly the case. The field of NRMs is so wide and includes such varied religious phenomena that it would be artificial to put forward a thesis which presupposes a common ground for all of these movements.

On the other hand, very many such movements do in fact operate on a basis of common cosmological assumptions, and it is my intention to describe, analyze, and interpret these assumptions. The movements which I will thus include are in many ways the most important ones, since my presentation will deal with those movements which have a Hindu-base or have their base in Buddhism. [1]

As the presentation will prove, such movements themselves point to the field of yogic ideology and practice as the most decisive ground for their conceptualizations. The yogic way of life is found at the bottom of all these movements, be they Hindu, Buddhist or generally occult in their self-presentation. I shall aim at penetrating the deep meaning of the yogic universe/cosmos, and I venture the hypothesis that this yogic cosmos is the fertile ground in which most of the new religious movements grow today. [2]

The yogic cosmos, however, is characterized by the important role the elements and the chakras play as expressions of the macro-cosmic and micro-cosmic reality respectively. In the different cosmological projects, which characterize the new religious movements, there is a common structure, a psycho-cosmogram, in which the elements and the chakras and many other secondary symbolizations related to the elements and the chakras are the determining factors. These elements and chakras are not just concepts and ideas. They are interpreted as powers of influence for human mental direction and psychic manipulation.[3] In the yogic world-view the elements and the chakras have become interior realities, whereby the exterior world is mastered and manipulated.

The modern worldwide yoga movement is probably one of the most decisive international movements of today. While 15-20 years ago the proliferation of Marxist or at any rate leftist "cells" could be seen as the decisive and most influential phenomenon among youth internationally, today the proliferation of yoga classes and meditational groups could be seen as the most interesting and challenging feature.

These yoga activities engage millions of people in all parts of the world, not just for relaxation purposes, which they may advertise, but with clearly religious aims and means. At the bottom of all or nearly all such activities one finds a more or less clearcut edition of the general cosmology which will be described in this presentation. The participants in the yoga classes may not know that all yoga is taught in the name of some yogi and on the basis of his instructions. They may also be ignorant of the fact that the yogic exercises *nolens volens* put them under the influence of this or that yoga tradition and make them objects of a yogic ideology which is taken into their bodies directly as the result of the various psychosomatic exercises.

The clarification of the ultimate meaning of such exercises may be reserved for a few "illuminati", but the yogic worldview/cosmology will gradually become part of the life-style of the participants.[4]

To an important extent the same observations are valid concerning the worldwide movement called alternative medicine or healing. Within this very manifold movement it is easy to localize and define yogic presuppositions. It is a fact that very many healers in the contemporary world are in fact operating on the basis of a worldview/cosmology which is deeply rooted in the Hindu- Buddhist-occult understanding. The analogical operations of elements and chakras constitute the frame of reference for many, maybe most of the healers of today's world.

Thereby again an important reason for the change in the general worldview of humankind is pointed out. Even if most of the believers in alternative medicine will remain in the churches or remain agnostics or atheists, the simple fact of their participation in the healing sessions and the growth-seminars does mean a gradual change of their outlook. The new elements of that outlook are the same elements as are operative in the NRMs in general.

It is thus my hope in this presentation to analyze the main pattern of the worldview which is basic to the NRMs in general and at the same time is decisive for the wider change in the international general worldview, which is coming into existence by means of yogic manipulations and the alternative approaches in healing.

The churches have up till now been able to operate within a sort of Christendom, the cosmological dimensions of which were related to Christianity. The missionary par excellence for this Christendom has been the English language. Simply by expressing oneself in English one expressed a "Christian" worldview. That this has changed has already given new perspectives to the self-understanding of modern people. Now a different type of international language is coming into existence. It is a language marked by occult and esoteric frames of reference and it is highly symbolic. [5]

New religious movements in the general meaning of that term are as a whole expressions of a new development that started in the middle of the last century, when the liberal movements brought forward new ideas of freedom of religion. Even if the freedom guaranteed in the new liberal constitutions generally helped develop the variety of Christian denominations and provided for freedom from religion, it was not long before the new ways of relating to the Eastern/Oriental world came to have important consequences in the former world of Christendom.

### The theosophical movement

The first or most important agent in this transmission of the Light from the East (*Ex Oriente Lux*) was the theosophical movement. It is easy today to underestimate the historical importance of Theosophy for the meeting between East and West, which today has created the possibilities for a world community in which all religions on equal terms can present their messages to the whole of humankind.

I therefore "take off" from the wide field of Theosophy, and I have chosen Charles Leadbeater (1847 [or 1854]-1934), known as "Bishop Leadbeater", as the spokesman. He was "the second" to Annie Besant, who again was the successor to the founding mother of Theosophy, Madame Blavatsky, who together with her "second", "Colonel Olcott", was the inventor of Theosophy. Among his many books the monograph *The Chakras* is an excellent guide to theosophical cosmology and ideology in general. This volume has been published in large numbers and is extremely influential even today in many parts of the world. Leadbeater represents Theosophy in a very wide sense. His reflections have had a great influence on the various trends of Theosophy today and on the New Age Movement in general. [6]

Leadbeater states thus the general principle of a psycho-cosmogram in the theosophical meaning of the word:[7]

> Each chakra is considered to be especially connected with one of the elements earth, water, fire, air, ether and mind. These elements are to be regarded as states of matter, not elements as we understand them in modern chemistry. They are thus equivalent to the terms solid, liquid, fiery or gaseous, airy and etheric and are somewhat analogous to our subplanes and planes — physical, astral, mental, etc. [8]

The "system" is strictly hierarchical. The world as the macro-cosmos and the body as the micro-cosmos have come into existence from above as an emanation of divinity into matter, and the liberation from human existence as matter caught in "time, space and causality" has to take place as a reversal — from below and upwards, moving from level to level, from chakra and element to the next and higher stage.

This "system" or cosmogram is intimately connected with the theosophical "system" of bodies, for the chakras are seen as points of connection at which energy flows from one body to another body.[9] "Man is a soul and owns a body — several bodies in fact."[10] It is important to notice that humankind has a body, but is a soul. Bodies are secondary and preliminary for humankind. But it is not as simple as it used to be in classical dualistic thinking, when soul and body simply had to be disengaged and soul (*Purusha*) had to get away from matter (*Prkriti*). There are several bodies — and the liberation takes place both from these bodies and by means of these bodies.

First of all humankind has "the etheric double",[11] through which the streams of vitality or energy flow, thereby keeping us alive and making the use of the brain possible. "The etheric double" is the bridge from the physical body to the astral body. It is important to notice that the chakras are found in this etheric body which is invisible, but can still be seen by clairvoyance. They are "saucerlike depressions or vortices on the surface of the etheric double".[12] They normally glow dully, but when awakened and vivified they are seen as blazing whirlpools, much increased in size and resembling miniature suns.

The Energy/the Force/the Primary Force/the Serpent Power is the life-stream, which enters our world from somewhere. It enters into the individual through "the open mouth" of each chakra. This Force is in itself sevenfold — like the colours of the rainbow, to which it corresponds. That is why the rainbow is the predominant symbol within the New Age culture. The seven rays of the Force operate in all seven forms in all seven chakras, whereby the inrush of the energy of life is made possible, according to Leadbeater. [13]

Theosophy operates within various frameworks, one of them being theosophical freemasonry, in which the theosophical fascination of ritual-initiation is manifested in a number of interesting ways.

In his *The Hidden Life of Freemasonry* [14] Leadbeater revealed some of the inner processes of this sort of freemasonry. We shall especially present his way of dealing with the elements.

In the chapter called "The Three Symbolic Journeys" we are presented with a series of imaginations, but in the form of initiations: "There are three portals or doorways, through which the candidate must pass. They are invisible to the physical eye, but nevertheless perfectly real, because they are made by thought." [15]

Through the first door one passes out of the physical world body into the lowest part of the astral plane body, and here the candidate is reminded of the fear, hatred, malice or revenge which is the result of the former life. The person has to recognize his or her bondage.

At the second portal the candidate is introduced to the elements of earth and water. Turning to the north he or she makes an offering to the earth elementals, and turning to the south, makes a similar offering to the elementals of the water. The nature-spirits thus pacified continue as his or her body-guard on the further journey. But if the candidate clings to the order of matter and will not give water to water and earth to earth, he or she cannot continue on the spiritual journey. But if one is ready to shake off matter from one's astral body, one can pass on to the higher levels.

At the third portal one is introduced to the elementals of the air and to the elementals of the fire, turning east and west respectively. Once more one gives to the elementals what belongs to them, and can then pass through as their friend. The giving up of all matter means to purify the astral body. Somehow the offering to the elementals of the four elements is also a worship offered to the Devas of the N.S.E. and W. plus to the zenith and to the nadir (which is the opposite of zenith), and to the centre, all in all seven orders.

The ritual takes place in the Masonic temple, and it is in fact another version of the "Book of the Dead", for being trained ritually beforehand, while still alive, the mason can, when in fact he or she has to go through the three portals after death, rapidly pass into the heaven-world.

It is important to notice that this ritual presupposes worship of factual Devas, or Devarajas, who are the four Rulers of the Elements, "the great

Rulers... who are the agents of the Law of Karma, which is always balancing and adjusting the affairs of man". [16]

These Powers can be appealed to only by the rightly initiating officials, who are the guardians of the candidates. But when appealed to in the right manner the Powers, who are also called Angels, can give support, for in this way "all the forces of the various planes are at the disposal at the right time". [17]

## The psycho-cosmogram of anthroposophy

Rudolph Steiner (1861-1925) was the general secretary of the German theosophical movement for a number of years, but he went his own way and created anthroposophy as an alternative to theosophy. He was also the inspiration behind the creation of "The Christian Community" (*Christengemeinschaft*), which is the church of anthroposophy, in spite of the fact that most anthroposophists are not members of this church. Steiner is today one of the most influential thinkers in the New Age Movement in general. His thought is operative far beyond the limits of the many Steiner institutions.

Steiner's most important book is probably his *Die Philosophie der Freiheit* (1894). But in the context of this analysis his fascinating book, *How to Attain Knowledge of the Higher Worlds, the Way of Initiation*, is more helpful. It is analogical to what we have already seen in Leadbeater. [18]

Steiner's main interest seems to be to reach that sort of knowledge which goes beyond the senses. Only by means of clairvoyance can knowledge in the true meaning become possible. Those who reach this sort of knowing are few, but they can communicate to others who do not have that ability.

In order to reach occult knowledge, i.e. knowledge beyond the senses, one has to go through a rather complicated schooling. Steiner describes a number of trials connected — similar to Leadbeater — with the elements. Steiner describes the fire-trial, the water-trial, the air-trial, whereby the candidate is tested and tried and trained in order to secure genuine occult insights. Only after such trials can the candidate enter "the Temple of Higher Wisdom". [19]

Upon arrival in that temple the candidate is served "the draught of forgetfulness", so that he or she is liberated from the veil of memory. After that the person is served "the draught of remembrance" whereby one can keep the higher secrets in one's soul in such a way that they can become part of oneself, whereby one breathes and sees with the soul and hears and speaks with the spirit, i.e., gets knowledge beyond the senses.

This being the initiation, Steiner also describes the ways and means of the training. This again takes the candidates to the manipulation of the chakras.

In order to understand these techniques one again has to remember the nature of the occult bodies. Apart from the physical body one can develop an etheric and an astral body. The etheric double is — as in theosophy — a bridge between the physical and the astral body, more or less of the same size as the physical body, while the astral body is much larger and penetrates both the other bodies.

The main part of the training seems to consist in moving the etheric body by moving the chakras, which are seen as organs of the etheric body. So by moving the organs one moves the body itself. How to do this is not explained, probably because it is part of the oral instructions. But somehow yogic exercises are presupposed, i.e. exercises in meditation and concentration, whereby the etheric body is moved in all directions. [20]

The Steiner understanding of the chakras is of special importance, for the movements of these chakras determine the movements of the etheric body, which is the bridge between the physical and the astral world. The wider influence of anthroposophy is therefore also determined by this understanding of the chakras. From the movements of the chakras the colours of the human aura are developed, depending on the speed of each chakra. By deciphering the colours by clairvoyance one can see what chakra suffers in which way, and healing can be sought for accordingly. The healing process seems to depend on the ability of the lotuses/chakras to open up for the influences from the astral world and mediate this influence via the etheric body to the physical body.

Steiner's understanding of the chakras is by himself referred back to the Buddha. It is quite clear, however, that he — as was the case with Leadbeater — in fact is dependent on the traditional hatha-yogic texts from about 1500 years after the Buddha. The various abilities or powers (*siddhies*) which Steiner wants to promote by means of his manipulations are simply his version of the traditional hatha-yogic quest for supernatural powers.

The chakras, as Steiner sees them, are identical with the classical hatha-yogic "lotuses". Steiner's chakras have respectively 4, 6, 8, 10, 12, 16 and 2 "leaves", similar to the Hatha-yogic understanding. We cannot go into detail, but remembering the hesitation of Leadbeater concerning the "sex-chakra", it is interesting to note that Steiner in a similar way tones down the nature of the second chakra. He does not mention its sexual nature, but underlines the necessity of finding a balance between the sensual and the spiritual ability of the human being in order "to allow for sensuality". He mainly emphasizes that by developing this chakra one reaches contact with powers of the higher worlds, that aim which is explicitly the name of the whole book. This centre, therefore, must have a priority in Steiner's system.

At the other end of the spine, the last chakra — with two "leaves" — seems to comprise both the eye-chakra and the final chakra, and thereby one reaches contact with spiritual entities. The means for that is "the inner light" which is developed in that chakra. This is considered a real new birth, not symbolically, but in fact. Only when this happens will concepts like karma and reincarnation become experiential realities, and now contact with the Great Initiates, the Spiritual Masters will become a personal experience.

## The psycho-cosmogram of yoga

We have seen that both Leadbeater and Steiner draw on the insight of yoga, and this is so with many other occult masters from the earlier generations. Yoga is not simply yogic exercises but is first of all a total cosmological interpretation of life in this universe. As such yoga has become the basis of nearly all New Age groups and therefore of most of the new religious movements of this time.

We therefore need to have a look at the operative issues of yoga. We shall begin with classical yoga, the so-called Raja-yoga.

Patanjali's Yogasutra with Vyasa's commentary has had a decisive influence on all yoga, probably for between 1500 and 2000 years. The cosmological basis of the Yogasutra therefore is of fundamental importance for our theme. This sort of yoga is generally called Raja-yoga. [21]

In the commentary to III, 43 of the Yogasutra this conclusion is drawn:

> Now from the Samyama (which is the term used for the three highest levels of the eight-step ladder of Raja-yoga) upon the appearance which exist in these five elements... the yogi, after conquering the appearance of the five elements, becomes the Master of the elements. On account of that mastery, the elemental powers become subordinate to his will like the cows following their own calves.

One should notice here that the basis of yoga is the mastery of the elements. Their appearance has to be "conquered" or mastered, in order that the elemental powers in the elements can become subordinate.

The commentary to III, 44 runs like this:

> The mastery... means that he (the yogi) becomes possessed of control over all the elements and elemental powers and is not subject to control by others. The creative Power... means that creation, destruction and aggregation all depend upon his will... As he wills, so becomes the position of the elemental powers... the earth does not resist the working of the yogi's body by its hardness; he can pass even through a stone. The sticky water does not wet him. The hot fire does not burn him. The air in motion does not carry him. His body becomes concealed even within the coverless ether and he becomes invisible even to the Sidhas (perfect beings).

One should notice here how precisely the magic dream of mastery over all the elements is expressed. One is immediately reminded of scientology and its dream of becoming superhuman operating thetans, who can operate with pan-determination. But the same magic dream is expressed in the Sidha Transcendental Meditation, which promises its candidates the same total power over the elements. In the development of such powers TM does in fact use verses from the Yogasutra as auto-suggestive means.

This main line from Raja-yoga is taken to its consequences in Hatha-yoga, probably some few hundred years after Raja-yoga was presented. The Hatha-yogic texts are at any rate from the high Middle Ages. [22]

Hatha-yoga has developed a know-how for the older Raja-yoga, but the two ways of yoga are not essentially different from each other. To separate Hatha-yoga from Raja-yoga, as is often done in these days by apologetic Hatha-yogis, is quite meaningless. The Hatha-yoga first of all aims at developing techniques for achieving the mastery over the elements, similar to the Raja-yogic aim.

In *Shiva Samhita* the emphasis is on "the five-fold dharana forms of concentration on Vishnu, by which the command over the five elements is obtained (III, 63). This is done by concentrating successively on the chakras. Thereby the elements cease to cause harm to the great Yogi" (III, 64). When the yogi in this way "conquers the six wheels", i.e. the chakras, the person conquers "all elements and the elementals" (III, 78) and in fact also conquers suffering and death of "this body".

### "This body" as the egg of Brahma

In order to understand what "the five-fold dharana" implies we will take a look at the cosmological dimensions in which the yogic enterprise understands itself.

In its first chapter *Shiva Samhita* demonstrates the nature of cosmos, all the manifold elements and powers which constitute the universe of human beings and all other beings. In the second chapter, *Shiva Samhita* puts forward the fundamental idea that the great cosmos manifests itself in the little cosmos of the body. In the little body ("this body") everything which is found in the great body (the cosmos) is at hand. [23]

"This body" is often called "the egg of Brahma", an expression with important connotations. In *Shiva Samhita* (II, 6f) it is stated: "In this body which is called Brahmanda (microcosm, literally the mundane egg) there is the nectar-rayed moon, in its proper place, on the top of the spinal cord." The various parts of the occult physiology are all found in this microcosmic body, structured by the six chakras as the macrocosmic body is structured by the six elements.

In *Shiva Samhita* (V, 160) one reads: "Let him contemplate on his own reflection in the sky as beyond the Cosmic Egg... Through that let him think on the Great Void unceasingly" — a formulation which reminds the reader of the affinity of Goraknath to the Buddhist teaching of his own master Matsyendranath.

The cosmic egg is a fundamental symbol, for from it the whole cosmos is projected, and to it the whole cosmos will return. All the secrets of the cosmos are therefore revealed in the microcosmos, which is at the same time the macrocosmos *in nuce*. The cosmic egg therefore is of the nature of a mandala. The egg is the mandala of Brahma in which the secrets are deciphered. [24]

A mandala expresses the macro-micro analogy "as above so below", meaning that the order (cosmos) "in heaven" is realized "on earth". In the drawing of the great magician and occultist Eliphas Levi, one reads: *Quod superius (sicut) macroprosophus*, which literally means: "As highest the face for the great, so lowest the face for the little." Interpreted this esoteric key could mean: "The reality which stands forth in the macrocosmic project is analogous to the reality which is found in the microcosmic project in this body." As above, so below means that the infinitely great is reflected in the infinitely small, the stars in the genes, the gods in humankind.

This approach has very definite methodological consequences for the worldview of NRMs. This correlation of the macro- with the micro-reality means that analogical thinking is the obvious way of arguing, when a statement has to be verified or falsified. Logic in this way of thinking is analogic!

This methodology opens up a meaningful interpretation of the quite obscure texts which are the points of reference of many NRMs with their yogic way of interpretation. An example from *Shiva Samhita* can illustrate this analogical way of thinking, the analogy here being that of India as the macrocosmic reality, mirrored in "this body" as the microcosmic base (the following is paraphrased from the beginning of chapter II).

The Sahasrara (the crown chakra) is the Mount Kailash, the abode of Shiva. The spine (Sushumna) is Mount Meru (the *axis mundi*). It is surrounded by seven islands (the seven chakras) and by rivers, seas, mountains, fields (the nadis). In "this body" are also found the lords of the rivers etc., and the stars and the planets are there too. There are shrines and pilgrimages and deities of such shrines and pilgrimages. In "this body" also move the sun and the moon and all the elements: ether, air, fire, water and earth (II, 3).

This body is the promised land, the divine realm, not only found somewhere in the Himalayas, but here and now in the human world. Most important is the analogy which comes to mean that the Ida-"nerve" which takes the moon-fluid of immortality downwards (V, 103 ff.) is Ganga, while Pingala, the opposite "nerve", which takes the sun-fluid of mortality upwards, is Jumna. The secret river, however, is also there, for Saraswati is found in the Sushumna, within the spine. The place where these three holy rivers meet is the Triveni, and it is the most inaccessible one (V, 132-133), but also the most holy spot, the centre of liberation, from which the elixir, the soma, the amrit, the drink of immortality, the fluid of divinization comes into existence.

The aim at this point is only to show how the idea of an operative mandala in the form of a cosmogram/psycho-cosmogram inherent in "this body" can come into existence and give meaning.

Such cosmological speculations are by nature soteriological, i.e. meant for liberating goals. Cosmology is not meant as a description of the cosmos, but as a way whereby cosmos can become a means for liberation. The cosmogram of Brahma's egg, the cosmic egg, is meant to be an instrument for identification, whereby one becomes what one concentrates on. Such a cosmogram is thus a transforming reality, in fact it is a machine (yantra) for divinization. The order of a cosmogram therefore is an *ordo salutis*.

### "This body" as a means for obtaining liberation

In the cosmogram one can integrate many elementals and deities. They will all belong to the same order, but there will be different roles for them to play in the order, and only one of them will be at the centre. The whole "pantheon" will seemingly be quite tolerant and enclose quite different religious trends, but since only one is at the centre, others will of necessity be relegated to the periphery. As such they are still parts of the cosmogram, but defined from the centre. This model should not, however, be interpreted as tolerance! In the first chapter of *Shiva Samhita*, the many ways of liberation are described. They are not accepted—as one should expect—as the many ways to reach the same goal. On the contrary. From I, 4 till 1, 14 the reader is taken to see the many ways as inroads to the delusion of the mind (15-16). The conclusion is in fact quite intolerant: the Yoga Sastra has been found to be the only true and firm doctrine (17), and the necessity of any other doctrines (18).

The only way out of the human dilemma is gnosis/Jnana Kanda (32), for only gnosis can make the difference between reality and unreality clear (I, 57, 58 and II, 54), and thus deliver humankind from the karmic necessity.

The specific understanding of gnosis, which is operative in this occult cosmology, is expressed *in nuce* in *Shiva Samhita* (II, 49): "When this body, obtained through karma, is made the means of obtaining Nirvana (divine beatitude) then only the carrying of the burden of the body becomes fruitful, not otherwise." "This body" is now a means of salvation, while it was — in the classical yoga — the decisive hindrance for salvation. While the body used to be part of the problem, it is now — in Hatha-yoga — part of the solution. The body is still, however, "a burden", not a gift. There is no "holistic" approach in this understanding.

One can interpret this understanding in the following way: The body is the karmic conclusion. Therefore the solution has to begin with the conclusion, from which access to the karmic premises can be had.

*When the idea of this body as the microcosm is combined with the idea of this body as the means of liberation, then the specific ideology of the contemporary NRMs may be found.*

### To master the elements in "this body"

The yoga of Patanjali (in Vyasa's interpretation) shows us the yogi as the master of the elements. By *samyama* on the elements, they are mastered (III, 43 f.). Thereby the yogi gets the elemental powers and achieves control over each and everybody. All depends on his will. He is pan-determining, to use a modern term.

The Hatha-yoga is on the same line. Instead of *samyama*, however, the *Gherand Samhita* emphasizes the dharanas, which means the practice of sense-withdrawal (III, 68 ff. s. 30 f.). That in itself does not make much of a difference between the two schools of yoga.

Before we ask the question about a possible specificum of Hatha-yoga, we must have some insights into the way in which elements in "this body" are manipulated. This is described in *Shiva Samhita* (I, 69 ff.) under the heading "Emanation or Evolution". When this world came into being, Avidya first came out from the Lord's will (I, 69) and this Avidya is the mother of the false universe, the cosmos of illusion.

The emanation then happened like this: From the conjunction of Pure Brahma and Avidya, or Shiva and Shakti came Brahma, from which came Akasha, from which came Air, from which came Fire, from which came Water, from which came Earth. "This is the order of subtle emanation" (I, 71). It is, however, made a little more complicated, for in fact (I, 72) Ether produced Air, but air and ether produced in combination Fire, and the triple compound of ether, air and fire produced Water, and from the fourfold combination of the mentioned elements came Earth.

This system is then combined with the qualities:
— the quality of Ether is sound, perceived through the ear;
— the quality of Air is motion and touch, perceived through the skin;
— the quality of Fire is form, perceived through the eyes;
— the quality of Water is taste, perceived through the tongue;
— the quality of Earth is smell, perceived through the nose.

But again in fact it is more complicated, for Ether has only one quality, namely sound, while Air has the quality of sound and motion and touch, and Fire has all these qualities plus form, and Water all the mentioned qualities plus taste, and finally Earth has all qualities, including its own smell.

This is the case, obviously, also when the elements are seen as the composition of the human body (I, 91). The fivefold combination produces all objects, including human objects. In human objects, however, intelligence is confined by karma, and this intelligence is called a Jiva (I, 93). "All this world is derived from the five elements. And the Jiva is the enjoyer of the fruits of action." Jiva is thus immaterial and is not of the elements, but in them. The task of liberation then is simply to deliver the Jiva from the karmic confinement in the elements. This is the only way out of the samsaric destiny.

Since the coming into being of the world is seen as a horrible and fatal illusion, the liberation from that illusion obviously means the turning of the tide and dissolving the elemental world. While the emanation or evolution of this world began "in heaven" and ended "on earth", the dissolution or devolution obviously must begin "on earth" and aim at "heaven".

Already in *Shiva Samhita* I, 78 the presuppositions for such dissolution are given:
— Earth can become subtle and dissolve in water.
— Water is resolved into fire.
— Fire merges into air.
— Air is absorbed into Ether.
— Ether is resolved in Avidya.
— Avidya merges into the Great Brahma.

As stated already, the Raja-yoga (Patanjali and Vyasa) aimed at conquering the elements and the elementals. The same is the case in Hatha-yoga (III, 78). It is dramatically expressed like this (V, 49):

> Having conquered all the elements, and being void of all hopes and worldly connections... the mind of the Yogi becomes dead and he obtains the spiritual power (siddhi) called Khechari, which means to walk in the air.

Or very explicitly (V, 153):

> By the practice of this Yoga, he gets the power of creating or destroying the creation, this aggregate of elements.

Finally then — at the end of *Shiva Samhita* — comes the real goal of yoga: Total Power in the form of control over persons, dominion over deities, command over the cosmic powers and the acquisition of all supernatural forces (V, 198 ff.).

This end, however, is only reached when the absorption of "the quadruple creation in the Paramathman" is reached (V, 157). This absorption is at the same time the final dissolution, called Laya. The final solution is the final dissolution!

The know-how of this yogic absorption or dissolution is Hatha-yoga. Fundamentally Raja-yoga and Hatha-yoga are the same sort of yoga, having the same goals and the same elementary ideology. But in Hatha-yoga a special emphasis on the technical ways and means is found.

The Hatha-yoga is the putting into practice of the idea that "this body" is the means of liberation. This does not mean, however, that the modern propaganda for yoga is true. Yoga is definitely not just another form for body gymnastics. Yoga is certainly not just a means of relaxation. In fact such statements are bluntly offensive in relation to yoga.

Dharanas — the five dharanas[25] — are the basis of the Hatha-yogic techniques. Dharana means the practice of sense withdrawal. In the texts mentioned the five dharanas mean the five main techniques by which one can get full control and mastery over the elements by manipulating the chakras. Therefore the term "five Dharana-mudras" is also possible.

Eliade underlines the importance of what he names "the physiological materialism of the explanation of the dharana",[26] and in fact the various dharanas are physical manipulations, which as a syndrome exercise pressure on the bodily system in order to stop or reverse its normal functions.

We cannot in this context describe and explain how this Hatha-yogic know-how operates; such detailed instruction is part of the guru's job and consequently is normally not set down on paper. This does not mean that this know-how is much of a secret. Many people have by now tried out this system and have reported the ways and means.[27]

In short the yogic process consists in the reversal of the cosmic evolution/emanation in the form of a well-planned devolution and dissolution. Various yogic techniques such as asanas, brahmacharya, mudras, pranayama, mantra-jap, shakti-pat are used in order to take control over the Force, the Kundalini-power so that it can "regain its lost empire" and gradually rid itself of "the human condition" and achieve divinity.

### The Kundalini-force as the Serpent-power

The possibility of arousing the Kundalini-power is the key to the functional aspect of yoga.[28] Without this perspective it is meaningless to talk or write about yoga and — since yoga is the key to the worldview of the NRMs — to talk or write about NRMs.

The literature about Kundalini is endless, but the heart of the matter is the sexual energy of humankind. The essence of Kundalini-yoga is the transformation of the sexual energy into occult energy. To interpret this approach as another sort of "sublimation" is as far from the real world as it is to interpret brahmacharya as "celibacy". Such analogies simply reveal a total lack of understanding.

The heart of the Kundalini-yoga is semen mystique, which again is the story about the transformation of the male semen into the soma, elixir, amrit, i.e. the drink of immortality and divinization.[29]

The result of all such "energies" is the gigantic power exercised in the "siddhies", the supernatural powers which are both the end of the Patanjali-yoga (Raja-yoga) and of the Hatha-yoga and of many of the NRMs.

Such powers, however, are not the final end of yoga. The final end is divinity for the yogi; it is the final dissolution into the one Parabrahman or Shiva. The relation to the various divinities is an important part of the whole power game, and the attitude to the "gods" and "goddesses" is similar to the attitude to the elementals, in fact a development from that attitude. In both cases it is a matter of mastering them, to make them manageable by means of yogic manipulations. On the way towards the ultimate divinization, the divinities as well as the elementals can be hindrances or they can be assistants in the realization of the divine state. Pacified, they are the most important instruments to one's own ultimate purpose.

## The *religio occulta* as the nature of the NRMs

Even if this presentation has had to limit itself to one perspective of the worldview of the NRMs, it should have become quite clear that there is in fact a common worldview, and a very profiled one, and that this worldview is basically of the nature of cosmological speculation and imagination and manipulation.

It has become a common attitude within the NRMs that all religions are fundamentally similar. The various religions are just so many roads to the same goal. This statement is not obvious to students of the classical religions, but it may be a verifiable statement, if it is taken to be a self-evaluation by the occult Hindus, the occult Buddhists and the occult Christians!

There are good reasons to see a *religio occulta* as the basic reality within the whole field of the NRMs of today. They do to a large extent share the same cosmological presuppositions and they do to a similar extent engage in the same yogic manipulations, and they nearly all share the same aim: to become divine.

I know well that this hypothesis will be unacceptable for most "experts" today, but it may still be true. The insight into the occult dimension of one's religion is normally not made a part of one's self-presentation, when Hindus and Buddhists or Theosophists communicate to researchers. Therefore many researchers are misled and never find their way into the operative parts of the religion they research.

In the good old days it was considered a necessary control for all researchers of religion to have their presentation verified by the people whom they researched. That is in fact rarely possible today, for if the researchers hit at some important esoteric part of the religion in question, it is the duty of the believers to deny the truth.

## A sort of conclusion

It cannot be the aim — after this analysis and interpretation of the worldview of the NRMs and their roots in the occult tradition — to enter into a lengthy discussion about the Christian response. Suffice it to say that it is necessary not to Christianize such occult traditions and go for a sort of *Heimholung* according to the attitude *so ein Ding müssen wir auch haben*.

Still it should have become obvious from these pages that the Christian tradition looks rather weak when it comes to cosmic imaginations! But it is probably not to be blamed for that reason.

The Christian cosmology is first of all determined by the Christian eschatology. If the churches today find themselves in a serious dilemma when they are confronted with the NRMs and their imaginative cosmologies, it could mean that they should take a second look at their own eschatological presuppositions and see if in them there is not enough substantial material for a relevant message to the occult religion as it is presented in the NRMs of the contemporary world.

A relevant eschatology must, however, be presented in the context of a genuine cosmology. There are good reasons to believe that a renewed interest in the traditional elementary theology of the old church could help us to see and interpret the cosmos in a way that might prove meaningful for today.

First of all, a serious study of the NRMs and their worldview could help us to understand the meaning of religious language. The fact that such language is not first of all informative but transformative is often neglected in the churches. The occult language makes us again aware of the way in which symbolic language changes people from within by means of identification and symbolization.

We should thereby also recognize the essential difference between the Christian version of religious language and the occult language in the form of "the secret script" or "occult writing systems". In occultism the "twilight language" consists of signs and symbols which correspond to powers, which actively involve people in processes they do not understand until they have taken place. Often the esoteric language, exactly because it is a veiled and hidden form of communication, directly misleads people and "takes them, where they in fact did not want to go".

The symbolic language of the Christian tradition is by nature different. It also has its code, the gospel itself, but this code is presented freely and publicly for each and everyone without any esoteric reservation of the mind.

Theology by definition is quite different from the various forms of *sophia*, which characterize the NRMs. *Sophia* anal *gnosis* are not in themselves to be rejected, but they are, in the Christian tradition, safeguarded by the *logia*, by the logic of theology.

Occultism as it functions in the NRMs is not logical, and it does not intend to be. It is analogical by nature. "The mystery-languages" or "the alphabet of occultism" cannot be understood by means of the sort of logic which has come into existence in the Christian tradition and has marked Western culture and science. The psycho-cosmograms which are the codes of the occult communication systems are all created on the basis of the analogical way of thinking, as we have seen in the foregoing pages.

But even when this fundamental difference is respected and upheld, Christian theology can remind itself that the way of logical thinking it has developed does in no way diminish the symbolic nature of its language. Also Christian communication takes place by means of a language which is not only informative, but first of all transformative. The specific nature of that transformation is at stake in each and every dialogue with members of the NRMs.

NOTES

[1] I therefore leave out all NRMs which have their origin in the Christian tradition, such as Mormons, Jehovah's Witnesses, Unification Church, The Love Family, The Way International, The Local Church, etc. I have introduced my area of concern in two articles in *Update* (a quarterly journal on new religious movements, edited from The Dialog Center, Katrinebjergvej 46, 8200 Århus N, Denmark); see Vol. IV, 3, 1980, "Who is Who in Guruism", pp.4-50. And Vol. V, 2, 1981, "Modern Syncretist Movements", pp.29-36.

[2] My approach implies that I leave out all those parts of the worldview of the NRMs which deal with social and political dimensions of the NRMs. I have dealt with such dimensions elsewhere, for instance in "Guruisme og Politik" in "Bortom 1984", *Nordisk Ekumenisk Årsbok 1984-85*, Sigtuna, Sweden, 185-201, and in *Nordisk Missionstidsskrift Mission*, Vol., 97, 1, 1986, pp.3-21.

[3] The term "manipulation" is here used in order to express the fact that the theoretical part of the story is not the important one. The decisive part deals with the power operations, whereby people are changed and transformed into new ways of life by means of certain ritual initiations and techniques.

[4] Publications from the Hindu world organization Visva Hindu Parishad (VHP) confirm that the yoga movements are seen as the spearhead of the worldwide Hindu expansion. I have presented this perspective in *Update*, Vol. IV, 1/2, 1980, pp.5-15, "Guruism — a Hindu Countermission", and in *Update*, Vol. VI, 3, 1982, "Hinduism's World Mission", pp.4-9. The problem in how far yoga in fact is changing people into Hindus mentally is a controversial question. It is a fact, however, that the present "explosion" of the number of people in the Western world who believe in reincarnation is related to the participation in yoga exercices. Most of these people remain — for the time being at any rate — as

members of the churches. Many of them maintain that they have become "better Christians" by means of yoga, since they include belief in karma and samsara in their Christian belief system.

⁵ About this language, see for instance Annie Besant and C. W. Leadbeater, *Thought-Forms*, Theosophical Pub. House, 1969, and Colin Wilson, *The Occult*, New York, Vintage Books, 1973.

⁶ The reinterpretation of yoga performed by the theosophists is expressed well by Annie Besant herself in her *An Introduction to Yoga*, 1908, reprinted in large numbers since then. Leadbeater continues Annie Besant's approach, and his influence is clearly seen when one reads such modern theosophical leaders as Alice Bailey and Elisabeth Clare Prophet. Most probably Leadbeater has also inspired such movements as transcendental meditation and scientology. It is obvious at any rate that most modern yoga schools owe a lot of their yogic insights to the reading of Leadbeater.

Behind Leadbeater, however, one has to recognize the influence of the scholarly works of Sir John Woodroffe (Arthur Avalon). Already in 1918 he began his translations of Tantric texts, whereby he gave rise to the modern fascination with Tantrism, which is today so mixed up with theosophy that a clearcut separation would be impossible. Authors like Ernest Wood and Christmas Humphreys, for instance, who are often considered the great authorities in the basic New Age thinking, represent such a mixture.

Leadbeater is aware that he operated on the basis of what he calls Laya-yoga. He does, however, refer to such texts as *Shiva Samhita, Gherand Samhita* and *Hatha-Yoga Pradipika*, which are normally considered the basic texts of Hatha-yoga. These texts are, so to speak, the technical aspects of the much deeper Tantra-yoga, which is the basis of the Tantric Tradition, which for instance Agehananda Bharati has presented to the world in his book of the same name (1965). There is now a whole library of books which present this worldview, which in fact is decisive for the worldview of the NRMs.

⁷ The chakras are psychosomatic centres, supposedly connected with body functions, but not simply physiological entities. They correspond to various parts of the body, where intense nerve concentrations are found, such as (1), the anus, (2) the sexual organs, (3) the solar plexus, (4) the heart area, (5) the throat, (6) the eyes. The seventh chakra is beyond the others, at the top of the skull, and is in fact not a real chakra, but "the beyond" of all chakras. For literature about the chakras see note 28.

⁸ In *The Chakras*, 1969, p.74. In his cosmogram Leadbeater also connects the elements and chakras with various forms and colours, Sanscrit letters, divinities, fairies, animals (vahanas) and various benefits.

⁹ *Idem*, p.3.

¹⁰ *Idem*, p.2.

¹¹ See for instance Arthur E. Powell, *Den æteriske Dublet og beslægtede fænomener*, Copenhagen, 1952.

¹² *The Chakras*, p.3.

¹³ Leadbeater's chakra system is not identical with Sir John Woodroffe's system. Leadbeater has dropped the chakra situated close to the generative organs. He does not deny its existence, but declares that "the arousing of such a centre would be regarded as misfortune, as there are serious dangers connected with it" (*The Chakras*, p.5, note). As a substitute Leadbeater — and also some of the later theosophists — introduces a "spleen centre", situated "over the spleen". This centre for him has to do with astral flights, levitation and other supernatural powers.

¹⁴ Madras, Adyar, 1926, but cited here according to the 1975 edition.

[15] *Idem*, p.197. The idea that creations "by thought" per definition are real is an important part of the theosophical heritage. One has to remember the difference between language as information and language as transformation mentioned in note 5 to be able to appreciate this idea.

[16] *Idem*, p.79.

[17] *Idem*, p.160f.

[18] This book was first published in the periodical *Lucifer-Gnosis* from 1904-5. I will cite from the 3rd edition, 1909.

[19] Steiner's main cosmological idea is the Gnostic understanding that all matter is a result of the descent of the Spirit. Now, however, at the turning point a respiritualization is taking place. Even matter can now be redeemed. The turning point is the redeeming descent of Christ.

[20] *How to Attain Knowledge*, 1909, pp.71ff.

[21] The text used in this interpretation is by Bangali Baba: *Yogasutras of Patanjali with the Commentary of Vyasa*, Delhi, Motilal Banarsidas, 1976.

[22] The text used in this interpretation is the edition of *Shiva Samhita*, translated by Rai Bahadur Srisa Chandra Vasu, 3rd edition, 1979. Similar citations can be found in *Gherand Samhita*, while *Hatha Yoga Pradipika* is somewhat different, since it ignores the elements.

[23] This important idea is developed by Goraknath himself as the basis of his Siddha-yogi school. Goraknath was the founding father of Hatha-yoga; and still the Mahant of Gorakpur is the spiritual head of all Hatha-yogis. The present Mahant is also the president of the commission on monastic communities within Hinduism. This commission is a leading body within the Visva Hindu Parishad, i.e. the World Mission of Hinduism. The importance of Goraknath is normally not known. He is, however, still a living reality and inspires directly or indirectly the self-understanding of yoga. The best book about Goraknath is by A. K. Banerjea: *Philosophy of Goraknath...*, 1961.

[24] More about the egg of Brahma, the golden egg, the mundane egg, the cosmic egg is found in *Encyclopædia of Religion and Ethics*, ed. James Hastings, Vol. IV "Cosmogony and Cosmology", for instance pp.126, 156ff. See also *Puranic Encyclopædia*, ed. Vettam Mani, pp.158f. The egg and the elements belong together, for the egg is covered by "shells" of water, fire, air, ether, etc.

[25] The five dharanas are described in *Gherand Samhita*, Lesson 3, verse 68-81, and in Theos Bernard's *Hatha-Yoga*, Rider, 1982, pp.81f., and in Mircea Eliade's *Yoga, Immortality and Freedom*, 1958, for instance pp.125f.

[26] Mircea Eliade, *Yoga*, p.125.

[27] There are many "schools" in this respect, but one of the most revealing is expressed by Jonn Mumford (Swami Anandakapila) in his book *Sexual Occultism, the Sorcery of Love in Practice and Theory*, Minnesota, 1975. The author is in the line of Swami Satyananda Saraswati, the "grandfather" of a number of the radical Tantric yoga-schools within the NRMs.

[28] Books and articles on the Kundalini power are numerous. As mentioned in note 6, Sir John Woodroffe's scholarly works were the beginning. And the theosophical leaders made his insights popular. In 1927 John Woodroffe himself wrote the foreword to the popular book *The Mysterious Kundalini* by Vasant G. Rele, 11th edition, 1970, much read and cited. In his foreword Woodroffe writes about the Kundalini-yoga: "What may be its value is another question, a matter upon which I am not so sure as I once was. That this form of Yoga has a parapsychic interest is very clear. That it is, from what is called

the 'spiritual' aspect, of equal value is not now so clear to me. That it may be dangerous is admitted by those who practise it... I am disposed to think that I underrated in my Serpent Power the value of some adverse criticism of this Yoga..."

M. P. Pandit's *Kundalini Yoga*, Pondicherry, 1979 (1959), is written as a more recent theosophical interpretation, and is connected with the Aurobindo milieu.

Most yogis and gurus use Kundalini-yoga. This is so in the Divine Life Society, where Swami Sivananda with his *Kundalini yoga*, 1935, set a pattern, followed for instance by his strong opponent Swami Narayanananda from N. U. Yoga in 1950 with his *The Primal Power in Man or the Kundalini Shakti*. Sri Chinmoy has a special approach in his *Kundalini: the Mother-Power*, 1974. And Yogi Bhajan has made the secrets of Kundalini into a "Meditation Manual" for his Healthy-Happy-Holy students, 1975. Even more on the popular side is Ajit Mookerjee's *Kundalini, the Arousal of the Inner Energy*, 1982.

No real medical psychiatric research on the Kundalini theme has as yet been done. The book which comes closest is Lee Sanella's *Kundalini: Psychosis or Transcendence*, 1976. Pandit Gopi Krishna's famous books are in fact so superficial that they give little help in understanding the phenomenon; see his *Biologische Basis der Glaubenserfahrung* (with Carl Friedrich von Weizsäcker as co-author!), 1971. Raymond Bernard's *The Serpent Fire, the Awakening of Kundalini*, 1959, has some useful insights. Swami Sivananda Radha (with a foreword by Herbert V. Guenther and an introduction by Stanley Krippner) has published *Kundalini, Yoga for the West*, 1978, in a way the most informative volume on this topic. Mary Scott's *Kundalini in the Physical World*, 1983, also gives valuable information, and so does the collection of essays, *Kundalini, Evolution and Enlightenment*, ed. John White, 1979.

Centred on the chakras one finds a series of books, which of course are also relevant for the understanding of the Kundalini, and the Kundalini books mentioned above are also helpful for the chakra understanding. Important ones are Werner Bohm's *Chakras, Lebenskräfte und Bewusstseinszentren im Menschen*, 1974, and the *Chakra-Physiologie, Die subtilen Organe des Körpers und die Chakra Maschine*, 1980, by Hiroshi Motoyama and Rande Brown.

Peter Schreiner has collected a bibliography on yoga: *Yoga, Grundlagen, Methoden, Ziele*, Brill, 1979f.

[29] Most alarming in this field is Swami Narayanananda's book *Brahmacharya, its Necessity and Practice for Boys and Girls*, 1960. I have analyzed Swami Narayanananda's teaching on this theme in *Update*, No. 3-4, 1977, Vol. 1, pp.4-33 in an article called "A Yogic Attitude to Sex".

# The Emergence of a New Religiosity in the Western World

## JEAN-FRANÇOIS MAYER

The world is entering a period of turmoil and upheaval when the old institutions and ways seem either woefully inadequate or totally irrelevant. Whichever way you turn, there are movements, groups, sometimes lonely voices counselling us to consider another way forward. [1]

These are the first sentences in a recently published *Guide to Alternative Living*. It goes on to list the various fields where new proposals are being heard: politics, education, diet, economics, medicine. The guide contains entries about Zen, parapsychology, mysticism, flying saucers and faith healing; spiritualism, dreams, Christian Science, charismatic renewal and yoga; Ayurvedic medicine, Lourdes, Theosophy, humanistic psychology and Kundalini; reincarnation, reflexology, vegetarianism, exorcism, telepathy and Transcendental Meditation, etc.

### A return to the sacred?

All this is perhaps somewhat difficult to digest, but whether we like it or not there is today a *link* between those various topics in the minds of a growing number of people. And after reading such a book, one gets a strong feeling that behind it all there is some diffuse or explicit spiritual quest. It is difficult to determine the extent of this quest but it is not by chance that books on such a variety of topics can be found in the *same* bookshops. A research group (commissioned by the French Roman Catholic bishops to study a pastoral approach towards sects) speaks of the spread of "a microculture with Eastern undertones", "ferment centred around esoteric topics and gnosticism, around spiritism, the occult and clairvoyance", a "taste for the irrational, the strange, and the mysterious". [2]

A group of academics in Belgium expresses its anxiety in view of the "irrationalist temptation" which it feels "is threatening the West from inside in a great variety of ways". They feel that they must warn the reader:

> In the most advanced areas of science, in physics (especially in quantum and relativistic physics), there are physicists who have become gnostics and use the strangest language in which they employ a monstrous mixture of scientific vocabulary and theosophic expressions... all is mixed up in confusion and chaos: Krishna, flying saucers, parapsychology, utopias, spiritualization of matter, return to the past and dreams of the future, creating a sparkling and fascinating system for those who lack information and whose critical faculties are not trained. [3]

Is it then legitimate to speak of a "return to the sacred" (whether with hope or anxiety would of course depend on one's perspective)? I feel that such a view is too absolutist and that to a historian a few years, and even a few dozen years, are not enough for measuring such trends. The collective mind of a society changes slowly and it is premature to pretend to know what the spiritual make-up will be in the third millennium. All we can make are prudent forecasts, especially since there are also signs of other potential developments. And before we speak of a "return to the sacred", we ought first to be sure that the sacred has indeed been abandoned. It seems better to speak of *the mutations of the sacred* because religious feelings are now being expressed — albeit with some scepticism and in a diluted form — in areas where this had not been customary in the West.

I think therefore that we must place NRMs in the much wider context of the phenomenon of a new religiosity and contemporary mutations of the sacred. Seen in that perspective, and excluding NRMs with a purely Christian background, they are only signs — rather like the top of an iceberg. Because they are organized and structured groups, they attract comparatively more interest from the media, sociologists and other observers, but realistically speaking many of those movements will probably be more or less short-lived. In the long run what matters are the ideals, concepts, worldviews, etc. which they help to spread *within the framework* of much more important developments that go far beyond the relatively small influence exerted by an individual movement and touch quite a number of individuals who are not affiliated to any movement.

## Moving beyond religions

James A. Beckford has remarked that, from a sociological viewpoint, the term "NRM" is relevant only in a *collective* sense and that the situation would be less confusing if one spoke in the singular of "*the* new religious movement".

> ...It is important to emphasize... that the term "NRM" was originally applied to a *plurality* of freshly observed groups. It did not refer to any particular group in isolation from the wider phenomenon. This means that, in its application to several movements in isolation, the term is problematic: it applies more appropriately to them collectively. [4]

In a different way I think that we can use Beckford's comments for our purpose as well. We must obviously emphasize strongly that there are important differences between the NRMs and must refuse to amalgamate them as many people are tempted to do. But on the other hand, although NRMs often have incompatible and contradictory beliefs and life-styles, they nevertheless contribute to an increasingly multicoloured atmosphere of "new religiosity", even if this consists only in making some countries more pluralistic in their religious life. Through the actions of different NRMs (which may well be hostile towards each other) and other less organized trends, our spiritual environment is being progressively and subtly changed and a new kind of religiosity created. [5] In some cases a constant exchange of ideas has started; for instance groups like the Lifewave Organization and Bhagwan Shree Rajneesh draw at least as much from the new religiosity as they contribute.

The "newness" of this religiosity is of course only relative.

> ...the dissatisfaction which is widely felt with today's orthodoxy is leading to a reappraisal of old ideas and systems. Thus Yoga, Zen, Buddhism and other ancient traditions are seen to have a contemporary message for the West. The key to the future may, indeed, lie in a deeper understanding of the past. [6]

There have been precursors in the West of this new religiosity and of NRMs. We need only think of the important role played by the Theosophical Society and related groups which in the nineteenth century spread some fundamental concepts such as reincarnation, karma, etc. in the West. Another example is the Baha'i faith whose programme already contained a universalist perspective and aimed to reconcile science and religion.

The universalist view is characteristic of quite a number of the new spiritual groups and is also expressed at the religious level by their belief in the underlying unity of religions. Many new groups feel that the older religions have lost much of their spiritual power; they are certain that they can contribute more than any of the religions, and that they could even become the supra-religion of the future. The "ecumenical" approaches and overtures of some NRMs are not without ambiguity.

According to Taisen Deshimaru "Zen is beyond the religions": it is "the middle way, the way of synthesis" — because this middle way "integrates everything"; the Zen practitioner is free to keep his/her religion or not — what matters is "to find the true essence of all religions". [7] According to Maharishi Mahesh Yogi, it is TM that will be found if we search for the essence of the scriptures of all religions; the religions have experienced so many failures that the modern world has turned away from them but fortunately the solution is available to the spiritual leaders: by accepting TM for themselves and for their faithful, the religions will be regenerated. [8]

But there is competition: the followers of Shri Mataji Nirmala Devi assert that it is Sahaja Yoga which "integrates and transcends all forms of meditation, prayers and yogas". [9] Sahaja Yoga "gives back the whole substance to many rituals of various religions, because it brings them into contact with the energizing phenomena of which they are the support": baptism as practised by today's churches is no more than a "semblance" or at best a "symbolic prefiguration" of the spiritual realization brought by Shri Mataji. [10] A spiritual master of Krishna devotees says that we must not condemn any religion. Jesus is an avatara. [11] God has countless names, let us chant them, whether they are the name of Krishna or of Jesus among the Christians, [12] but "Prahbupada used to say that other scriptures may be compared to a pocket dictionary, whereas the Vedas are like the unabridged dictionary". [13] Members of Sukyo Mahikari are not turning towards India and the Vedic tradition but rather towards Japan, a country they see as "the cradle of *all* major religions" and of humankind; [14] "Jesus Christ is crying because of the way his followers have misinterpreted his teachings and the way Christianity has degenerated." Fortunately, "Mahikari teachings and practices clarify and give deeper understanding of the basic doctrines of Christianity"; [15] anyway, "Mahikari is the basis or core of all religions." [16] As its name indicates, the Unification Church also wants the unity of all religions; under the patronage of the Rev. Moon, the first session of the Assembly of the World's Religions was held in New Jersey in November 1985 and will culminate in 1993 to mark the hundredth anniversary of the World Parliament of Religions in Chicago. (This was an important event in the introduction of Eastern religions in the West.) At the same time Moonies believe that there is some kind of process going on in the spiritual world through which the founders of all the religions are linked to the Rev.

Moon, making the dream of the unity of religions around the messianic figure come true even though there might not be visible external unity.

I think we can say that the aim of most NRMs is not to oppose existing religions but rather to move beyond them.

In another study, [17] I have emphasized how members of the NRMs often associate traditional Christianity with the idea of something rather old and moribund. They respect the figure of Christ but the "folly of the cross" is not a popular doctrine in their circles. For Bhagwan Shree Rajneesh "Christianity is not Christianity, but Crossianity. Its symbol is the cross, not Christ." [18] "It became death-orientated. It became anti-life." [19]

For the Unification Church, as we know, the crucifixion was not God's original plan nor the divine means of saving the world but rather a "secondary course of salvation" in view of the impossibility of establishing the kingdom of heaven completely on earth at that time. When speaking about the eucharist, a spiritual master of Krishna devotees notes: "It is very hard for devotees to appreciate a ceremony that celebrates the death of the guru. Actually, devotees rarely even discuss the disappearance of the Lord from his earthly pastimes. It is too painful." [20] Mahikari affirms that its message does not invalidate the Christian message but simply that "the doctrine that 'people's sins are washed away by Jesus' blood on the cross' can no longer be upheld." [21] According to the founder of Mahikari, Jesus did not die on the cross but was replaced there by his younger brother. It is said that Jesus then went to Japan where he lived until a fairly advanced age and that you can still see his grave. [22] This story reminds us of the somewhat similar theories of the older Ahmadiyya movement which located Jesus' grave in Srinagar, Kashmir.

The NRMs propose more than a new religious synthesis. They also see themselves as the heralds of a New Age, a regenerated world and purified humankind. As the leader of one movement explains: "Sekai Kyusei Kyo (World Messianity) is not exclusively a religion; religion is only a part of it. What kind of title would then be more appropriate for our church? I believe it would be more fitting to call ours a 'New World Construction Project'." [23] "After thousands of years of darkness or of semi-darkness, a great turning point has arrived, the turning from the Age of Darkness to the Age of Light." [24] Moonies are so dynamic because they are certain that the restoration of the kingdom of God on earth is imminent, even if the form which this is to take is only vaguely described. And even the Krishna devotees — who think that we are only at the beginning of Kali-yuga (Dark Age) which will last for another 400,000 years — believe that there will first be a kind of "parenthesis" lasting 10,000 years, during which "this congregational chanting will become dominant all over the world and usher in a worldwide social change that will affect all areas of corporate society". [25]

At their meetings, Universal Life devotees sing "Now is the great moment, humanity is ready", but according to spiritual messages the Tchernobyl nuclear catastrophe was only the beginning of the end of the world. And there will be more and more and ever graver disasters; forests and plants will soon die. Many movements are announcing major upheavals as a prelude to the wonderful transformation of the world; in this way they create a synthesis between an optimistic vision of the New Age to come and a catastrophe-oriented atmosphere. This is less contradictory than it seems and in fact expresses once again the perpetual vitality of millenarian hope in various forms: catastrophe and redemption go hand in hand in a messianic perspective.

### Towards a syncretistic future and new worldviews

In many groups we find that some technique is used to support the spiritual experience of individuals and that this can also be a means of introducing, foreshadowing and preparing a better world. It is often forgotten that even groups which appear to be oriented towards the self-realization of the individual may also quite often aim for what could be called "collective redemption" — and maybe it is this feature that distinguishes them from purely therapeutic groups. We have all heard how TM claims that its technique is able to have a positive influence on the situation of a city, a country or even the world, thanks to the practice of TM by a certain number of people. Scientology is sure to have the necessary "tech" in order to improve any society and make it "clear". "By having the clouds removed from our spiritual bodies" thanks to Johrei (as practised in Sekai Kyusei Kyo) we are preparing for the advent of paradise on earth. [26] And in Mahikari (whose founder had been a member of Sekai Kyusei Kyo) a similar practice of Okiyome — purification by the True Light — is supposed to allow the greater part of our problems to be solved, whether of individuals or groups. [27] Through "raising the Kundalini of other people", the Sahaja Yogis believe that they are participating in a "grandiose plan for redemption" so as to avoid "the final disintegration of the universe" and to prepare for the Golden Age. [28] It may also be appropriate here to mention the use of Holy Salt in the Unification Church: any object or place sanctified through this Salt is no longer part of Satan's dominion but belongs instead to the sovereignty of God.

> When we use Holy Salt, we become participants in building the Kingdom of
> Heaven on earth... We take things from the world and ask God to accept them
> under his dominion. [29]

Many NRMs are aware too of a link between the individual and the
environment and the world around him or her: anything we do will have
consequences and we cannot escape them. This is rather similar to
present-day attitudes and developments in the ecological and therapeutic
fields. The founder of Sekai Kyusei Kyo even asserts that human thought
can affect the climate. [30] And the concept of "karma", whether correctly
understood or not, has become widespread today.

Since many observers have already pointed out that NRMs insist on the
importance of *experience*, I need not deal with this topic here. But it is
probably this emphasis on experience which is responsible for the shift
from the religious to the therapeutic mentioned by a number of authors.
The fact that one can speak about a "shift" (though I am not sure that this
is the best way to describe it) shows clearly that there is a link. Perhaps it
would be better to speak about an attraction for new therapies. This is a
field where — as in NRMs — there is much moving from one group to
another by people "in search" of something and may well be a kind of
spiritual quest or a substitute for it.

It is the area of the "crypto-religious fashions" described by Carl A.
Keller:

> ...The religious need, the deep and inescapable necessity to cling to some
> Truth, felt and confirmed as absolute, is indistinctly manifested in various
> ways. The fundamentally religious nature of such trends is hidden behind a
> non-religious language, or even behind a polemical and derisive behaviour
> towards the religion. [31]

Perhaps the various "shifts" and other disconcerting phenomena are
simply attempts to adjust to new situations in a changing world. For
instance, the structural similarity between Melanesian "cargo cults" and
UFO cults has often been pointed out; both are attempts to respond and
adjust to new facts and situations. And in the same way as the UFO cults
and their adherents or those new prophets called the "contactees", [32] the
contemporary belief in astrology is part of a "wide syncretism at the
border between the rational and the irrational" and "offers a compromise
between science and mystery". [33]

In one of the last interviews he gave before his death, Mircea Eliade
warned all of us that we must be able to recognize what could be
unexpected manifestations of the sacred:

It is quite possible that some day we will see absurd, strange things appearing which may well be new expressions of the experience of the sacred... I believe... we will experience difficulties in recognizing immediately the new expressions of the experience of the sacred. [34]

In our encounters with NRMs or other disconcerting phenomena, we should remember Eliade's stimulating remarks. They might help us to be open in our approach and willing to enlarge our perspective beyond the venerable heritage of the great religious traditions and they might enable us to understand the views of others, however strange or even irritating they might be at times.

I hope that this short paper will make us see NRMs (or "the" new religious movement) as one aspect of a variety of religious or crypto-religious trends. On the cover of the book *A Pilgrim's Guide to Planet Earth* there is a Khmer temple, an Egyptian pyramid, a Celtic megalith, a Japanese landscape, a Gothic church, the enigmatic statues on Easter Island and a flying saucer. Although no one knows to what kind of syncretistic future the pilgrims of the New Age are heading, we can be sure of one thing and that is that the challenge to the Christian churches will not come from this or that new religious movement but rather from new worldviews which will have an impact on an ever-growing number of people in the Western world who are not necessarily members of an NRM.

NOTES

[1] David Harvey, *Thorsons Complete Guide to Alternative Living*, New York, Thorsons Publishing Group, 1986, p.9.

[2] *S.N.O.P.*, No. 519, 2 November 1983.

[3] Gilbert Hottois ed., *Aspects de l'irrationalisme contemporain*, Brussels, Ed. de l'Université de Bruxelles, 1984, p.8.

[4] *Cult Controversies: the Societal Response to the New Religious Movements*, London/New York, Tavistock, 1985, p.14.

[5] We look at NRMs and the new religiosity mainly from the point of view of a "break" with traditional Western Christianity in its various expressions but there are of course groups which could be defined as being on the border (see my book, *Sectes nouvelles: Un regard neuf*, Paris, Cerf, 1985, pp.11-14).

[6] Harvey, *op. cit.*, p.9.

[7] *Questions à un Maître Zen*, Paris, Albin Michel, 1984, pp.13-20.

[8] *La science de l'être et l'art de vivre*, Paris, Ed. de l'Age de l'Illumination, 1981, pp.198-306.

[9] Lotus Heart, *L'Avènement*, Paris, Ed. PubliSud, 1985, p.139.

[10] *Ibid.*, p.130.

[11] Swami Bhaktipada, *Christ and Krishna* (n.p:), Bhaktipada Books, 1985, pp.2 and 4.

[12] *Ibid.*, p.48.

[13] *Ibid.*, p.133.

[14] Andris K. Tebecis, *Mahikari. Thank God for the Answers at Last*, Tokyo, L.H. Yoko Shuppan, 1982, pp.389-390.

[15] *Ibid.*, pp.363-364.

[16] *Ibid*, p.380.

[17] *Sectes nouvelles*, pp.68-69.

[18] *The Rajneesh Bible*, Vol. 1, Rajneeshpuram (Or.), Rajneesh Foundation International, 1985, p.142.

[19] *Ibid.*, p.147. A characteristic actually shared by all the religions, according to Rajneesh.

[20] Bhaktipada, *op. cit.*, p.147.

[21] Tebecis, *op. cit.*, p.362.

[22] *Ibid.*, pp.351-361.

[23] *Foundation of Paradise: From the Teachings of Meishusama* (n.p:), Church of World Messianity, 1984, p.7.

[24] *Teachings of Meishu-sama*, Vol. 1, Los Angeles, Church of World Messianity, 1979, p.33.

[25] Bhaktipada, *op. cit.*, p.131.

[26] *Teachings…*, pp.3-5.

[27] Tebecis, *op. cit.*, pp.48-49.

[28] Heart, *op. cit.*, p.295.

[29] *The Tradition. Book One*, New York, The Holy Spirit Association for the Unification of World Christianity, 1985, p.48. Once a country has been "restored", there will be no further need to use Holy Salt there, "all things will be sanctified". The use of Holy Salt is also connected with the individual experience of the members, "striving to live spiritual lives, each of us is desperate to become free of Satan. Using Holy Salt, in a very basic way, we obtain some of that freedom."

[30] *Teachings…*, pp.59-60.

[31] "Tradition, innovation et imitation dans la vie religieuse", in *Le phénomène de la mode*, Lausanne, Payot, 1985, pp.75-89 (p.76).

[32] People claiming to have met extra-terrestrial beings and (usually) to have received messages, instructions, information from them.

[33] Jules Gritti, "L'astrologie et ses adeptes", in *Universalia 1986*, Paris, Encyclopaedia Universalis, 1986, pp.365-369.

[34] *Construire* (Swiss weekly), 19 March 1986, slightly different version in *Le Monde*, 4-5 May 1986.

# Bringing Them In

*Some Observations on Methods of Recruitment Employed by New Religious Movements*

## EILEEN BARKER

The first, and one of the most important things that must be said about the new religions is that they differ enormously from each other in a number of ways, including the ways in which they try to gain new recruits. The movements may be more or less (or not at all) actively involved in the task of recruitment; some may be trying to bring about conversions only, others may be also trying to secure a commitment from their converts to dedicate their lives to the movement (by living in special centres and/or working full-time for the movement); the methods they use in their mission work may involve exerting more or less pressure on the potential recruit — and so on. In this paper I shall make no attempt to describe the full range of recruitment practices of the new religions, but, after a very general introduction, I shall try to suggest some of the ways in which the methods of recruitment of the new religions might be *approached*. In doing this, I shall be raising some rather obvious points, which do, despite their obviousness, frequently get forgotten, but which it might be helpful to keep in mind in our discussions.

### The environment

It is, of course, obvious that recruitment does not (cannot) take place in a social vacuum. There have been situations in which a particular truth is assumed to be so self-evidently The Truth that no one even thinks of questioning it — any more than one would think of questioning the fact that night will fall and be followed by another day. Muslim (or Catholic) parents living in an exclusively Muslim (or Catholic) environment would be extremely unlikely even to consider whether or not they ought to bring up their child in the Muslim (or Catholic) faith. We might wish to note that in such a society "mission" is unnoticed, but, sociologically at least, it could be said that an exceptionally efficient method is being employed.

In a social environment in which there is more than one religious option available, there might be a "live and let live" philosophy in which those of different faiths accept that "many are the ways"; alternatively, there might be strong divisions, with each side convinced that they alone hold the truth and that people on the other side are not only wrong, but ought to be shown to be wrong and, by one means or another, brought to their senses. In the contemporary West, there are numerous societies that enjoy both religious pluralism and a political democracy that is dedicated to the principle of freedom of belief for all citizens. In some of these societies (in England and in Scandinavia, for example), there is an established church; in other countries, although there is no establishment, there are long-established ties with a particular religion (such as the Catholic Church) and/or political parties strongly associated with a Christian denomination; in some countries evangelizing is or has until recently been forbidden (as in the case of Spain, and, of course, many non-Western societies and most of Eastern Europe); in other countries (such as the United States) the constitution demands that there be no interference into or promotion of religious beliefs on the part of the state. There are, in short, a number of different social environments within which new (or old) religions have more or less freedom to try to convert others to their faith.

The openness of the social environment to proselytizing endeavours will have some effect on the number of ways that a movement will make the first contact with potential recruits — and the kind of response that missionary activities will receive. In California, one can see posters on every street corner advertising meetings or phone numbers that will lead us to some new truth (I was once offered six different truths in the course of one crossing of San Francisco's Union Square); in several Arab and Eastern Bloc countries, Moonies and International Society for Krishna Consciousness (ISKCON) devotees have been imprisoned for speaking of their faith (as have been Jehovah's Witnesses, Baptists, Catholics and others).

**A variety of methods**

Other things being equal (which, of course, they seldom are), movements that are offering obviously religious beliefs and/or ways of life are likely to focus on making personal contacts — either in a public place, or by knocking on people's doors or, quite commonly, through previously existing networks of friends and relations; while movements that are seeking to sell courses in self-enlightenment and/or self-development are more likely to advertise impersonally. This is not, however, an invariable rule (*est* relied almost exclusively on word of mouth to attract new guests to its seminars and the Unification Church has frequently looked for new members through posters and small ads — although with very little success).

Again, speaking very generally, the self-development/spiritual fulfilment types of movements (Scientology, Transcendental Meditation, the School of Economic Science) are likely to offer "guests" (or "clients") a series of meetings, seminars, classes or courses, the first one of which may be free or available for a token fee. The guest, having obtained a flavour of the group's beliefs and/or practices, may then be prevailed upon to proceed to further levels — each level frequently involving not only more of the person's money, but also more of his or her time and commitment. Movements (such as ISKCON, the Unification Church, the Children of God) that are looking for a religious commitment to a communal way of life, in which it is people's full-time dedication (or, in rather crude economic terms, their earning-power rather than their earning) that is being sought, are more likely to press the potential recruit to join the members for a residential visit (often referred to as a workshop or a seminar) in which they can not only learn about the movement's beliefs and aims, but also gain first-hand knowledge of the everyday life of the movement — although, not surprisingly, these residential introductions are rarely held in "normal" working centres, but in special places that are used exclusively or primarily for recruitment purposes. Several movements (such as that founded by Bhagwan Rajneesh, or the Way International) offer both courses and a communal life-style.

The methods used by the various movements will differ to some degree according to what it is that the movement is trying to offer the potential recruit, but most movements will employ some sort of combination of carrots and sticks. There will be the promises of novel revelations of, perhaps, ancient truths, of a deeper understanding of the way God, people, and/or the cosmos work, promises of closer relationships with God, with one's fellow beings, and/or with one's innermost self, promises of playing a role in creating a new kingdom of heaven on earth, changing the world, setting up a utopian enclave, and/or promises of communicating with the deep mysteries of the beyond and/or the within. There will be warnings of lost opportunities, of opening oneself, or abandoning oneself (or the world) to dark forces and/or Satan, of not realizing one's full potential, not being truly free, but forever bound by the conventions or accretions of society, of letting down oneself, one's family, one's new friends, the world and/or God. Testimonials (in the form of letters from transformed and grateful customers or talks from bright-eyed "born-again" members) tell of the wonderful changes that can take place in a person's life once they have accepted the new truth; and, at the same time, stories may be whispered of fearful happenings that have befallen those who were offered but rejected the opportunities given by the new truth.

Movements that employ techniques (such as chanting, meditation, yoga, or "auditing") are likely to give the prospective recruit an introduction to these at an early, if not the first, meeting. There is often an atmosphere of intense excitement or reassuring calm in introductory sessions. Those in charge may exude authority or love or, quite often, both. Often the guest will undergo some quite grilling questioning about his or her beliefs and aspirations, but however demanding such sessions may be they are usually experienced as exhilarating by the convert — they are, after all, focused on the individual, and he or she is unlikely to have been the subject of such interest on many other occasions. Sometimes the guest is invited/cajoled into "letting yourself go — completely". This can appear quite a frightening "method". During an extremely intensive weekend with the Rajneeshee, I became very worried when one of my fellow-guests seemed to have lost control of himself and was screaming hysterically at a cushion with which he was bashing up an already battered mattress. "That's beautiful, let it all come out," cooed our instructor into a microphone. I was anxiously checking that the second-floor windows were firmly closed and the door to the roof barred when she continued: "But don't forget that your saliva may be contaminated." Whereupon a helper proferred a box of Kleenex to the apparently possessed guest, who obediently reached out a hand, took a tissue, wiped his mouth, and then continued with his hysteria. I relaxed.

### Brainwashing techniques?

Several of the movements have leaders who are labelled charismatic. I have, however, found little evidence that many members actually *joined* because of any Svengali-like powers of the leader. Furthermore, the movements tend to attract people on an individual basis — there are few, if any, reports of mass conversions as a result of revival-type evangelical meetings.

Despite the allegations that have been presented in the media and elsewhere, neither I nor any serious student of the better-known new religions has ever come across any use of *physical* coercion in recruitment practices. Some groups (possibly Synanon and certainly the People's

Temple, the Manson family and the SLA) have prevented people from leaving their premises — but such instances do not fall under the heading of recruitment into the new religions.

But lack of physical coercion certainly does not mean that some other kind of coercion and/or deceptive method may not be used.

The movement with which I have had the most contact is the Unification Church, about which it has often been said that it employs both deception and brainwashing in order to obtain its recruits. In 1981 a popular British tabloid, *The Daily Mail*, won a libel case that the Unification Chuch brought against it on account of an article that it had written in 1978, accusing the movement of brainwashing and breaking up families. It was partly because I was so disturbed by the evidence and deliberations that I heard in court during this case that I ended up by devoting a 300-page book to the question of whether or not the Moonies do, indeed, use brainwashing techniques. [1]

Let me make it clear, my concern was not because a court could decide that it was legitimate for a newspaper to accuse a new religious movement of brainwashing. I happen to believe that people *can* use unacceptable means of persuasion; and I happen to believe that if they do so then it is permissible — even desirable — for newspapers (academics or whomsoever) to reveal/expose such practices. I happen, for example, to believe that "flirty fishing", the use of sexual intercourse as one of the recruitment techniques of the Children of God (or Family of Love, as they are now known), is an undesirable method of obtaining converts to any religion. But I also happen to believe that, on the one hand, religious beliefs cannot be judged as true or false by the courts — largely on the ground that, epistemologically, most of the claims they make are not susceptible to empirical testing and, thus, there is no way in which disagreements can be resolved. (Inconsistency is frequently celebrated as paradox in theological discourse.) *And*, on the other hand, I happen to believe that there are ways of judging the truth or falsity of statements about behaviour that *are* amenable to empirical (and logical) scrutiny.

What worried me in *The Daily Mail* case (and in innumerable other claims that Moonies are brainwashed) was the apparent disregard for these two positions: on the one hand, there was the implication that anyone who could believe the "gobbledy-gook" of the Unification theology must be brainwashed — or mad — because it was "so obviously wrong"; on the other hand, the methodology of the "scientific expertise" called upon by *The Daily Mail* was about as unscientific as one could imagine.

There is no time to go into details concerning all the fallacies (as I see them) that are invoked by those who claim that new religions employ brainwashing techniques, but I would like to address just a few of the most common.

At the most crude level, there is the purely tautological assertion that anyone who believes that sort of rubbish and/or who is prepared to live that sort of life *must* be brainwashed — otherwise, why would they believe and/or do such things? This, of course, is no more than an assertion posing as an explanation. A slightly more elaborate version of the tautology is that it would be impossible for a particular person to change in such a way because he or she was so different before the conversion. The problem with these sorts of "explanations" is, as the Moonies themselves continually complain, that there is no way in which they could prove that a genuine, voluntary conversion could have taken place. When the Moonies protest that they have chosen to be members of the Unification Church, they are merely told that they have been brainwashed into believing that they had made a free choice. (It is, however, possible that members of the new religions will be convinced that something did happen *to* them which, in fact, they could not resist — but in such a case they are likely to insist that it was God, not other people, who was responsible for the outcome.)

Arguments purporting to substantiate claims that brainwashing takes place frequently include both statements about the processes to which the potential recruit is subjected at the Unification workshops, and statements about the state the person was/is in after he or she became a Moonie. In the first category (which concentrates on the process), one finds accusations of such things as hypnosis, sugar-buzzing and/or inadequate diet, sensory deprivation, sensory over-stimulation, an overly controlled environment, deception and "love-bombing". In the second category (which concentrates on the state of the convert), one hears of glassy-eyed robots with such characteristics as inability to concentrate, loss of interest in former friends, hobbies, career, etc., changed physical appearance, an uncritical passivity *and* a tendency to be hypercritical.

Now, *of course*, someone who has experienced a genuine conversion will change. St Paul was hardly the same man after his experience on the road to Damascus. It is possible to argue that *anyone* who converts or, to put it in more secular terms, radically changes his or her mind about the way things are, must have been brainwashed (had their mind changed) — or become definitely peculiar. I am assuming, however, that this is not a point at issue, that is, I am assuming that we can allow for the possibility of "genuine" conversion. I am also assuming that those who accuse the new religions of using brainwashing tactics believe that free choice and genuine conversions are possible, as they are claiming that something which could be termed free will has been removed from the "victim".

But what do we mean by free will? How is it possible to determine whether or not it is being exercised? In particular, is there any way in which we can try to judge whether or not people who themselves assert that they are making freely-chosen decisions are, in fact, mistaken? Is there any way out of the sterile deadlock in which one person insists that he or she made a free choice and another person insists that he or she did not?

A common approach is to point to ex-members who say that they now realize that they were brainwashed or under some kind of mind-control while they were in a particular movement; during the time that they were members, they assert, they believed that they were doing what they wanted, but now that they are no longer members, they realize that this was not really the case.

There are several problems with this as a "proof" of brainwashing. First of all, it is quite possible that the ex-members are using concepts such as mind-control to explain what they now feel was a mistake. Secondly, research has shown quite clearly that it is those who have been deprogrammed who are most likely to say that they now realize that they were brainwashed, while those who leave voluntarily are very unlikely to make such a claim — and, it may be noted, part of the deprogramming process involves *telling* deprogrammees that they have been brainwashed.

Thirdly, however, I am not convinced that the persons themselves — as either believers or as ex-believers — can be the final arbiters when others who knew them before the event insist on an alternative account of their ability to judge what has been happening — although, of course, what converts and ex-converts say has to be taken into account. We cannot *just* accept the word of those who disagree with the members of the new religions without any further substantiation.

Furthermore, to a sociologist who sees people as being part of a social context throughout their lives (we are — need to be — born into an environment in which certain beliefs are assumed and transmitted to us from the cradle), it seemed obvious that no actions could be said to be reduced to being *either* the result of a free, autonomous will *or* brainwashing; almost all situations are the result of more or less influence (positive acceptance or negative reaction) by others, be they parents, teachers, priests, peers, the media or smiling new friends offering a new Truth.

In trying to arrive at some solution to such difficulties, I came to the conclusion that, although we would certainly have to listen to what everyone was saying, and to observe the processes of recruitment in action (pontificating from an armchair certainly could not be relied upon to produce any reliable resolution), it was necessary to approach the problem by looking not just at each individual case on its own, but also at a number of cases, taken together.

But, first of all, it was necessary to decide what might be meaningfully implied by such concepts as brainwashing, coercion, mind-control and free will — all of which are used in a variety of ways, and most of which are, philosophically, extremely slippery, and, methodologically, not readily amenable to empirical investigation. I did not want to *start* from an assumption that people were either active or passive participants in conversion (as much of the literature in the sociology of religion does). I decided to start from the concept of choice. Bearing in mind the need to "operationalize" the concept (that is, to devise a practical way of being able to recognize and test for the presence, or absence, of an abstract concept), it seemed helpful to think of choice as involving three inter-related ingredients: (a) reflection (in the present), (b) memory (of the past), and (c) imagination (of possible futures).

This led to the formulation: *A person can be considered to be making an active choice between two or more possible options when he or she can anticipate their potential existence and, in reflecting on these, is drawing upon his or her previous experience and previously formed values and interests to guide his or her judgment.* It is, of course, still possible for people to have been strongly influenced (by, say, their parents) in the values that they hold at any particular time, but my suggestion was that, in so far as people can *actively use or draw upon* their accumulated "input" (and genetic dispositions) *at a particular time*, we can talk meaningfully of their making a choice. Conversely, if other people somehow manage to prevent their making a decision in the light of their previous experiences and dispositions, or prevent their considering an otherwise available future alternative (such as continuing at university), then we might say that the person's capacity to choose had been reduced — or even removed.

Following from this definition, it is possible to isolate four variables that would have to be considered if we were to attempt to assess the extent to which a person is making a choice. First, there is the *person* (the potential recruit) with his or her predispositions; secondly and thirdly, there are the *alternative futures* (joining the new religious movement or continuing, as before, in the "outside" society); and, fourthly, there is the *social context* within which the decision is reached — in this case, a Unification workshop.

If a movement were to lie about its beliefs and practices, then a decision, based on inaccurate knowledge about one of the alternatives, might not be the same as one based on more accurate knowledge. This in itself would constitute *deception* rather than mind-control. We might talk of brainwashing, mind-control, or undue influence occurring according to the extent to which the fourth variable, the social context, is instrumental in determining the outcome. If, *whatever* the previous beliefs, dispositions or expectations about their future happened to be, people inevitably became Moonies once they were successfully lured to a Unification workshop (as has, indeed, been frequently claimed to be the case), then we might seriously consider that it was not they who were making the choice (unless we were to believe that the alternative that the movement was offering was irresistibly attractive — which most of us do not).

In fact, I found (and other researchers have come up with similar findings[2]) that 90 percent of those who got as far as attending a Unification workshop did *not* become Moonies — that is, the workshop was at least 90 percent ineffective. The workshop guests were perfectly capable of deciding that the movement was not for them. The range of both positive and negative reactions to the movement, its teachings and its members clearly indicated that each guest was capable of reacting in his or her own special way to the alternative that was on offer — and by far the most common reaction was rejection, although only a minority expressed strong dislike or disapproval of the movement (in fact, several of the non-joiners claimed that they had developed a greater understanding of God and/or their own religion through their experience of the workshop).

In other words, the large number of people who seemed immune to the Unification offer and the impressive variety of their reactions suggested that the social context was not sufficient to account for the outcome of a stay at a Unification workshop. It seemed clear that it was, rather, something that the potential recruits "brought with them" that was to be responsible for the decision whether or not they would become Moonies.

It might be proposed that there was a biological difference separating the joiners from the non-joiners, the former being more susceptible to lack of sleep, variations in diet and such like. I could, however, find no evidence that people's *brains* were being affected to the extent that they would no longer be able to reflect on the possibilities open to them in the light of their past experiences, hopes, values and so on. A more difficult question concerned a differential susceptibility of their *minds* — whether the Moonies were somehow able to control the thoughts of some of their guests, even if they were unable to control the thoughts of those who rejected the movement.

There are several traps that people are likely to fall into when considering the practices of apparently strange groups. These are traps which, if we wish to be honest and fair, we must try to avoid in our assessment of the new religions, whatever our personal preferences may happen to be. I have already briefly mentioned the epistemological confusions that can arise out of assuming that we can, on the one hand, prove religious beliefs to be true or false, or, on the other hand, that observable behaviour is not amenable to systematic inquiry and that anyone's *opinion* on such matters is equally valid. Related to these confusions is the belief that some kinds of behaviour are necessarily more "natural" and/or God-given than other types of behaviour. I am not suggesting that we cannot decide that we prefer one kind of behaviour or set of social customs to another set, but to insist that our own behaviour is more *natural* than other people's is usually to display (at least) an ignorance of anthropological and historical knowledge. We certainly know that people from other cultures have often considered the beliefs and actions of the conventional Christian missionary to be extremely unnatural.

The assurance that one's own behaviour is both natural and right can lead to the most blatant use of double standards in judging the behaviour of others. This is often revealed in the use of evaluative concepts that laud the behaviour of "us" and denigrate exactly the same behaviour in "them". Examples used by both the new religions and their opponents are too numerous to list, but it is interesting to note the disparate ways in which the hands of God and Satan are seen to work from the points of view of the antagonists.

A final trap that I wish to mention is that of assuming that the differences between them and us are far greater than they may, in fact, be. Quite often "bad" actions/beliefs are noted and assumed typical of members of "it", and not noted and/or assumed atypical of "us". An obvious example would be that a suicide by a member of a cult would almost invariably be reported *as* a suicide by a member of a cult; a suicide by a Lutheran is unlikely to be reported in headlines proclaiming that the victim was a Lutheran.

The point I wish to make is that, if we want to learn about the characteristics of a particular group, unless we make direct comparisons between the new religions and the population as a whole (or, more helpfully, those of a similar age and social background), we are not going to get information that we can *relate* to the group *per se*. If we read about cultists committing suicide more frequently than we read about Lutherans doing so, it is not altogether difficult to understand why we might grow to suspect that the new religions induce suicide in their members. If, however, we find that a smaller percentage of cultists commit suicide than do non-cult members of the same age and social background, we may wonder whether there is something about the movements that *prevents* people committing suicide. Of course, it may be that the movements attract those who are unlikely to commit suicide, but now the question is at least raised to be answered.

One reason for my making this point at such length is that it is frequently asserted that the new religions are particularly successful in recruiting people who are, in some sort of way, particularly suggestible — perhaps because they are rather pathetic, inadequate or passive persons, or those who have had unhappy experiences and are looking for a refuge from the difficulties of the world.

## Findings of research

When I began my research, I admit that I did suspect that this could, indeed, be the case. I compared four groups: the population as a whole, a "control group" of young adults of the same age and from roughly the same background as the Moonies, a group of people who went to a Unification workshop, and the Moonies themselves. I hypothesized that I would find the control group most "normal", the workshop group "slightly peculiar", and the Moonies the most "peculiar". "Peculiar" is not, of course, a very scientific term, but I was concerned to look at a number of variables such as unhappy childhood, divorced parents, a history of psychiatric disturbance (including, perhaps, a suicide attempt), being unemployed, doing badly or erratically at school, or having no prospects for the future. What I found was, however, that so far as most of these variables were concerned, it was a sub-group of the workshop attenders who did *not* join — or who joined for a very short time (a week or so) and then left — who turned out to exhibit the most "pathetic/ peculiar" characteristics. In other words, those who might seem particularly susceptible to suggestion might get as far as investigating the Unification Church, but they were very unlikely to actually commit themselves to full-time membership for anything but a few days — when they would be perfectly capable of deciding that they did not want to continue their association with the movement.

Who, then, were the people who joined? Their average age was 23; men outnumbered women by 3:2; they were disproportionately from the middle-middle and upper-middle classes; from "good" families in which the values of duty and service to others were more likely to be found than those of earning money; they tended to be of above average intelligence and to have done well, although not brilliantly, at school; many had started, completed, or were planning to attend university or some kind of further education. They were more likely than either the control group or the non-joiners to have been brought up in homes in which religion was important, and to have believed in God at the time of their visit to the workshop. And they tended to be extremely idealistic. But they were doers, not drifters. They wanted to *do* something to make the world a better place, but had been unable to find a way of playing such a role in the wider society. Among the characteristics that seemed to offer the greatest "protection" were atheism and (to a lesser extent) a strong commitment to another belief, and/or a happy and stable relationship with a partner.

I do not want to suggest that the workshop does not play an important part in persuading recruits to join the Unification Church; few (but, nevertheless, a few) join without attending one. At the workshop they offer them a loving community of like-minded "brothers and sisters"; they make utopian promises about the restoration of the kingdom of heaven on earth and the role that the guest can play in this procedure. I am not even suggesting that converts deliberate rationally about what they are doing — they are quite likely to be swept along by the enthusiasms of the occasion — but *only* when there is some kind of "fit" between the sort of things that they were *already* predisposed to be looking for or to feel at home with. They may not all make a choice in a hard, calculating sense, but, I believe, they do make a choice in a softer sense; they feel "at home" — that at last they have found the answers that they have been looking for — that they have been *brought up* to look for — and that the conventional churches had seemed to be unable to give them. And, let it be remembered, if the alternative that the Unification Church is offering its guests does not seem to make sense to them in the light of their predispositions and previous experiences, they simply do not join.

* * *

There have always been those who, having discovered a new truth (or rediscovered an old truth) want to share their important knowledge with others. This, in itself, is not necessarily a "bad thing". So far as my personal experience goes, I have certainly felt myself under pressure from several of the groups whom I have studied. Moonies have quite definitely tried to influence me and some have dropped rather ominous suggestions about what might happen to me if I do not take advantage of the opportunity which I have been lucky enough to have to learn about the movement. But evangelical Christians have chased my soul with just as much ardour and have warned me, with just as much foreboding, of Satanic repercussions if I do not give myself to Jesus — *their* Jesus.

Although both movements would vehemently deny any similarity, it is possible that the recruitment methods of another very visible new religion that has been (successfully) accused in the courts of brainwashing, the International Society for Krishna Consciousness (ISKCON), have been fairly similar to those of the Unification Church with respect to intensity. [3] It is also the case that, for some time now, both movements have been increasingly selective about whom they are prepared to accept as full-time members — partly because they have learned through bitter experience that unstable recruits can lead to their being blamed for the instability and any unfortunate occurrences that might subsequently happen as a result (they would say) of that prior instability. Both movements (especially ISKCON) have also become more insistent that potential members should wait some time before they finally commit themselves to a full-time membership. At the same time, both groups (and several of the other new religions) have recruited a growing number of members who, while sympathetic to the movements' beliefs and goals, do not dedicate their whole lives to the movements. These "home church" or "associate" members are more like members of a congregation, while the more fully committed members can be likened to priests, nuns or ministers.

A further aspect of the mission of several of the movements that should, perhaps, be mentioned is that they will frequently make contact with people, not in order to try to convert them, but in order to win their friendship or sympathy either for the movement or for one or more of its ideals. An increasingly popular method for this kind of mission is the sponsorship of conferences on a variety of subjects, but very commonly, on the themes of peace and of the unity or synthesis of science and religion. Examples of movements that have organized such conferences within the last decade would be the Brahma Kumaris, the Church of Scientology, the Divine Light Emissaries, Sai Baba, the International

Society of Krishna Consciousness, and, perhaps most frequently, conspicuously and successfully, the Unification Church, which has built up networks of scholars, theologians, ministers, journalists, politicians and military personnel who share and hope to promote certain common interests — even if they do not agree with the movement's theology.

Of course, what applies in the case of the Unification Church and ISKCON does not necessarily apply in the case of other new religions, but the *method* of assessing their method is, I believe, a valid one — or, at least, more valid than that used by many so-called specialists who have, in my opinion, caused a lot of unnecessary anxiety and harm through their sweeping, and frequently inaccurate, descriptions of the new religions and their recruitment practices.

Some of those who read this paper may come to the conclusion that I have been irresponsible by playing down the potential problems that may be inherent in the practices of the new religions. Let me repeat that I do believe that it is possible for people to use unacceptable methods in order to further their own organization's beliefs and/or goals, and that these beliefs and goals (and the means used to obtain them) ought to be scrutinized and, in some cases, controlled by the wider society. However, I also believe that those of us who wish to sit in judgment over the beliefs and practices of others should be as honest with ourselves, let alone with them, as is possible, given (and recognizing) both the limitations *and* the potentials of our knowledge.

It is understandable why the parents of those who join the new religions might be highly suspicious of the movements' motives and their methods, but if a democratic society wants to ensure that its young adults continue to lead a more conventional life, it might like to look at some of the reasons why a few of the movements do manage to persuade a few young people that they have something to offer them that society has not, for little that is constructive will result from merely accusing the new religions of using unfair methods in their recruitment. The same advice might be given to the conventional churches.

NOTES

• I would like to thank the Social Science Research Council of Great Britain and the Nuffield Foundation for financial assistance for the research from which this paper is drawn.

¹ Eileen Barker, *The Making of a Moonie: Choice or Brainwashing?*, Oxford, Blackwell, 1984.

² See, for example, Marc Galanter, "Psychological Induction into the Large Group: Findings from a Modern Religious Sect", *American Journal of Psychiatry*, Vol. 137, No. 12, 1980.

³ E. Burke Rochford, Jr, *Hare Krishna in America*, New Brunswick, NJ, Rutgers University Press, 1985.

# A Response

## RÜDIGER HAUTH

In my view, I should not respond to Eileen Barker's paper by giving a description of the recruitment practices used by the sects in question based on my own experience. A sufficient number of books have by now been written which deal with this concern. Among these, let me cite John G. Clark, Michael D. Langone, Robert E. Schecter, *Destructive Cult Conversion: Theory, Research and Treatment*. I would prefer to respond by commenting on some of the points Dr Barker has made. But I should like first to describe briefly my personal and professional relationship to the problem of the NRMs and to clarify the point of view from which I make my response.

It was in 1969 that I first met a group of young people belonging to a questionable group; they belonged to the Moonies. Shortly after, many other communities made their appearance, such as ISKCON, Children of God, Scientology, Divine Light Mission (Guru Maharaj Ji), to name only the most important. At first I thought that this was a variation on the phenomenon we had seen in the 60s, when we had had the beat generation, hippies, flower power, etc. But once I looked more closely at the background and intentions of these "new religious movements", it soon became evident that here was something quite different from hippies and flower power.

In the summer of 1968, I was appointed by the Evangelical Church of Westphalia as Secretary for Sects and Ideologies and asked to observe and collect information on the activities of sects and ideologies. This information was then made available to anyone interested among the public and was also used as the basis for counselling and pastoral care in acute cases.

In order to obtain materials used internally in the sects, and also to learn more about their structures and psychological techniques, my col-

---

● Translated from the German by M. Noetzlin, Department of Studies, LWF.

league Pastor Friedrich-W. Haack (who is responsible for work related to cults in the Bavarian church) and I have travelled extensively in many countries around the world. We also wanted to meet leaders and members of sects, to take part in their different activities and training courses, to dialogue with gurus, to become initiated, etc.

Against a background of nearly twenty years' intensive work with the problem of controversial sects, I should like to start by asking what Eileen Barker in her paper means when she speaks of "so-called specialists". We should be very careful in the use of this term because it is part of the characteristic "cult" terminology used by Moon, Krishna, Scientology and similar groups which attempt in this way to discredit and disqualify their critics. Eileen Barker also says of the "so-called specialists" that "... they caused a lot of unnecessary anxiety and harm through their sweeping, and frequently inaccurate, descriptions of the new religions and their recruitment practices". I cannot agree with this opinion because I think that "anxiety and harm" are produced exclusively through the harsh and unacceptable practices of the sects, and not through such "descriptions", even if they are inaccurate in some places. And we should remember that people whose lives have been affected by the sects, such as parents, sisters and brothers, friends, etc., have gathered much experience over a number of years on the activities of sects and have become "specialists" in their own ways, even if such experience is not always based on academic knowledge.

I should like to add a word here about the basic description of the controversial communities (and this would apply also to the general theme): "new religious movements" is a term which all the sects in question find most satisfactory, since it sounds neutral, harmless and innocent and says nothing abut their true structures, intentions and practices. We should therefore drop this concept because it makes the sects sound harmless and is certainly misleading, and replace it by something more adequate. It really is not possible to use the same concept to describe both shady and often semi-criminal organizations and such bodies as the Salvation Army, YMCA, Taizé, the charismatic movements, etc. who were also seen in their time as "new religious movements".

Here are some other aspects of Dr Barker's paper. The title is "Bringing Them In — Some Observations on Methods of Recruitment Employed by New Religious Movements". But her "observations" are limited to general remarks, as would seem to have been her intention, since she says that "in this paper I shall make no attempt to describe the full range of recruitment practices of the new religions..." But our discussion here has shown that a number of participants in the consultation are not as familiar with the subject as some others and they would have been helped if two or three examples had been given of methods of recruitment. For instance, one might have taken the Moon movement: how are young people generally approached? What precise techniques are used to enlist them? What step by step processes do "candidates" have to go through until they are fully integrated in the group? What kind of parallel changes take place in a candidate's personal and mental make-up?

Another example might be that of Scientology. It would have been possible to describe briefly but meaningfully and impressively what happens to a new recruit on his/her way from the first approach via the communication courses until the core of the psycho-cult is reached.

Dr Barker does point out that difficulties might arise in regard to methods of recruitment: "... the methods that they use in their mission work may involve exerting more or less pressure on the potential recruit..." "Movements (such as ISKCON, the Unification Church, the Children of God) ... are more likely to press the potential recruit to join the members for a residential visit..." but only concrete examples would have brought to light the real extent of the harsh problems. This is not the case in her paper.

She is right when she remarks that the individual sects do not apparently use "physical" coercion when recruiting and she concludes logically: "... but lack of physical coercion certainly does not mean that some other kind of coercion and/or deceptive method may not be used". Why does she not then give concrete examples and cite specific publications which are certainly available in order to illustrate those "other kinds of coercion"?

Another aspect of Dr Barker's paper could be described as "criticism of the critics". She asserts that someone who criticizes the dubious activities of sects could "fall into a trap" since there is allegedly no neutral or objective means to judge their activities. It is a subjective point of view, she claims, to describe the behaviour of "normal people" as "natural": "... to insist that our own behaviour is more natural than other people's is usually to display (at least) an ignorance of anthropological and historical knowledge". I cannot accept this line of argument. In my view it is precisely the knowledge of history and anthropology which provides us with the criteria on which to judge the behaviour of the sects, enabling us to contrast this with the "natural" behaviour of "normal" people and to identify where there is divergence from an agreed norm.

Dr Barker's subsequent comparison with conventional Christian mission which, according to her, has also been felt to be "extremely unnatural" by people of other cultures does not help to clarify the point since we are talking about sects which operate in our Western part of the world. This world is moulded by Christian concepts and its standards are based (at least in theory) on humanism, freedom, democracy and self-determination and sects operating in it must be measured against those standards, in the same way as any other secular or religious institution.

Dr Barker observes quite rightly in this context that the suicide of a member of a cult would be judged in another way than that of a "Lutheran". This differentiated view makes sense because in all the known cases of suicide of a member or former member of a sect it was triggered by the ideology of the sect in question. If a former Moonie commits suicide because he or she cannot get over the feeling of having betrayed the "Messiah Moon", or if a member of TM commits suicide because he/she is terrified of inadvertently revealing the "secret mantra", such suicides really cannot be compared to the suicide of a Lutheran or a Roman Catholic whose motives, as we know from experience, have hardly ever anything to do with their confession. Dr Barker's subsequent arguments contribute little to the clarification of the issue.

I also feel that Dr Barker is ambivalent when she speaks of "criticism of the critics". On the one hand she concedes that "I do believe that it is possible for people to use unacceptable methods in order to further their own organization's beliefs and/or goals, and that these beliefs and goals (and the means used to obtain them) ought to be scrutinized and, in some cases, controlled by the wider society"; on the other hand, she relativizes this when she demands that "those of us who sit in judgment should be as honest with ourselves as is possible" and recognize the "limitations and potentials of our knowledge". If someone has spent many years observing the cult scene intensively and coming to grips with it, then we can surely assume that this person has gathered sufficient information and knowledge, including knowledge of the sects' internal structures, to be able to arrive at a reasonable judgment. The advice to the observer and the "conventional churches" to look critically at themselves is unnecessary, since it is surely true that hardly any other organization looks at itself and its traditions in such a critical way as do most of the mainstream churches. Anyone who really knows something about internal church structures will confirm this.

Dr Barker has contributed mainly a sociological approach and used sociological criteria for our dialogue. However, I feel that the churches as organizational bodies as well as individual Christians have to defend a point of view in their discussions and analyses of alien religions, cults and ideologies which is based on the proclamation of the New Testament and our Christian faith. The same principles should guide us as we reflect on possible forms of dialogue.

# Religious Liberty and Socio-political Values

## Legal Threats to Conversion in the United States

### DEAN M. KELLEY

Everyone has the right to freedom of thought, conscience and religion; this right includes freedom to change his religion or belief, and freedom, either alone or in community with others and in public or private, to manifest his religion or belief in teaching, practice, worship and observance.

Article 18, *Universal Declaration of Human Rights*

Thus reads one of the world's greatest unattained ideals, violated every day and hour in every quarter of the globe, and nowhere more than in the treatment of *new* religions and their members. It is not a theological ideal — though many would find it consonant with their theologies. It is a social and political ideal, adopted by the parliament of nations in the middle of the twentieth century (1948), and almost nowhere fully realized in practice, not even in the Western industrial democracies (such as the United States) which pride themselves on their devotion to religious liberty.

Why should it be important — from a social and political standpoint — that the "human right" to "freedom of thought, conscience and religion" be recognized and protected? It is a social good, in and of itself, to respect the dignity and autonomy of every human being. In addition, there are utilitarian reasons for respecting individual conscience. For instance, a citizen conscientiously opposed to war does not make a very "good" soldier. Any moderately prudent manager tries to find capacities in which individuals can serve that will not generate strong resistances, not just for the sake of the individuals but for the sake of the whole enterprise, whatever it may be. Sometimes the range of accommodations available may not be great, but any accommodation is better than none, since trying to force round pegs into square holes benefits neither the pegs nor the holes.

## The secular importance of religion

But beyond the value of accommodating individual commitments of
the most central and intimate kind, society has a prudential *secular*
interest in the encouragement of religious behaviour and — within the
broad spectrum of religious behaviour — a special concern for the
flourishing of *new* religious. Why is that?

> It is widely held by students of society that there are certain functional
> prerequisites without which society would not continue to exist. At first
> glance, this seems to be obvious — scarcely more than to say than an
> automobile engine could not exist, as a going system, without a carburetor...
> Most writers list religion among the functional prerequisites. [1]

What function is religion performing that is as essential to society as a
carburetor is to an automobile? It is providing an *explanation of the
ultimate meaning of life*.

Of course, in most societies today there are several religions fulfilling
this function. (Even in those societies that try to limit the field to one
favoured faith there are also usually one or more "underground" or
"folk" religions). And any one religion does not necessarily perform that
function for everyone, however much it may seek or pretend to do so,
but only for those who are its (voluntary) adherents. (The term
"voluntary" is crucial, since no one can be *made* to believe something,
even though people can often be compelled to *say* they believe or to *act
out* certain gestures of fealty, but the exercise of coercion itself can
generate doubt and negativism under the surface of compliance. "Man is
a volunteer", declared Milton Mayer, and neither man nor woman
functions well under duress, least of all in embracing or endorsing the
source of "operant conditioning" — B.F. Skinner to the contrary
notwithstanding.)

> What each religion is doing for its adherents... is to help them to "make
> sense" of life, especially of their own lives, and particularly of those aspects of
> their lives which are both unsatisfactory and unalterable: failure, handicap,
> defeat, loss, illness, bereavement, and the prospect of their own death. Those
> are the experiences that pose most sharply the question of "what is the
> meaning of life?" and religion tries to provide answers to that question,
> offering the widest and deepest concepts the human mind can grasp, so that
> the suffering or perplexed individual can see the pain or difficulty of the
> moment in a broader perspective of greater good or longer purpose or firmer
> reality.
>
> Such "explanations" of the ultimate meaning of life may be theistic or non-
> theistic, naturalistic or supernaturalistic, activistic or quietistic, conventional

or bizarre. If they help believers to rise up each morning with hope, to get through the day somehow with purposefulness, and to lie down at night with some sense of satisfaction, they are performing — for *them* — the function of religion, whatever outsiders may think. Not all churches, synagogues, mosques or temples perform that function well for all believers all the time, and many people may get what ultimate meaning they have from other sources, including some that are not conventionally religious. Yet whatever the source, the function being served is still essentially *religious*.

Not all people feel an equal need at all times for ultimate meaning, and some may go for years — or perchance a lifetime — without experiencing the profound inward pang of desperation to know "what's it all about", "whether I really *matter*", or "what's the use of it all, anyway?" But for those who do experience it, this threat of meaninglessness can be frightening. Unless most people, most of the time, can find moderately satisfactory ways of answering the ultimate questions... the society of which they are a part will be in peril. Persons who cannot find some kind of more or less satisfying answers are apt to succumb to despair, bitterness, resentment, anomie, or to fall into one or another of the escapisms, derangements, and addictions which are the increasingly prevalent "maladies of meaninglessness" besetting our society today. Such persons are often a hazard to themselves and others, sometimes resorting to impulsive or desperate violence or suicide.

Some people in this plight find a religion which relieves their distress, others do not. The same mode of "explanation" does not work for all. Some resonate to a mystic appeal, others to an ascetic one; some to an otherworldly call, others to a summons to earthly service to humankind. Fortunately, there are many varieties of religion..., and almost anyone should be able to find one that suits. But the test of the functional adequacy of a religion is not just in its content or in its initial appeal.

Strange as it may seem, the quality which enables a religion to satisfy the need for ultimate meaning does not appear to be the cogency, reasonableness, plausibility, or even attractiveness as wish-fulfillment of its doctrinal affirmations, but rather the intensity with which they are advocated and embodied by a devoted community of adherents. Intellectual propositions in the abstract do not seem to fill the hunger for meaning, but rather the continuing, reinforcing experience of a supportive company of fellow believers bound together by strong commitment to the faith. It is for this reason that there is — properly speaking — no individual religion, no "instant" religion, no invisible or disembodied religion. Religion exists as a functioning reality only to the degree that it is embodied in an ongoing community — a "church".

That religion will be most *convincing* whose community of faith is most *serious* about its beliefs. Their seriousness may be manifest in various ways; by strictness of doctrinal unanimity, by rigor of behavioral or attitudinal conformity, by intensity of emotional investment, by depth of commitment of time, energy, money (a relatively "cheap" commodity in religion), and self.

There are many ways of carrying out the religious function, each with its own characteristic mode of being serious, and they are not all equally attractive to outsiders who are not at the moment seeking ultimate meaning for their lives... In fact, it may be the very difficulty, "peculiarity", or bizarreness of the religious behavior exhibited that is most compelling in convincing potential converts that "their faith must be true, or they wouldn't *do* such things!"[2]

\* \* \*

If the function of religion is as important for the survival of society as this analysis suggests, how can society make sure that that function is effectively performed? Historically — and *pre*historically, for that matter — the answer has been for the rulers to favor the functionaries of one or more existing religions with high rank, wealth, power, and other material rewards, while at the same time penalizing or suppressing upstart new religions — the "impious" and "unpatriotic" cults that keep springing up among the "lower orders" of society. Yet somehow these privileges, perquisites, and emoluments (collectively termed the "establishment" of religion) have not insured the effective performance of the religious function — quite the contrary. They have instead contributed to its deterioration. Why should that be?

Religious movements begin, as a rule, among the "have-nots" and have their greatest impact there, perhaps because the "have-nots" know a disproportionate share of miserable yet unavoidable experiences. Having less in the way of material resources to shield themselves from adversity, they have a more acute and continuous need to "make sense" of their lives... Actually, among the "have-nots" there are fewer individuals in proportion who are religious adherents, but their involvement with religion is more intense than is that of the "haves", among whom a much larger proportion have a veneer of religion, while few have as intense an attachment to it.[3]

## Conventional religions do not reach those who need religion most

It is not just the economic "have-nots" who may experience intense needs for a religious explanation of the meaning of their lives but those who for other reasons (in the words of Eric Hoffer) "feel their lives to be irremediably spoiled" — not only "(a) the poor", but "(b) misfits, (c) outcasts, (d) minorities, (e) adolescent youth, (f) the ambitious..., (g) those in the grip of some vice or obsession, (h) the impotent..., (i) the inordinately selfish, (j) the bored, (k) the sinners".[4] Meaning-needs are intensified for these and for others by the recently-attained awareness of the perpetually impending and imminent threat to all earthly life of nuclear doom. The point of this analysis is that the religion that satisfies the "haves" — the people whose meaning-needs are not acute — is not satisfying to the "have-nots" — the people who need a sense of ultimate meaning most. That is one reason that "establishment" of religion doesn't work.

The people who arrange the "establishment" and whose religion is the one to be favored with privileges and benefits, prestige and the official sponsorship of the state are, of course, the "haves". Their religion is not only unusable to the "have-nots"... because it doesn't "explain" their lives, but the very act of "establishing" it as official and respectable and "required" makes it part of the problem that needs to be "explained". In addition, the "established" religion loses much of its persuasiveness even among the "haves", since the quality that makes it convincing is its *cost* to the believer, and the effect of "establishment" is precisely to take the cost out of religion...

As the "established" religion prospers, its functionaries demonstrate the paradox first pointed out by C. Northcote Parkinson ("Parkinson's Paradox") with respect to governmental occupations: *the more secure their situations, the less productive they become.* They come to feel that their stipends and emoluments are given in recognition of their *being* rather than their *doing.* They tend to wax fat and indolent. They neglect their duties, or delegate them to apprentices and underlings. Under these circumstances, it is not surprising that the religion these functionaries serve begins to lose adherents, actual and potential, to competing religious bodies whose diligence and zeal have not (yet) suffered the debilitating rewards of official favor — the new cults of the "have-nots"!

The response of the "establishment" to such competition from below is seldom increased vigor and productivity. Instead, the effort is invariably made to suppress the competition, and the heavy hand of the state is called into play to protect the favored faith from "unworthy" rivals. Persecution follows, the devotion of the non-established groups is stimulated by danger, the cost of adherence among them is increased — and with it the convincingness of their beliefs — while the "establishment" is debased by having had to call in the state to defend it... (It) is not invigorated but rather confirmed in its pretensions and sinks further into that characteristic blend of arrogance and debility that "establishment" fosters.[5]

Although this analysis is focused on the effects of establishing religion (by law), it casts some light on informal establishment as well, in which the flaccid and complacent religion of those who benefit from the status quo and do not want it criticized or disturbed is not attractive or satisfying to those in search of ultimate meaning that will make sense of an unacceptable status quo. They turn instead to newer, more fermentative, more demanding faiths, which are then denounced as "cults" by the conventional religions.

To recapitulate the argument thus far:

1. It is important to society that the function of religion (explaining the ultimate meaning of life) be available to those who need it.

2. Since different modes of explanation are needed to meet the variety of individual readinesses, the widest range of religious offerings should be encouraged through freedom of religion.

3. It is the new, unconventional and demanding religious movements that appeal most effectively to those who for a variety of reasons experience the most acute needs for meaning and who find the older conventional and avocational religions unsatisfying.

4. Yet it is precisely those new "upstart" religions that incur the animosity and resentment of the older religions and their adherents, and the result can be various forms of persecution of the newcomers.

## Opposition to new religious movements in the United States

The remainder of this paper will be devoted to exploring some of the tactics used — particularly in the United States — against new religious movements and the dangers these pose to religious liberty and to the entire spectrum of religious bodies.

Thus far in the United States the major religious bodies have not been active in initiating or encouraging measures against new religions, either because of commitment to religious liberty, belief that they do not pose a significant threat, reluctance to dignify them by attention, inertia, or a combination of the above. Indeed, in some instances they have been commendably resistant to persecutory measures advocated or initiated by others. The main impetus for restrictive or suppressive actions has come from lay organizations composed mainly of (1) the parents, spouses, other relatives and friends of converts to new religious movements, (2) apostate ex-members of such movements, and (3) persons who advise or assist the organizations in their work, often for pay, such as mental health professionals, "exit-counsellors" and a variety of specialists in "rescue" operations, to whom we shall return in a moment.

The principal modes of attack on the activities of new religious movements, however, have been more directly focused on specific problems, often invoking various laws against them that were not originally intended for such application. Thus legal prosecutions have been instituted, not because of excessive zeal on the part of public officials, but as a result of complaints and goadings by irate citizens. (This pattern is extensively documented by Lee Boothby in "Government as an Instrument of Retribution for Private Resentments" in *Government Intervention in Religious Affairs, II.*[6]) Among the main lines of attack are the following:

1. Denying or revoking tax exemptions
   *(Holy Spirit Association for the Unification of World Christianity v. Tax Commission of New York City* (1982), *Church of Scientology of California* v. *Commissioner of Internal Revenue* (1984), etc.)
2. Regulating or restricting solicitations of charitable contributions
   *(Heffron v. International Society for Krishna Consciousness* (1981), *Larson v. Valente* (1982), *Scientology Flag Service Org. v. Clearwater*, etc.)
3. Prosecutions of leaders of new religious movements for "crimes" not normally prosecuted as rigorously
   *(U.S. v. Mary Sue Hubbard* (1980), *U.S. v. Sun Myung Moon* (1984), etc.)
4. Enforcement of other regulations
   *(Alamo Foundation v. Secy of Labor* (1983) minimum wage; *Moon v. Immigration and Naturalization Service* (1982?) immigration laws; etc.)
5. Attacks on conversion

## The anti-cult movement and attacks on conversion

Many of these attacks on new religious movements have created or threatened to create precedents that would apply equally and injuriously to other religious bodies, and for this reason some of the older religious bodies have entered friend-of-the-court briefs in some of the above-mentioned cases, not so much in "support" of the new religious groups as in opposition to the government's tactics. But the fifth category involves litigation and proposed legislation that strikes even more directly at one of the central concerns of most religions, particularly Christianity: the validity of *conversion*, the right pointed to in the Universal Declaration of Human Rights as "freedom to *change...* religion". Conversion is an essential element in the New Testament, from the summary of Jesus' message — "repent and believe in the Gospel" (Mark 1:15) — to Paul's sudden conversion on the road to Damascus (Acts 9). Throughout the subsequent centuries Christianity has sought the turning of hearts to the Lord that is the beginning and the *sine qua non* of salvation.

Yet it is this very threshold act that is a source of deep antipathy towards religion, since it precipitates and evidences a change of life and loyalties and may suggest a repudiation — or at least abandonment — of old ways and attachments. Family and former associates resent the implied reproach of such a change, that the previous patterns and commitments were not good enough and so were left for something better. Family have been split and friendships broken over conversion and intense antagonisms generated which seem able to fuel far-reaching vendettas against the religious group(s) thought to be the cause. In addition, some older traditions look upon conversion to more recent faiths as a deadly threat to their survival. Procuring conversion from the "official" religion is a serious crime in Greece and some Muslim countries. The Jewish community is particularly distressed by the threat of loss by (out)conversion and intermarriage, and it is one of the main elements fuelling the anti-cult movement in the US and elsewhere.

Attacks on conversion have taken three main forms in the United States:

a) private "self-help" efforts to reverse conversions by force, called "deprogramming";

b) efforts to use existing "conservatorship" statutes or to enact broader ones to legalize deprogramming;

c) litigation by apostates against unpopular religious groups for torts allegedly arising from membership in the group (i.e., from conversion).

## A.  "DEPROGRAMMING" BY THE NEW VIGILANTES

Beginning with the efforts of one Ted Patrick in the early 1970s, a tactic has been developed to reverse conversions by force. It is called "deprogramming" after the argument that converts to new religions have been "programmed" — like computers — by insidious techniques that require stern and intrusive measures to reverse the process. Deprogramming, like the anti-cult movement that promotes and protects it, proceeds from the presupposition that new religious movements gain their adherents by deception and "coercive persuasion" to overcome the will of the unwary and subject them to the dominance of the "cult" so that they can be exploited for the aggrandizement of cult leaders. The entire panoply of anti-cult methods depends upon this axiom of "brain-washing" or "mind-control" — the insistence that intelligent, upwardly mobile young people would never join such bizarre groups or remain in them of their own free choice and therefore must have been tricked or coerced. It may be questioned whether such an exotic new explanation is needed. Most of the behaviour changes described can be adequately accounted for by the age-old phenomenon of conversion.

Another axiom of the anti-cult movement is that the "cults" — or at least the "destructive cults" (whatever those may be) — are not really *religions* but merely economic or political scams disguised as religions in order to claim the privilege of religious liberty. It is crucial to anti-cultists to insist that the cult which a loved one has joined is not a legitimate religion and that one could not have experienced a genuine and voluntary conversion to it. Thus is it not an invasion of religious liberty or a violation of the adherent's free choice, but a high duty and obligation, to "rescue" the adherent from the cult, by force if need be, on the supposition that the cult member will eventually be grateful for deliverance when the hold of the cult is broken. In fact, the hold of the cult is not thought to be broken until the former adherent *is* ready and willing to thank the deliverers and to help deliver others from similar subjection.

Thus the anti-cult movement has its own faith-commitments, theomachies, rites, gurus, and crusades to which it seeks to counter-convert those it rescues; it is a sort of anti-cult "cult", with its missionaries and propaganda networks, such as monthly newsletters that seem to urge, "Be the first family on your block to hold a successful deprogramming!" (At least that was the case a few years ago. More recently the movement has tried to take on a more genteel veneer, assuring critics that deprogramming is crude and passé, "we only do 'cult-awareness education' now". Unfortunately, this message has not yet reached all of the faithful, and deprogrammings still go on.)

*A description of deprogramming*

The praxis of deprogramming usually includes some or all of the following elements:[7]

1. Parents or other relatives of a young person who has joined a "cult" contact a deprogrammer and employ him or her to "rescue" the convert. (Fees for this service may run from $20,000 as high as $80,000 *plus expenses*, whether "successful" or not.)

2. The convert is located (sometimes the hardest part of the job) and the situation is scouted to determine times and places of vulnerability to seizure.

3. A plan of action is formulated, helpers are hired and briefed (sometimes part-time practitioners or relatives of the convert or both), and the routes and means of transportation and place or places of detention arranged.

4. Gaining control of the person of the convert (kidnapping) is often brought about by a ruse — if there is still any relationship between the convert and relatives — such as taking the convert out to lunch or home for a visit or to the hospital to see an ailing parent (said to be recovering from a seizure brought on by the convert's absence); if deception is not practical, reliance must be placed on surprise and/or superior force (assault).

5. At some point, in any event, deception is replaced by force. The convert is seized, often by several strong men, bundled into a car or van, and transported (often across state lines)[8] to a place where he or she can be kept in isolation for an

extended period of time: a motel, a relative's home, a deprogramming centre (of which there are several in the US) or a combination of the above in succession.

6. Keeping the convert under control (unlawful imprisonment) is the next problem. Often the place of confinement is an impromptu prison with windows boarded up, furnishings removed except for a bed and a chair or two, doors locked, guards outside, isolated from outsiders. Sometimes the victim is tied or handcuffed to the bed. He or she is seldom left alone, even when using the toilet, and is told that this detention will continue as long as necessary to attain the desired result: restoring "freedom of choice" to the victim, which can be evidenced in only one way — by deciding to leave the cult.

7. The main activity during this detention is intensive counter-indoctrination (which often involves menacing, intimidation, assault, etc., but apparently not torture, or the use of drugs). Various techniques are used, including the following:

a) Essential to the process is getting and retaining the victim's attention, which may require knocking hands away from covering the ears, gripping the cheeks to prevent turning the head away, twisting the arm, tying in a sitting position, shouting, shining a bright light in the eyes, etc.

b) A second tactic is removing any vestiges of cult-identification (to instill a feeling of isolation and weaken the will to resist) by taking away cultic garb, prayer-beads, amulets, literature, cutting off cultic hair-do, etc., stripping the victim down to underwear (which also inhibits escape and intensifies a sense of vulnerability), disrupting prayers or chanting.

c) A major effort is devoted to "overloading" the victim with the deprogrammer's messages so that other thoughts, memories and messages are crowded out: the victim is subjected to a continuous barrage of round-the-clock argument, reproach, beration, cajolery and abuse by "helpers" who work in shifts, keeping the victim awake as long as possible to prevent leisure for reflection or regaining composure, keeping the victim perpetually "off balance", as it were: denunciation alternating with pleading, kindness with harshness, accusations with entreaties by tearful parents, etc.

d) Attacks on the victim's new religion are a central ingredient in the process and include ridicule of the cult's teachings and practices, atrocity stories about the cult, exposes by apostates (ideally former members of the same cult), defacing of cult scriptures, symbols or pictures of its leaders, and never-ending argumentation from the Bible and other sources to "prove" the convert's religion false.

e) The victim is pointed to "the (only) way out", the new doctrine to be accepted in place of the (not very) old. Sometimes videotapes are shown of the "breaking" of other deprogrammees — the capitulation, the reconciliation with parents, the expressions of gratitude for being "rescued" from the cult.

The "explanation" is provided of "how the cults work", which also provides a formula of exoneration if the victim will only accept it: "they tricked you; you were duped; they just wanted to use you for their own ends; but now you're free to make up your own mind (to leave the cult, of course); soon you will be able to help rescue other victims of mind-control", etc.

These efforts continue until the victim gives in, escapes, or is rescued from the self-appointed "rescuers" by the police, the cult or other third parties — or the parents' money for paying the deprogrammers gives out.

In a "successful" deprogramming, the victim eventually "breaks" and comes over to the Right Side, when all is forgiven, the Family is Reunited, the battle is won. (Sometimes, since the cults have their own self-defence programme of *anti-cult* awareness training that recommends pretending to "break", the victim feigns capitulation in order to turn off the pressure, so the process culminates in a final phase: "floating".)

f) After capitulation or deconversion (or frequently re-conversion to a new, anti-cult faith), the deprogrammed person is kept under close observation for several weeks or months (during which he or she is said to be "floating") to prevent reversion to the cult, often in one of the several "halfway houses" such as "Unbound" in Iowa City or Carla Pfeiffer's "Enrichment Center" in Norfolk, Nebraska.

(Notwithstanding these precautions, many victims eventually go back to their chosen faith-group anyway.)[9]

It is instructive that this methodology of forcible deconversion resembles in many respects precisely the same techniques which the anti-cult movement accuses the cult of using: deception, coercion, sensory overload, sleep deprivation, repetitive indoctrination, emotional pressure, etc. Whether or not the *cults* use these methods as diabolically as their accusers allege, there is no doubt that the *deprogrammers* do — by their own admission.[10] Perhaps it is another instance of "fighting fire with fire", which often produces remarkable resemblances between the supposedly benevolent and the allegedly malevolent, so that it is sometimes hard to tell which is which. The most striking likeness, however, is that both sides rely upon the most penetrating reagent in human experience: intense, protracted one-on-one attention such as few people experience except for a few minutes at a time, and that rarely. Whether it be "love-bombing" or "reproach-bombing" may be less significant than that it is close, interpersonal, saturation "attention-bombing" that goes on for hours, days, even weeks. Very few people can resist that influence, though — like the physical coercion of Chinese "brainwashing" — once it ceases, the effect can quickly wear off, therefore, the long period of "decompression".

This deliberate, concerted, protracted, violent assault on religious faith is probably the most serious infringement of religious liberty in the United States in the second half of the twentieth century, and the agencies of law enforcement and the courts have been rather dilatory and uneven in their efforts to apprehend and punish its perpetrators. (In the US, there is an important distinction between state action v. private action, and the latter is more difficult to reach by law.)

Local law enforcement and prosecution efforts have been spotty at best. There are instances in which local police have ignored or even *aided* deprogrammings. [11] But in some other instances they have been prompt and effective in apprehending and prosecuting deprogrammers, only to have grand juries refuse to indict or petite juries to convict. But there have been some significant criminal convictions. And where criminal prosecutions fail — or are not even attempted — civil actions have sometimes been brought and sometimes have succeeded.

### Two states case

State courts have been mixed in their treatment of deprogramming complaints. The first deprogramming case on record arose in Queens County, New York, where a young woman brought suit against her mother and a deprogrammer because they had held her captive for four days in an effort to reverse her conversion to the Krishna Consciousness movement. The grand jury refused to indict the mother or the private detective she had hired and turned its attention instead to the religious group, indicting ISKCON and two of its leaders for unlawful imprisonment, [12] which shifts this case to class C, below.

In 1977 on the West Coast an effort was made by the parents of five members of the Unification Church to obtain a conservatorship order to allow a *legalized* deprogramming. In this instance — unlike many other such efforts (i.e. Baer v. Baer and Taylor v. Gilmartin, above) — the offspring were given advance notice and allowed to present evidence and argument in opposition, which they did in a hearing that continued for eleven days. Despite "expert" testimony on both sides, the judge was in no doubt as to the solution. Judge Lee Vavuris granted the parents custody of their (adult) offspring with these classic comments:

> (W)e're talking about the very essence of life here, mother, father and children... This is the essence of civilization. The family unit is a micro-civilization. That's what it is. A great civilization is made up of many, many great families, and that's what's before this court.
>
> One of the reasons that I made this decision, I could see the love here of a parent for his child, and I don't even have to go beyond that.
>
> The child is the child even though a parent may be 90 and the child 60. [13]

(Sharon Worthing has termed this, appropriately, the doctrine of "perpetual religious infancy". [14])

The court of appeals reversed on an appeal brought quickly against the superior court. It noted that judge Vavuris had not found the conservatees insane, incompetent or unable to manage their property, which are the only grounds on which guardians (conservators) can be appointed under the California statute. It held that the conservatorship orders interfered with the conservatees' constitutional right to religious freedom and that courts have no competence to judge the validity of anyone's chosen religion or the process by which one chooses a religion. But the damage had been done. Although the appellate court had ordered that no deprogramming be done until it could review the case, the deprogrammers had started to work as soon as the lower court's order was granted, and the day after the appellate court reversed it, three of the five conservatees renounced their membership in the Unification Church. [15]

### A Minnesota state case

Two cases of civil suits against deprogrammers from the state of Minnesota will round out this section. One was brought by a young woman who had joined The Way, International, and had been subjected to deprogramming by her parents, but after feigning deconversion she escaped, returned to The Way and sued her parents and the hired deprogrammers. The jury exonerated the defendants. She asked the court for a judgment in her favour notwithstanding the verdict, and when it refused she appealed to the supreme court of Minnesota, which decided the case *en blanc*. The court noted that she had been in alleged captivity for 16 days, but that for the last 13 of them she "willingly remained in the company of defendants". It announced that "(d)amages may not be assessed for any period of detention to which one freely consents". But how about the first three days? The appellate court agreed with the jury's conclusion that her later acquiescence served as a waiver of any lack of consent during the initial period of captivity.

> Because, it is argued, the cult conditioning process induces dramatic and non-consensual change giving rise to a new temporary identity on the part of the individuals whose consent is under examination, Susan's volitional capacity prior to treatment may well have been impaired. Following her readjustment, the evidence suggests that Susan was a different person, "like her old self". As such, the question of Susan's consent becomes a function of time. We therefore deem Susan's subsequent affirmation of defendants' actions dispositive. [16]

The court's logic at this point seems obscure. If her apparent acquiescence on the fourth day cancelled her resistance on the first three days, why then did her subsequent change on the sixteenth day — after her "treatment" and "readjustment" — when she decamped and instituted suit against her captors, not cancel the acquiescence? Apparently the process only works one way. Coming out of the "cult" wipes the slate clean, but going back in doesn't.

Not content simply to affirm the jury verdict, the court expatiated upon society's interest in thwarting "cult indoctrination".

> Although carried out under colorably religious auspices, the method of cult indoctrination... is predicated on a strategy of coercive persuasion that undermines the capacity for informed consent. While we acknowledge that other social institutions may utilize a degree of coercion in promoting their objectives, none do so to the same extent or intend the same consequences. Society, therefore, has a compelling interest favoring intervention. The facts in this case support the conclusion that plaintiff only regained her volitional capacity to consent after engaging in the first three days of the deprogramming process. As such, we hold that when parents, or their agents, acting under the conviction that the judgmental capacity of their adult child is impaired, seek to extricate that child from what they reasonably believe to be a religious or pseudo-religious cult, and the child at some juncture assents to the action in question, limitations upon the child's mobility do not constitute meaningful deprivations of personal liberty sufficient to support a judgment of false imprisonment. But owing to the threat that deprogramming poses to public order, we do not endorse self-help as a preferred alternative. [17]

This belated caveat did not noticeably detract from the court's manifesto for deprogramming as a public service, and the decision has been lauded by the anti-cult movement from coast to coast as a kind of judicial signal for "open season on the cults". It did not go unchallenged, however. Two judges filed vehement and commendable dissents. Justice Wahl wrote:

> In every generation, parents have viewed their children's religious and political beliefs with alarm and dismay if... different from their own. Under the First Amendment, however, adults in our society enjoy freedom of association and belief. In my view, it is unwise to tamper with those freedoms and with longstanding principles of tort law out of sympathy for parents seeking to help their "misguided" offspring, however well-intentioned and loving their acts may be...
>
> Any imprisonment "which is not legally justifiable" is false imprisonment; ... therefore, the fact that the tortfeasor acted in good faith is no defense to a charge of false imprisonment. [18]

Justice Otis joined Justice Wahl's dissent and added his own:

> If there is any constitutional protection we should be slow to erode, it is the right of serious-minded people, young or old, to search for religious or philosophical fulfillment in their own way and in their own time without the interference of meddling friends or relatives, however well-intentioned they may be.
>
> At age 21, a daughter is no longer a child. She is an adult. Susan Peterson was not only an adult in 1976, but she was a bright and well-educated adult. For whatever reason, she was experiencing a period of restlessness and insecurity which is by no means uncommon in students of that age. But to hold that for seeking companionship and identity in a group whose proselytizing tactics may well be suspect, she must endure without remedy the degrading and humiliating treatment she received at the hands of her parents is, in my opinion, totally at odds with the basic rights of young people to think unorthodox thoughts, join unorthodox groups, and proclaim unorthodox views. [19]

### A federal case in Minnesota

The second case followed four years later in federal district court, with Peterson v. Sorlien (Sorlien was a Lutheran pastor who assisted in the deprogramming) as the leading decision in the forum state, looking over the judge's shoulder, as it were. It involved two young people, Bill Eilers, 24, and his wife, Sandy, 23, who lived in Wisconsin. The wife was pregnant, and they were in Winona, Minnesota, for a prenatal check-up on 16 August 1982, when they were seized by several men and thrust into two vans and taken to the Tau Center on the campus of the College of St Theresa operated by the Roman Catholic Sisters of St Francis. Here they were kept prisoner in separate rooms for six days while persistent efforts were made to break their adherence to a small fundamentalist Protestant group called Disciples of the Lord Jesus Christ led by a convert from Hinduism, Rama Behera, which was viewed by the Eilers' families as a "cult". Bill was kept handcuffed to a bed in a third-floor room with windows boarded up and guards at the door. He was periodically roughed up when he refused to listen to deprogrammers explaining the evils of cults or playing for him tape-recordings of Jim Jones's last speech at Jonestown, Guyana. On the sixth day, Bill decided that the only way out was to feign deconversion. The deprogrammers then decided to take him and his wife to a retention centre in Iowa City. As they were being put in a car, Bill broke free and ran to a nearby house shouting for help. The householder let him in and he called the police, who caught several of the perpetrators and arrested them for false imprisonment, but the grand jury declined to indict them. So Bill Eilers filed a civil suit against them in federal court in Minnesota, which came on to be heard in March 1984. After a jury trial of several days, the judge took the unusual step of granting a directed verdict (the first directed verdict he had ever issued, he said) finding the defendants guilty of false imprisonment.

First he dealt with the Peterson v. Sorlien precedent. (He had remarked in chambers during the trial that he considered Peterson unconstitutional and would not enforce it in his courtroom, which as a federal judge he was not obliged to do.) The defendants had contended that there was no actual confinement because the plaintiff, at least by the fourth day, had consented to the defendant's actions.

> Many people would feign consent under similar circumstances, whether out of fear of their captors or as a means of making an escape. But in this case, unlike the *Peterson* case relied on by the the defendants, it is undisputed that the plaintiff was at no time free to leave the Tau Center during the week in question, nor were any reasonable means of escape available to him. Under these circumstances, the Court finds, in agreement with many other authorities, that the plaintiff's apparent consent is not a defense to false imprisonment. [20]

There remained the claimed defence of "necessity", that the actions taken, though illegal, were done to prevent even more serious harms.

> They claim that the confinement and attempted deprogramming of the plaintiff was necessary to prevent him from committing suicide or from otherwise harming himself or others... (T)he right to confine a person in order to prevent harm to that person lasts only as long as is necessary to get that person to the proper lawful authorities...

> \*     \*     \*

> The defendants' failure to even attempt to use the lawful alternatives available to them is fatal to their assertion of the necessity defense... (T)he defense of necessity eventually dissipates as a matter of law... In this particular case... where the defendants held the plaintiff for five and one-half days with no attempt to resort to lawful alternatives available to them, the Court could not sustain a jury verdict in the defendants' favor on the issue of false imprisonment. Accordingly, the Court rules as a matter of law that the plaintiff was falsely imprisoned without justification. [21]

The court left to the jury the determination of the amount of damages, and the jury awarded the plaintiff the rather meagre amount of $10,000. (Fortunately, he had already collected over $50,000 in out-of-court settlements from the two families and the Sisters of St Francis!)

In these two Minnesota cases — one state and one federal — we see two very different understandings of the deprogramming situation. Which way the jurisprudence of the United States will move remains to be seen.

## *An overview of deprogramming litigation*

One of the foremost legal commentators on church-state issues in the US, Prof. Douglas Laycock of the University of Texas Law School, has summarized this situation:

> The resulting litigation has produced mixed results. Most appellate courts have recognized the threat to free exercise rights and have been reluctant to legitimate abduction, involuntary "deprogramming", or guardianship orders against adults not proven to be mentally incompetent. [22] But some courts have assumed that brainwashing by new religions is a serious threat and have tolerated, or even assisted parental intervention by force and threats of force. [23] Even in some cases where the deprogrammed convert won, juries have rarely returned substantial verdicts.
>
> *The right to convert to a new religion deserves better protection than this. The right to choose one's own religious beliefs is the very essence of religious liberty.* Courts and families might legitimately intervene when a conversion is involuntary. The importance of the right to convert, and the likelihood that the majority's perceptions of new religions will be distorted by hostility, requires a strong presumption that conversions are voluntary. Such a presumption is not rebutted by evidence of an intense emotional experience and a sharp break with the past; these often accompany wholly voluntary religious conversions. Little more than that has been offered in most of the reported cases. In most of these cases, there has been no evidence that proselytizers for the new religion used physical force and little evidence of brainwashing, but there has been largely undisputed evidence of physical force by the parents and deprogrammers. [24]

### B. LEGALIZING DEPROGRAMMING THROUGH CONSERVATORSHIP LAWS

Recently the anti-cult movement has apparently sought to distance itself from the cruder forms of deprogramming and has sought to legalize it wherever possible. (Perhaps the threat of being sued, with the attendant stigma of illegality — "mixed" though the court results have been — was not an inviting prospect.) We saw above that an attempt to proceed under existing guardianship laws was not (legally) successful in California in Katz v. Superior Court (1977), [25] nor has it generally been elsewhere. One reason is that conservatorship of the person is equivalent to civil commitment, and the supreme court of the United States has said that civil commitment is justifiable only if and only so long as a person is clearly shown to be a danger to self or others[26] — not an easy standard to meet and one not met in Katz. Since existing guardianship or conservatorship laws have proved inadequate for their purposes, the anti-cult movement has pressed assiduously for amendments to authorize a kind of custodianship arrangement that *would* meet their purposes by allowing legalized deconversion under court order. Since none of those proposals has been adopted, we need not treat them here.

## C. TORT SUITS AGAINST UNPOPULAR RELIGIOUS GROUPS

A far more fertile field of legal redress has opened up since People v. Murphy suggested the way in 1977.[27] As was noted earlier, that case began as a complaint against deprogrammers, but a Queens County, NY, grand jury turned it around and instead indicted the leaders of the local Krishna temple for unlawful imprisonment. Judge John J. Leahy of Queens supreme court (the lowest court of record in NY State) stated the problem thus:

> The entire crux of the argument propounded by the People is that through "mind control", "brainwashing" and/or "manipulation of mental processes" the defendants destroyed the free will of the alleged victims, obtaining over them mind control to the point of absolute domination and thereby coming within the purview of the issue of unlawful imprisonment.[28]

He noted that no evidence had been adduced to show that the ISKCON members had been subjected to physical coercion or deception. Like other converts, they had chosen this mode of life of their own free will. He rejected the prosecution's contention that daily ritual chanting and other communal activities of the Krishna group were a form of intimidation or restraint.

> Religious proselytizing and the recruitment and maintenance of belief through a strict regimen, meditation, chanting, self-denial, and the communication of other religious teachings cannot under our laws — as presently enacted — be construed as criminal in nature and serve as a criminal indictment.[29]

Therefore, he dismissed the case.

This was a case of first impression, and the judge had little precedent to guide him.[30] It was the first time that the anti-cult movement's characterization of the problem had surfaced in a court of law as the gravamen of a criminal prosecution, and — though unsuccessful in that role — it soon found wider appeal in civil actions.

We will now focus on the leading successes and failures in this burgeoning new field of litigation arising out of conversion to unpopular religious groups. It is apparently seen as a growth industry; one attorney in Boston has filed seven tort suits against the Church of Scientology alone, and others in other states are equally enterprising. It has come to be a standard riposte of the anti-cult movement. As soon as a convert is deprogrammed, the idea is explored of launching a retaliatory suit against the religious group involved, charging fraud, breach of contract, outrageous conduct, libel, and other torts, even — where plausible — wrongful death! As in litigation against deprogrammers, the results have been mixed.

*The Christofferson case(s)*

One of the longest-running serials in this genre is that initiated by Julie Christofferson Tichbourne against the Church of Scientology in Portland, Oregon. In 1975, Julie Christofferson became involved with Scientology briefly, took several courses, worked for the Delphian Foundation, an institute related to the Church, to pay her tuition, leaving college to concentrate on her studies in Scientology. In April 1976 her mother had her deprogrammed, and she turned against the Church, suing it for outrageous conduct or "intentional infliction of emotional distress" and fraud. The jury awarded her damages of $2,000,000! But the appellate court reversed with respect to the first cause of action and remanded for retrial with respect to the second. It also dismissed the Church of Scientology of Portland and the Delphian Foundation as defendants, leaving only the (Scientology) Mission of Davis and its president, Howard Samuels. The appellate court held that Scientology was a religion (because the plaintiff had not claimed otherwise) and that its teachings were entitled to protection by the free exercise of religion clause of the First Amendment of the US Constitution *if made for a religious purpose.*

> (D)efendants could be held liable if the jury found that the courses and services offered by the Mission to plaintiff were offered for a wholly secular purpose. A wholly secular purpose means that... the statements were made for a purpose other than inducing plaintiff to join or participate in defendants' religion. A wholly secular purpose, in this regard, would include, but not be limited to, the intention solely to obtain money from plaintiff... A jury could find that the courses and services were offered on a secular basis and that a religious designation had been merely "tacked on".[31]

On remand, after a lengthy and heated trial, the jury did so find, and awarded even vaster monetary damages to Ms Christofferson:

$39,000,000! But the court declared a mistrial because of prejudicial and improper statements made by Christofferson's attorney during argument to the jury.[32] This case and the ones awaiting trial in Boston were all settled out of court by the Church of Scientology late in 1986.

### Two New England cases

In 1978 one Shelley Anne Turner sued the Unification Church of Sun Myung Moon in federal court in Rhode Island, charging that she had been held in involuntary servitude and peonage to the Church, but the court held that she had not shown "physical restraint and complete psychological domination" necessary to prove involuntary servitude nor a relationship of bondage based on indebtedness essential to peonage, and so dismissed the complaint.[33]

LaVenda Van Schaick sued the Church of Scientology in federal court in Massachusetts. With respect to her complaint of intentional infliction of emotional distress, the court observed that complaint was based on allegations that

> the church exhorted her to sever family and marital ties and to depend solely on the Church for emotional support. (T)hese alleged courses of conduct (do not constitute) the kind of extreme and outrageous action which will support a claim for intentional infliction of emotional distress... They are similar to the demands for single-minded loyalty and purpose that have characterized numerous religious, political, military and social movements over the ages.[34]

With respect to the allegation of fraud, the court thought they would pose First Amendment problems *if* the Church was entitled to protection under the "free exercise of religion" clause. The parties were directed to submit briefs on that subject for the court's consideration. What might ultimately have been the outcome of this litigation in the courts is not known, since the parties reached a settlement out of court.

### Molko and Leal v. Unification Church

Tracy Leal and David Molko were members of the Unification Church for four and six months respectively until they were forcibly abducted and deprogrammed, after which they sued the church for false imprisonment, fraud and intentional infliction of emotional distress in a California state court in San Francisco. Molko and Leal claimed that they had been recruited under false pretences by persons who concealed their connection with the Unification Church until they were so bound by social constraints as to be unable to leave. The court stated that the tort of false imprisonment "requires direct restraint of the person for some appreciable length of time", and that this had not been shown.

> From the uncontroverted facts in this record, it is clear that neither Plaintiff was falsely imprisoned as conventionally understood... (B)oth Plaintiffs have acknowledged that they were never physically seized or restrained by the Defendants. At no time were they held by force of any kind; nor were their family members... prevented from gaining access to them... Indeed, during the period of his alleged "imprisonment", Mr. Molko commuted back and forth to San Francisco to prepare for and then to take the examination for admission to the California State Bar. [35]
>
> Similarly, Plaintiffs have acknowledged that Defendants made no threats of force or of other unlawful conduct. Plaintiffs do state that they were subjected to threats of harm, but the tendered evidence makes plain that these were entirely threats of divine retribution... Plaintiffs also suggest that they were prevented from leaving by their fear of disappointing the other Church members... But threats of social ostracism are not impermissible and, indeed, are constitutionally protected. [36]

But the plaintiffs contended that they were imprisoned by bonds of "mental control", that their consent to remain with the group had been "obtained when they were incapable of exercising independent judgment to leave", and they introduced testimony by Dr Margaret Singer, a psychologist who has been active in support of the anti-cult movement and has testified as an "expert" witness in many such trials. But the court considered that the proffered evidence was not sufficient to create a triable issue.

The trial court's opinion contains an insight that is particularly cogent for our purposes, having to do with the implications of this kind of case for the ability of *anybody* to "belong" to *anything*.

> If the church were subject to liability for damages whenever it were determined retrospectively that its attempts to influence a non-gravely disabled individual to join its faith — not by force or a threat of force or other unlawful conduct — had been so successful that the individual had lost his ability to decline, a substantial restraint would be placed on the ability of the Church and its present and prospective adherents to practice their religion. The testimony proffered by Plaintiffs does not identify any objective conduct engaged in by the Church which in itself is unlawful, or any conduct engaged in by the Plaintiffs which would have alerted Defendants to the fact that Plaintiffs' consent to remain with the Church was no longer being freely given. Thus, if Plaintiffs could proceed to trial on the evidence tendered in this action, the Church would be required to act at its peril, with no objective criteria to guide its conduct and subject to liability whenever it were later

determined that an individual who had agreed to remain with the Church had lost the capacity to decide that he or she really wanted to leave.

The decision in *Katz* rests on the principle that an adult who is not shown to be gravely disabled must have the personal and individual right to determine for himself or herself whether to associate with a religious group. Despite the possibility of coercive persuasion or "brain-washing", the right of the individual to make such choices is so important that it cannot be removed absent a showing of grave disability. In *Katz*, it was recognized that permitting the appointment of a guardian of the person absent such a showing would impermissibly infringe upon that right. So too would rendering that person's consent subject to repudiation if it were later determined that... the consent did not reflect the exercise of the individual's free will and judgment. If that could be done, in order to avoid potential liability, *neither the Church nor any other association could ever rely upon a person's agreement to join, and the individual's ability to consent to joint would be severely compromised.* [37]

In view of such considerations, Judge Pollak granted summary judgment to the Church, and on appeal his decision was unanimously affirmed on all points. [38] This decision has been taken on appeal by the supreme court of California.

## *Eden v. Moon (1982)*

A Michigan state court disposed of a similar suit brought by Eve Eden against Sun Myung Moon and the Unification Church for fraud, etc. Though unreported, the opinion of Judge Sharon Tevis Finch of the circuit court of the county of Wayne contains some trenchant colloquial insights as cogent as those of more polished higher court decisions. "These sorts of religious movements appear to take over the whole being of the person who is a member. It's much different than our idea of a traditional religion where the church is lucky... if they can get the member there once a week." [39]

> (T)his case is pled in the form of fraud, (and) it has been stated from time to time that the freedom of religion will not protect someone from committing a tort such as fraud... (But) I think that one reason we are here altogether is because Ms. Eden is too quick to believe.

> \* \* \*

> The law of the State of Michigan allows for a cause of action to exist where there is a failure to present all the facts, material facts, with the purpose of misleading a person to enter some activity, commercial or otherwise... It must, however, be extreme, since people are basically on notice, human beings are — well, in our system people are on notice to make their own

investigations when they are entering into commercial transactions, which is where most of the fraud law comes from.

I think that the law would not say that it is that much different in entering into a way of life or a personal belief. People are on notice to inform themselves of the facts. And if they are lied to, then that's actionable...

My difficulty here... is that there is an allegation that it was false and misleading that she would be able to live on a 600 acre ranch operated by this foundation, which would help further her work as a weaver...

Then it's also stated that the purpose of this was to have her join the church, to recruit her. Now, I don't think that purpose has anything to do with fraud..., that there is anything in our law... whatsoever which requires someone to tell another person the purpose that they have in mind when they are trying to get the other person to do something. They have to tell them the truth about what it is that they are trying to get them to do... And I tend to agree with counsel that if that were actionable, then there would be very little in our lives that would not be actionable, because people... frequently have hidden agendas of one type or another, sometimes known to them and sometimes not.

The Plaintiff, I think, is bound to understand that while the purpose to her may be to live on the ranch and be a weaver, that the purpose to the ranch may be something else. The naivete of this whole situation is extremely difficult to deal with, because I think probably most of us know that there are no free lunches in life...

(T)here is no way that her testimony could be read... that she got into the church to the depth she did because she was still believing that she could live on a ranch and be a weaver. What really I see here is that... this was the bait that happened to first draw her attention to this church...

Now... the actions complained of slide over into the Constitutional area, because, what happens, once her attention is gotten, is that the religion, the church, starts performing its religious activities and its method of recruiting and its method of causing belief to occur, converting, whatever we want to call it, and it's those methods that the Plaintiff is saying worked to her detriment.

Now, I don't think that there can be a civil action for those methods. And I think there cannot be for Constitutional reasons... (T)he courts cannot inquire into... the practices of religion, the beliefs, the activities, and, I think, the methods of conversion, unless they constitute independent torts...

I don't believe that the church or any church is required to disclose fully its identity, et cetera, before it starts to try and convert a person. I don't think that the law allows us to control churches in that way...

(O)ur law does not permit us to police thoughts and does not permit us to police religions... And it's because we have a lot of freedoms that people can do things that other people do not approve of. And it may work to the detriment of people at times, and it may have worked to her detriment, as she now believes it, but I don't think the conduct of the (church) as alleged here constitutes a cause of action. So the complaint against all Defendants is dismissed with prejudice. [40]

The court may have been somewhat influenced by the fact that the alleged fraud — the offer of living on a ranch and being a weaver — seems to have occurred in 1971, and the complaint was coming on for decision in 1982, and somewhere in between, the two-year statute of limitations had surely run. This opinion is noteworthy for its sagacious observation that people must bear some responsibility for what they get themselves into, and that a reasonable degree of caution should precede entry into any new situation, including conversion to a new religion.

*George v. ISKCON*

The last case in this series, and the most striking, arose in California, where in 1974, a girl named Robin George, just as she turned 15, began to frequent a temple in Laguna Beach of the International Society for Krishna Consciousness (ISKCON), accompanied by her mother. At the end of that year she left her parental home and wound up in New Orleans, where she lived in a Krishna temple until April 1975, when her father located her and took her home. In May she ran away again and went to Canada, where she lived in a Krishna temple in Ottawa until October, when she returned home. She was then placed in a juvenile detention facility for a year during which time her father died. A year later, she and her mother filed suit against ISKCON for false imprisonment, intentional infliction of emotion distress, libel, invasion of privacy, and the wrongful death of her father, which was alleged to have been brought on by anxiety over Robin, though the defence showed he had been suffering from a number of serious maladies, including chronic alcoholism. [41]

The defence contended that ISKCON had been acting within its rights.

The very nature of this action is anathematic to the free exercise of religion under the United States Constitution... (The Krishna movement), like the Seventh-day Adventists, the Jehovah's Witnesses, and many evangelistic Protestant denominations, engages in proselytizing, and as a result, gains numerous converts to its faith. One of them was Robin George. She now alleges that her conversion somehow constituted an actionable civil wrong, entitling her to substantial money damages. The First Amendment simply does not suffer religion to exist under such legal restraints. To say, in practical effect, that religious conversion should be recognized as a tort for which (action) may be brought by virtually any later diseffective (disaffected?) believer would result in an intolerable chill upon free exercise. [42]

Nevertheless, the jury awarded Robin and her mother damages of $32,000,000! The trial judge reduced the award to $9,700,000, still an astronomical amount. In order to stay execution of the judgment upon its assets, ISKCON would have had to post a stay bond of at least $14,550,000. Unable to put up that amount, ISKCON applied to the court of appeal for a protective order pending appeal, but the court of appeal instead appointed a receiver to take custody of any assets which ISKCON wished to protect from levy and sale to satisfy the judgment. The receiver has since taken a very vigilant and oppressive role in supervising every day-to-day transaction of the religious group, and it is struggling to maintain its existence while working to perfect its appeal of this appalling judgment.

A unique and perplexing aspect of this case is that — unlike the "cult" members involved in the cases discussed above — Robin George was a *minor* during the period of her membership in ISKCON. The defence argued that she had voluntarily consented to become a member of the religion, but the plaintiffs insisted she was without capacity to consent because she was under age. Defendants replied that the supreme court had unanimously settled the question of the age of consent in 1946 in the curious case of Chatwin v. US which provides a suitable conclusion to our survey of the law of the United States bearing on "cult" conversion.

### *Chatwin v. US (1946)*

Chatwin was an elderly widower of 68, a member of a fundamentalist cult of the Mormon faith which still believes in, preaches, and — where possible — practises plural or "celestial" marriage. Chatwin employed as a housekeeper a girl under 15 who had a mental age of 7. He and others in the household continually taught her that plural marriage was essential to salvation. "As a result of these teachings, the girl was converted to the principles of celestial marriage and entered into a cult marriage with Chatwin." She became pregnant, and her parents had her declared a ward of the Juvenile Court, but she escaped, obtained money from two of Chatwin's daughters (who were probably older than her mother), and went to live with him in another state.

He persuaded her to go with him to Mexico, where they were married civilly, and they then settled in Arizona until he was apprehended by federal authorities two years later and convicted of kidnapping. The US supreme court unanimously reversed the conviction on the ground that the girl had voluntarily chosen to go with Chatwin.

> There is no proof that Chatwin or any of the other petitioners imposed at any time an unlawful, physical or mental restraint upon the movements of the

girl... (S)he was perfectly free to leave the petitioners when and if she so desired. In other words, the government has failed to prove an act of unlawful restraint... Finally, there is no competent or substantial proof that the girl was of such an age or mentality as necessarily to preclude her from understanding the doctrine of celestial marriage, and from exercising her own free will. [43]

The Supreme Court did not characterize this series of events as a "conversion" nor refer to the religion clauses of the First Amendment in deciding it, but it appears to be pertinent to the facts of the Robin George case and to the legal capacity to make one's own choice of religion at age 15.

Whether that capacity prevails against a parent's or guardian's wishes to the contrary if the minor remains in the parent's or guardian's custody does not yet appear from the cases, but we may learn more if and when the George case reaches the higher courts.

*An overview of litigation against "cults"*

It is instructive to compare the amount of money damages awarded the victims of deprogrammers, of which only two are on record — $10,000 for Eilers, and $7,000 for Paula Dain against Ted Patrick [44] — with the amount awarded the purported "victims" of "cults" — $2,000,000 in Christofferson I, then $39,000,000 in Christofferson II; $32,000,000 in George, reduced to $9,700,000 — a differential of 1000 to 1! This ratio perhaps represents the "tilt" of disfavour against new religious movements among juries in the United States, but it is important to remember that neither Christofferson nor George has collected on a judgment and if the appellate courts are at all cognizant of the Free Exercise protections for conversion, they never will.

If the analysis with which this paper began is valid, society as a whole needs to be more solicitous of the new religious movements which offer attractions to the drifting and dissident souls unreached by more conventional religions. And it needs to be more protective of the threshold act of conversion by which those "tempest-tossed" souls enter the haven of a supportive religious community and begin to appropriate for the stabilizing of their lives the ultimate meaning offered there.

NOTES

[1] Milton Yinger, *The Scientific Study of Religion*, NY, Macmillan, 1970, p. 21.
[2] D.M. Kelley, *Why Churches Should Not Pay Taxes*, NY, Harper & Row, 1977, pp. 48-50 *passim*, summarizing a much longer exposition in Kelley, *Why Conservative Churches*

*Are Growing*, NY, Harper & Row, 1972, 1977, Mercer Univ. Press, 1986, chapters III-VIII.

[3] *Ibid.*, pp. 50, 52.

[4] *The True Believer*, NY, Harper & Bros, 1951, p. 24.

[5] Kelley, *op. cit.* (1977), pp. 55-56.

[6] D.M. Kelley ed., NY, Pilgrim Press, 1986, ch. 6.

[7] Derived from the autobiographical account of Ted Patrick in *Let Our Children Go!* (with Tom Dulack), NY, E.P. Dutton, 1976, and the descriptions by numerous victims from the author's files.

[8] Thus violating the Federal Anti-Kidnapping Statute, which, however, is not enforced by the US Justice Department against "family" actions.

[9] D.M. Kelley, *The Law of Church and State*, Book II, B, 2 (forthcoming).

[10] See Patrick and Dulack, *op. cit.*

[11] *Ibid.*, p. 263.

[12] *People v. Murphy*, (1977) discussed below.

[13] Le Moult, "Deprogramming Members of Religious Sects", *Fordham L. Rev.*, 46:599 (1978), p. 254.

[14] "The Use of Legal Process for De-Conversion", in D.M. Kelley ed., *Government Intervention in Religious Affairs*, New York, Pilgrim Press, 1982, p. 166.

[15] *Katz v. Superior Court*, 141 Cal. Rptr, 234 (1st Dist. 1977).

[16] *Peterson v. Sorlien*, 299 N.W. 2d 123 (1980).

[17] *Ibid.*, at 129.

[18] *Ibid.*, at 133.

[19] *Ibid.*, Otis dissent.

[20] *Eilers v. Coy*, F. Supp. (1984).

[21] *Ibid.*

[22] Citing *Taylor v. Gilmartin*, 686 F.2d 1346, *Ward v. Connor*, 657 F.2d 45, *supra*, and *Colombrito v. Kelly*, 764 F.2d 122 (1985) (attorney fees denied to a deprogrammer after the suit against him was dropped).

[23] Citing *Peterson v. Sorlien*, 299 N.W. 2d 123 (Minn. 1980), and trial courts in cases mentioned in previous note.

[24] Douglas Laycock, "A Legal and Constitutional Survey of Religious Liberty in the United States", in *Reformed Faith and Religious Liberty*, a special issue of *Church and Society*, May/June, 1986, NY, Program Agency of the Presbyterian Church (USA), p. 71, emphasis added.

[25] 141 Cal. Rptr. 234 (1st Dist. 1977), *supra*.

[26] "(A) State cannot constitutionally confine without more a nondangerous individual who is capable of surviving safely in freedom by himself or with the help of willing and responsible family members or friends." *O'Connor v. Donaldson*, 422 US 563, 576 (1975).

[27] *People v. Murphy*, 413 N.Y.S. 2d 540 (Sup. Ct. 1977), referred to in IV A5 above.

[28] *Ibid.*

[29] *Ibid.*

[30] He had his law clerk collect what little literature was available on the subject, among which was this author's manuscript later published as "Deprogramming and Religious Liberty", *Civil Liberties Review*, July-August 1977, pp. 23-33, reprinted in Bromley and Richardson, *The Brainwashing/Deprogramming Controversy*, 1983, pp. 309-318. Whether it played any part in forming the judge's conclusions is unknown, but his opinion was consistent with the views expressed therein.

[31] *Christofferson v. Church of Scientology*, 644 P.2d 577 (1981).

[32] Or. Cir. Ct., Multnomah County, Ore., 19 July 1985.

[33] *Turner v. Unification Church*, 473 F. Supp. 367 (1978).

[34] *Van Schaick v. Church of Scientology*, 535 F. Supp. 1125 (1982).

[35] He was assisted in this effort by taking a "refresher" course, the tuition for which was paid by the Unification Church!

[36] *Ibid.*, citing *NAACP v. Claiborne Hardware Co.*, 102 S. Ct. 3049 (1982), upholding the right to picket and boycott business alleged to be racially discriminatory.

[37] *Ibid.*, emphasis added.

[38] *Molko and Leal v. Unification Church*, P.2d (1986).

[39] *Eden v. Moon*, Wayne County Circuit Court, No. 77-736-880 NO, 3 December 1982, Court Reporter's transcript, pp. 2-3.

[40] *Ibid.*

[41] Conversation with David Liberman, ISKCON attorney, 28 May 1986.

[42] Defendant's Trial Brief, *George v. ISKCON*, Orange County Superior Court, Case No. 27 75 65 (1983).

[43] *Chatwin v. US*, 326 US 455 (1946), at 457.

[44] *Dain v. Patrick*, (C.D. Cal. 1984), No. CV82-1443-WMB, filed 11 June 1984, appeal pending.

# Part III:

# Responding
# to New Religious Movements

# Churches' Response to Innovative Religious Movements of the Past

## REENDER KRANENBORG

### Introduction

It can be argued that new religious movements always contain some form or degree of innovation. In their ideas and ideals, their practice and way of life, one can identify a more or less strongly pronounced element of searching. The founders and adherents of these movements clearly feel that their church or religious culture lacks something; their intention is either to bring about innovative changes in the traditional institutions or to offer an alternative they consider to be better. It is also evident that the Christian church may not ignore this phenomenon, not only on pastoral grounds but also for theological reasons, because these movements represent questions addressed to the church: What is your identity, what are your goals? And what are you doing, or failing to do, to achieve them?

In this paper I want to examine the manner in which the Protestant churches in the Netherlands reacted to the so-called sects during the period between 1860 and 1960 (I should add at this point that I will be using the concept NRM instead of the term "sect"). The reasons for this choice of locus and time are as follows. I limit myself to the Netherlands because of its reputation for tolerance in the past and present and because it has always been in some sense a pluralistic country. Never wholly Lutheran or Catholic or Reformed (although the latter category became predominant), the Netherlands has always legally recognized and toler-ated religious groups (Jews, Mennonites, Armenians, etc.). I have taken 1860 as a *terminis a quo* because it marked the end of the state church situation in the Netherlands, and 1960 as *terminus ad quem* because from that year onward many profound changes took place within the churches. They underwent radical revision, secularization began to grow exponen-tially; they became more open, their views on mission became different from those in the past and many new religions came into existence.

I am proceeding on the assumption that the situation in the Netherlands will be representative, and that the situation in other countries with respect to church-NRM relations will show similarities to that which obtained in the Netherlands.

What was the reaction of the churches during this period to the NRMs and in particular to their innovational drives? Of course we cannot exhaustively cover all Dutch NRMs. We have to limit ourselves to certain groups. We shall deal, accordingly, with the Jehovah's Witnesses (an example of a genuinely Christian "sect"), Christian Science (a group with a Christian background, but accepting other revelations as well), Theosophy (a movement of Western origin, but containing many Eastern influences as well), the Sufi Order (an Eastern group) and finally the Dutch movement of the Divine Lou. These movements differ widely from each other and have no common history.

## The innovation the groups stand for

*The Jehovah's Witnesses:* The movement began in 1872 as a small group led by Charles Taze Russell. This group was characterized by a longing for a new earth in which justice would dwell, not in a spiritual but a very concrete sense. They were a group of simple people who began reading and interpreting the Bible themselves. They did not feel the need for theologians trained at seminaries and universities. They raised many objections against the church, one of the most important being that it was too closely connected to the established order and that it identified itself with power and the state, forgetting that the kingdom of God is not of this world. An important feature of the movement is the great stress it places on community: its members form a very closely knit communion. Great store is set by individual, personal responsibility and the necessity of hard work.

*Christian Science:* In 1875 Mary Baker Eddy published her *Science and Health with Key to the Scriptures*, containing her views on health and sickness. Illness, she taught, is not real, nor are sin, evil and death. The human spirit is the only true reality, not the material world. People can heal themselves by means of spiritual power, through their insight into the true nature of existence. Humankind has fallen away from God by reason of its materialism and needs to become spiritual once again. Here we see a strong protest against evil, against the bad world in which we live, but one is capable of overcoming these.

*The Theosophical Society:* It was founded in 1875, by Helena P. Blavatsky. This society aims at the companionship and community of all people, encourages comparative study of religions, and seeks to discern the hidden powers of humankind and nature. It teaches an esoteric doctrine which is viewed as the true heart of all religions. The Society strives to supplant all contrasts between people with a higher human unity, with a view to achieving a deep inner knowledge and vision of the divine. An important concept in the theosophical teaching is that of Karma-Reincarnation, which is used to explain sorrow, ill-fortune and disaster, and is considered to be more agreeable than other common forms of theodicy. People are thought to be capable of taking their destiny in their own hands. We also find the idea of evolution in Theosophy, i.e. the conviction that humankind is steadily ascending to ever higher states of being, and an emphasis on contact with true Masters living in the Himalaya mountains. Finally, one might mention the great interest Theosophy has shown in European unity.

*The Sufi Order:* It was established in 1910 by Hazrat Inayat Khan. It places a great deal of emphasis on the unity of religions. At the centre of all religions is the religion of the heart or mystical experience. Doctrine is of no significance compared with the experience of oneness with God. The aim of the Order is to teach people to understand their own religion better so that they may become one. The goal is the universal community of all people, Unity or Oneness in all things is the essence: one God, one Master, one holy scripture, one religion, one moral principle, one law, one subject of praise, one truth, one way. What is important is the non-dogmatic and the non-rational, such as nature, the inner world, feelings, vibrations, music, sounds, love and forgiveness.

*The Lou Movement:* It was initiated in 1950. The adherents of this Dutch NRM are simple people who have suffered considerably from various kinds of illness. Lou preached that people can be liberated from sickness and even death. Anyone who "is in Lou" will not die. In the group everybody is equal, and this even applies to the godhead Lou. Until the death of Lou in 1972, the group had a deep sense of community, was imbued with a strong faith that Lou would protect his people against all disaster and evil, and was extremely negative in its attitude towards the church. The true meaning of the Bible is to be found in the real presence of the godhead Lou. Rational thought and technology are believed to be satanic. The movement often registered protests against civil law, and its members rejected marriage in favour of an arrangement whereby people simply lived together. After the death of Lou the movement lost many of its members.

## Church and new religious movements: the reaction of the churches

What was the reaction of the church and Christians to the innovational impulses of the NRMs? We will analyze the publications of a number of authors, some of which have had three or more printings. This analysis will be made with the following questions in mind.

— Did the authors involved have personal contact with adherents of the NRM they were writing about? Did they listen honestly to these groups and take the trouble to read their literature carefully?

— Did they describe the group and its positions fairly or did they mention only the strange and negative aspects of its teachings and practices?

— Did they display any understanding of the motives of people who joined these groups?

— Did they show any recognition of the innovational aspects or intentions of the NRMs? Did they engage in self-criticism? Did their encounter with the NRMs result in any change in their thinking, attitude or practice?

— Was the criticism of these authors only theological or also philosophical and scientific in nature?

*Jehovah's Witnesses*

Leaving aside the many brief and very negative leaflets written against the Witnesses, we shall review only the larger works published on this group. The first of these was written by H. Bakker, a Dutch Reformed minister, in 1923, and was entitled *Sekten en Stroomingen van onzen tijd* (Sects and Trends of our Time). Bakker's assessment of the Jehovah's Witnesses is entirely negative; what they say, he argues, is pure fantasy. They obscure the Triune nature of God. They consider themselves and their group to be superior to Christians and the church. They misuse the Bible. Bakker has, in fact, nothing good to say about the Witnesses. In 1939 a pastor of the Reformed Churches in the Netherlands, A.B.W.M. Kok, published a book called *Verleidende Geesten (Deceiving Spirits)*. He argues that the Witnesses are fanatics, erring spirits with dangerous ideas, propagators of lies, misusers of scripture who read their own wrong-headed, misbegotten ideas into the Bible. They do not believe in the Trinity and in Jesus as God. Nor do they have any knowledge of redemption, grace, the love of God or submission to God. They are anarchist; they live in darkness, are characterized by intolerance, and suffer from the delusion of self-sufficiency. The only positive thing Kok says about them is that they are prepared to give of themselves sacrificially in the service of their faith.

The year 1939 saw the publication of another book on the so-called "sects" written by the Dutch Reformed minister C. Aalders and entitled *Lot en Illusie (Destiny and Illusion)*. In all the NRMs he sees a protest against destiny and an attempt to exercise human control over it. On the other hand, he also sees something of God's work in the movements. In this connection he even goes so far as to argue that the Witnesses are a "reaction of Christian hope against the unfaithfulness of the Christian church". According to Aalders a great problem remains, namely that the Witnesses want to shape their own destiny. They seek to discover God's plan in the Bible and use the Bible as a weapon. They are not content to live by grace alone but wish to realize their own salvation. In this way they are brought even closer to the humanistic position and represent an increasingly troublesome problem for the Christian faith.

A fourth publication on this subject is the interesting book written by the Dutch Reformed sociologist F. Boerwinkel, *Kerk en secte* (Church and Sect) in 1953. It is Boerwinkel's purpose to make a careful analysis of the dynamics of the NRMs and to try to determine where the church has failed. He speaks of the "sects" as "unpaid bills of the church" and even of the "ministry of the sects". He refers to the NRMs as a "reaction to the failures of the church in the areas of faith, hope and love". In assessing the NRMs he employs the notion of "complementary thinking". He is particularly interested in the Witnesses. He is and remains the only commentator who defines the fundamental character and dynamics of this group in terms of innovation, expressed in the longing of its adherents for the new earth, their strong sense of community, the way they distance themselves from the world, the state and power, their willingness to assume active responsibility and their emphasis on the unity of the Lord. But he also puts a number of critical questions to the Witnesses. He wonders whether their eschatology is not too materialistic and why they lack a sense of solidarity with humankind. He perceives a strong tendency towards parochial legalism among Witnesses and judges their views on the state to be too negative. He deplores their refusal to come to terms with the cross of Jesus Christ and their narrow interpretation of the Bible.

### Christian Science

Here we turn once again to Bakker (1923). In Bakker's view Christian Science is pantheistic, entailing the undervaluation of the material world, the negation of sin, the failure to come to terms with the notion of punishment and judgment, the abrogation of the categories of redemption and forgiveness and the repudiation of the fundamental distinction between God and God's creation. According to him, Christian Science misuses the Bible and subordinates it to the writings of Mary Baker Eddy. But Bakker is also very appreciative of the emphasis Christian Science places on the human spirit and on the idea that the spirit can influence health and sickness. He values this protest against materialism.

In 1929 three Dutch Reformed theologians published a book called *Christus-prediking tegenover moderne gnostiek* (The Gospel of Christ Against Modern Gnosticism). The section dealing with Christian Science was written by M. Kromsigt, who takes Christian Science seriously and bases his analysis on solid arguments. His criticism parallels that of Bakker: Christian Science is deficient in terms of the perception of sin, redemption and judgment. It is unitarian, monistic and spiritualistic. It negates the material world and creation and is auto-soteriological. Nevertheless, he also sees many positive things in this NRM: its position on the relationship between faith and science and mind and matter; its emphasis on the power of the mind and the insufficiency of materialism; its rejection of fatalism, and the assertion that it is possible to do something about evil; its belief in the power of prayer.

Kok (1939), too, writes about Christian Science. He maintains that Christian Science lacks the notion of a personal God, has no real perception of prayer and is entirely bereft of the idea of sin. The movement, he argues, is pantheistic and its interpretation of the Bible is in fact a non-interpretation. It is fraught with superficial optimism, contains no concept of atonement or substitutionary salvation and is auto-soteriological. Its views on matter and the world are objectionable and unbiblical. To his mind the one positive thing in Christian Science is the idea that spirit is superior to matter and that the spirit has much influence on the body.

Aalders (1939) also finds Christian Science a religion of self-redemption. That this is true is clearly demonstrated by the Christian Science teaching that knowledge and insight are capable of conquering all things. Aalders terms this "the big lie". Even Christian Scientists are subject to death. Death and destiny are conquered only in Christ.

In 1940 another symposium on the NRMs was published, this time by a group of authors of the Reformed Churches, entitled *Op Occult gebied* (In the Sphere of the Occult). The author of the essay on Christian Science offers a very negative assessment of the movement. He characterizes Christian Science as a "labyrinth of aphorisms" and complains that it is difficult "to find one's way in the tangle". The terms he uses to define Christian Science are: spiritualism, monism, unitarianism, pantheism. He asserts that this movement has no respect for the Bible but only engages in biblical criticism. Its teaching consists of lies and leads to delusion. It leaves no room for the incarnation of Christ or redemption and is auto-soteriological. Though this commentator is not really prepared to accept the existence of anything positive in Christian Science, he does admit that people are sometimes healed by it. He goes on to explain this, however, in terms of auto-suggestion and psychosomatics. While he agrees that the spirit is capable of more than we often think, he also raises the possibility that these healings are not of God but the antichrist.

Another interesting book on our subject is that by the liberal Dutch Reformed professor of theology, M.C. van Mourik Broekman, *Geestelijke stromingen in het christelijke cultuurbeeld* (Spiritual Trends in Christian Culture Image) which appeared shortly after the Second World War. Broekman wants to listen and learn and come to an understanding of how the church could improve itself. But for him Christian Science is one of the more difficult groups to deal with in this regard. He considers this movement to be high-handed and its Bible interpretation arbitrary. He refuses to view it as science and finds it to be severely unbalanced in that it negates one whole side of reality, namely the material. Nevertheless, Mourik Broekman refrains from applying the term "pantheistic" to Christian Science and admits that it often does work.

Boerwinkel (1953) deals only briefly with Christian Science and remarks that such movements can exist only by virtue of the church's failure to connect the word of Jesus with healing, a failure which to his mind is beginning to be redressed.

### The Theosophical Society

In the groups we are dealing with, Theosophy has always held the greatest interest for Dutch commentators. Many books contain detailed descriptions and analyses. This interest began with the Dutch Reformed minister J.T. de Visser, whose book on Theosophy, *De nieuwere theosophie* (The Newer Theosophy) was published in 1906. De Visser is deeply concerned to represent Theosophy correctly and honestly. He begins with words of praise: Theosophy is characterized by enthusiasm and serious study; it engages in exemplary social work. He sees in Theosophy a protest against materialism and considers its accent on the spiritual to be important and necessary. Although de Visser rejects the idea of karma and reincarnation, he agrees with the theosophical position that one is responsible for one's own deeds and is required to bear the consequences. In the end, however, he remains fundamentally critical of

Theosophy. To him it is "one of the most destructive systems of our time". His critique contains some general elements, for example the observation that the so-called Eastern wisdom of Theosophy is not really Eastern and the Theosophical teaching fails to make a distinction between suggestion and real departure of the spirit from the body. For all that, however, the main part of his criticism is of a theological nature: Theosophy is pantheistic; it does not form the heart of all religions; it destroys individuality; it clouds the distinction between spirit and matter; it is gnostic; it amounts to worship of the mind; it has no perception of forgiveness, of the love of God or redemption.

In 1907 another Dutch writer, P.D. Chantepie de la Saussaye, addressed himself to Theosophy in the book *Geestelijke stromingen* (Spiritual Movements). To Chantepie the old form of Theosophy, advocated by Goethe and others, is the only real one. He is convinced that Blavatsky's new Theosophy has no genuine knowledge of God and recognizes no reality other than that of the empirical world. Karma and reincarnation are unscientific and non-Christian. Theosophy's negation of grace and forgiveness creates a vacuum which will inevitably be filled by fatalism. Blavatsky's books, in addition to containing foolish and nonsensical elements, are also characterized by a spirit of deception. Chantepie firmly rejects the idea that Christianity is outdated.

Bakker (1923) repeats this criticism. He too accuses Blavatsky of deceit. Further, he warns that acceptance of Theosophy means loss of the Bible; that its teaching is pantheistic and auto-soteriological, leaving no room for the substitutionary atonement of Christ; that it amounts to a subtle form of materialism; and that the notion of karma is destructive of faith in God. On the positive side Bakker mentions Theosophy's reaction against open materialism and industrialism, its pursuit of unity, and the prominence it gives to the function of conscience in consequence of its acceptance of the concept of karma.

In the book *The Gospel of Christ against Modern Gnosticism* the chapter dealing with Theosophy was written by H. Schokking who gives this movement very low marks indeed. He rejects the notion that all religions are one at heart and takes Theosophy to task for its optimistic view of evolution, its lack of a personal God, and its teaching that Jesus is merely a master. He argues that the concepts of reincarnation and karma, so central to the theosophical position, are both unscientific and un-Christian and further that Theosophy precludes any perception of sin, forgiveness or redemption. Schokking admits the presence of a number of positive elements in this NRM (for example, the protest against materialism, the idea of communion, etc.) but for him these are of such a general character that one certainly need not be a Theosophist to adhere to them.

It comes as no great surprise that Kok (1939) not only shares Schokking's negative assessments of Theosophy but even provides a number of additional elements. He accuses Theosophy of being mystic-pantheistic, speculative and evolutionistic; of leaving no room for a personal God; of viewing evil only as a passing phase in the evolutionary process; of holding to fantasies; of being anti-Christian; of replacing atonement with retaliation; of misusing the Bible. The only positive thing Kok sees in Theosophy is its emphasis on love and communion.

The same negative image is presented in the chapter on Theosophy in the book *In the Sphere of the Occult*. The author has little that is good to say about this movement, and in fact adds a number of new arguments to those already used by other commentators. Theosophy, he maintains, holds to a view of revelation which differs from that of Christianity. The Bible, contrary to what Theosophists say, contains no esoteric doctrine; the idea that matter is the origin of evil is false. Theosophy is neo-platonism, teaches self-redemption and leads to egoism. Other adjectives he uses to qualify this NRM are: functionalistic, rationalistic, subjectivistic, non-ethical and blasphemous. Theosophy's idea of internationalism is also wrong because each nation has a special place in God's plan for the world.

Aalders (1939) views Theosophy more positively. He too recognizes its auto-soteriological tendencies but, beyond that, sees positive elements in it as well. It ought not to be forgotten that the West has its own occult tradition, which includes magical, a-rational and irrational components. Aalders argues that the church cannot get along properly without a positive occultism, an occultism that takes serious account of prayer, angels, demons, spirits, stars, visions of the past and the future. He is attracted by Theosophy's accent on the religious nature of the human being and the interest it manifests for the mysterious and the infinite. Eastern wisdom can serve as a very useful and necessary corrective to Western rationalism and scientism. Van Mourik Broekman stands in this same tradition of moderate criticism. He does have reservations with respect to Theosophy but they are mostly of a non-theological nature. One of the difficulties he sees is that esoteric teachings do not permit any kind of acceptable verification; one simply has to accept them blindly. He is also averse to the idea of universal religion because it is precisely on the variety in religions that he places great value. He also raises questions about the identity of the Wonderful Masters spoken of in Theosophy. No one ever sees them and yet people are called simply to believe in them. On the basis of an extensive discussion of reincarnation Broekman comes to the conclusion that it would be inadvisable to adopt this notion. His final judgment is that Theosophy is too eclectic, too highly influenced by nineteenth-century optimism.

### The Sufi Order

This NRM is generally less prominent in the literature we are discussing because it was less familiar to most of the authors. Nevertheless, this group does not go entirely without comment.

Bakker wrote in some detail about the Sufi Order in 1923, but his assessment was purely negative. The Sufis do not recognize the Bible as the only source of life, nor do they have any knowledge of redemption. Sufism cannot be termed wisdom, for the only true wisdom is found in the cross of Christ.

Kok's description of Sufism (1939) is very brief, as is his assessment of it: this movement is pantheistic, universalistic and has no perception of Jesus as the Way.

The essay on the Sufi Order in the book *In the Sphere of the Occult* is exceptionally detailed. It is interesting that this author's description of Sufism includes sections on the practices and liturgy of the movement, something very rare in the books we have been examining. The essay concludes with a short critical commentary unrelieved by any appreciative remarks. The Sufi Order adheres to the doctrines of universalism which thoroughly informs and shapes its liturgy, thus making it impossible for those who participate in the liturgy to maintain their own identity. Further, Sufism must be recognized for what it is: a pagan ideology which dishonours God; a self-willed, merely human religion; a form of modern paganism in league with Belial (Satan).

Van Mourik Broekman's comments on the Sufi Order contain no theological arguments. As was the case in his treatment of Theosophy, his main objection arises from his rejection of the notion of the universal religion on the grounds that every religion is unique.

### The Lou Movement

Since the Lou Movement only came into existence in 1950, it is obvious that not much can have been written about it in the period and literature under review. There is a brief section on this NRM in the fourth edition of Kok's *Deceiving Spirits*. It is clear that Kok considers it quite unnecessary to take Lou and his movement seriously. To him Lou is impossibly irritating, speaks dark gibberish, uses empty words, proclaims foolish doctrines. In short the Lou Movement is "monumental nonsense".

Lou is also dealt with in a book we have not yet mentioned, written in 1957 by T. Delleman, a pastor of the Reformed Churches, and entitled *Tussen kerk en tegenkerk* (Between Church and Counterchurch). Delleman has nothing positive to say about this movement. He considers its leader to be a representative of darkness and finds him unintelligible, blasphemous, strange and irritating. Delleman indicates that he is intrigued by the fact that certain people are drawn to Lou.

## Conclusions

What conclusions can we draw from this survey of Dutch literature of historical Christian reaction in the Netherlands to the innovational dynamics of NRMs? A preliminary observation that needs to be made is that it is impossible for the church to meet all the needs of all people. It must also be understood that some people will not feel at home in the church because the truth and ethics for which they are searching are different from those held by the church. Thus the church does not necessarily have to feel guilty when people leave it to found a new faith community. Nevertheless, the church ought always to be aware of what is taking place in terms of the rise of NRMs and be prepared to engage in self-examination, and it must also take an interest in and be aware of what people are seeking.

1. Our first conclusion is that real interest in NRMs has been minimal in the Netherlands. Some authors have taken a genuine interest but they are in general critical. It is only since the Second World War that we observe the rise of a more sympathetic approach, especially in the writings of Van Mourik Broekman and Boerwinkel.

*Recommendation*: In dealing with the NRMs our attitude ought to be one of genuine interest and not an *a priori* rejection.

2. Most of the authors reviewed never actually met any adherents of these groups. Some of them have never read any of the literature produced by the movements, only secondary literature about them. Only Boerwinkel and Van Mourik Broekman differ from this pattern: the former had many contacts with Jehovah's Witnesses and the latter with Theosophists.

*Recommendation*: We should meet and speak with the adherents of the NRMs directly and read carefully the literature they themselves produce.

3. Many of the arguments in the literature we have surveyed are exclusively theological. Most of the authors have an eye only for that

which differs from Christianity. Some of the arguments are simply repeated time and again: the NRMs are pantheistic, auto-soteriological, have no perception of grace, of the cross, forgiveness or Trinity, reject Jesus as the only way. Even the more open authors such as Aalders, de Visser and Delleman come down clearly on the side of judgmental rejection in the end. Only Boerwinkel and Van Mourik Broekman can be said to refrain from judgment and offer genuine criticism.

*Recommendation*: Our discussion should not be limited to theological issues alone; we ought not to point only to differences but also try to discover unifying elements and points of agreement.

4. It is striking that in nearly all the publications reviewed only the doctrinal teachings of the NRMs come up for discussion. The practical and liturgical life of these movements seems to be of little interest. The only exception is the essay on the Sufi Order in the book *In the Sphere of the Occult*.

*Recommendation*: We should not fail to study the rituals, the way of life, meditations, liturgies, etc. of the NRMs, because these are in many cases more important than doctrine.

5. It is also noteworthy that none of our authors — with the exception of the sociologist Boerwinkel — seems to have any awareness of the sociology of religion. Not one of them mentions Troeltsch, Weber, Niebuhr or Wach, which would have been an obvious thing to do.

*Recommendation*: We should take careful account of the sociological, psychological and cultural backgrounds of the NRMs.

6. The non-theological aspects of the NRMs are rarely mentioned in the analyses of the commentators we have surveyed, with the exception of those of Aalders and Boerwinkel. There is also very little interest shown for members of these groups or for the question why they became adherents.

*Recommendation*: Any proper analysis of the NRMs must include an investigation of the motives that lead people to join such groups.

7. The innovational aspects of the NRMs was rarely remarked upon by the authors in question. If there was any awareness of those aspects, it was only of a general nature. There was appreciation for the reaction against materialism, for the insight that the spiritual is superior to the material and for the emphasis on individual responsibility and the necessity for hard work. In some cases specific innovational points of strength were mentioned. Christian Science makes us aware that the spirit is capable of much more than we often think and that healing is important. Boerwinkel clearly had some genuine understanding of the innovational

intentions of the Jehovah's Witnesses, and the same may be said of Aalders and Van Mourik Broekman with respect to Theosophy. Aalder's views regarding the NRMs of Christian origin are interesting in this connection. Aalders referred to such sectarian groups as reactions of "Christian faith, hope and love to the unfaithfulness of the church". Boerwinkel termed them "reactions to a shortage of faith, hope and love in the church".

Thus in general the accent is placed not on the innovation of these groups but rather on the failure of the church. In this way the reaction has no particular significance as such but becomes important only inasmuch as it urges the church to reform itself.

*Recommendation*: The innovative intentions and aspects of the NRMs must be carefully examined both because they are significant in and of themselves and because they can help us better to understand the church.

8. Even those authors who recognized the innovational aspects of the NRMs did not really go deeper into this matter. None of them seriously pursued the notion of sickness and health in relation to the spirit, or attempted through analysis to discern that which is of value in the occult tradition. It would have been possible to address such themes theologically. Apparently it never occurred to these writers to do so.

9. Our Christian commentators did not use the instrument of self-criticism to any great degree. The Reformed authors did not work with it at all. The Dutch Reformed writers, from Aalders through Van Mourik Broekman down to Boerwinkel, did, however, show a progressively greater awareness of the need for such criticism.

*Recommendation*: We must be prepared through our encounter with NRMs to engage in self-criticism, not in the normal general terms of sin and failure, but in terms of the concrete and specific life and practice of the church.

10. It is very interesting to see that no attempt is made in Dutch literature to "demonize" the NRMs in contrast to some contemporary Christian groups that categorize these movements as totally demonic and warn that even casual contact with them is fraught with danger. We noticed a few isolated references to the anti-christ and even one to Belial, but the idea of demonic occult contagion does not occur in Dutch literature. It would be interesting to make a comparison on this point between the Dutch and the relevant German literature, with its tradition of Blumhardt and Möttlingen.

*Recommendation*: We must refrain from any kind of "demonization" of NRMs not only in a theological sense but also in sociological terms such as "brainwashing groups", "destructive cults" or "dangerous to public health".

11. In general the Dutch authors reviewed do not provide much insight in regard to the background and structure of the NRMs. The classification of these movements is global and arbitrary and has little connection with religions such as Islam, Hinduism and Buddhism. The only exceptions are Van Mourik Broekman and the author of the chapter on the Sufi Order in *In the Sphere of the Occult*.

*Recommendation*: We should always be aware that most of the NRMs have arisen out of an older religion. In dealing with an NRM we are dealing implicitly with its mother religion. Any statement about such a movement implies an indirect statement about the religion of its origin.

12. It is clear that the groups which are nearest to Christianity meet the strongest opposition in Dutch literature. The Jehovah's Witnesses and Lou are dismissed as totally unacceptable. Christian Science and Theosophy are usually viewed as interesting, and sometimes described in detail but they also are finally rejected. The authors are rather neutral about Sufism. In general Boerwinkel is an exception here.

13. These authors never pose the question of the relation between Christianity and other religions. It seems that they consider the NRMs to be in an entirely different category from that of the great religions. But is there a real difference between a great and a small religion? The only thing said at the level of *theologia religionum* is that Christ is the only way. But there is no reflection in this literature about the possibility of divine revelation in other religions.

*Recommendation*: The theological question of the relation between Christianity and other faiths and the presence of God's revelation outside of Christianity should be applied to the NRMs as well as to the great world religions.

Our general conclusion must be that in the period surveyed there was no encounter between the church and the NRMs. There was virtually no interest in the innovative significance of these movements and what little interest there was was never developed theologically. The only real exception to this was Boerwinkel and in general Van Mourik Broekman. It is clear that Christians have never really listened to the NRMs and that genuine dialogue between the church and these movements has yet to take place.

# A Response

## FRIDAY M. MBON

As I understand it, the objective of Reender Kranenborg's paper is to discuss the significance and implications of the unprecedented proliferation of new religious movements in the Netherlands in the nineteenth and twentieth centuries. Dr Kranenborg has chosen to enter into that discussion through the back door of history and has presented us with an interesting and informative review of the literary reactions to new religious movements in Dutch ecclesiastical history during the period 1860-1960.

In discussing the significance and implications of new religious movements in the Netherlands, Dr Kranenborg points out that those movements emerged there in response to what the founding members felt to be a lack in the spirituality of established churches or, perhaps, their materiality. This supports the social scientific theory that, almost invariably, the precipitating condition for a new institution (e.g. a new religious movement) is to be found in the failure of existing institutions (e.g. mainline Christian churches) to provide for or meet the needs of their members or supporters. According to Dr Kranenborg, some of the needs of which the Dutch new religious movements felt "deprived" are in the area of sickness and spiritual healing; he sees this as one of the main emphases and "innovations" of those new religious movements and castigates Dutch church historians for failing to pay deserved attention to this particular contribution of the new movements.

I should perhaps add a long footnote here. This whole question of new religious movements coming into existence as a result of the church's failure and inability to provide for the needs of its members — whatever those needs may be — should not necessarily make the church feel too guilty. We must always remember that the diversity of human needs, wants and aspirations is almost infinite and that a church cannot be so ambitious as to think that it can always meet this plethora of needs. The church will of

course be expected to meet some of the needs and aspirations of some of
its members but certainly not all the needs of all of them. Thus those
members whose needs and aspirations cannot be met immediately by the
church might seek other ways of solving their problems. I feel that there
will always be people who will feel "deprived" in regard to what they
want from the church and that consequently there will always be church
members who leave the church in order to join new religious movements
or found new ones where they expect to "feel at home" and have their
needs and wants met. Quite often these are not merely material or
physical but, more importantly, spiritual and emotional.

Dr Kranenborg further points out that the negative attitude of Dutch
mainline churches and clergy towards the new religious movements stems
from the theological and doctrinal differences between them and the new
movements. The issue which seems to be at stake here is the theological
question of the precise content and colour of "pure" Christianity; if the
new religious movements regard themselves as Christian through and
through while mainline churches contest this, then it seems that the
question on hand is one that has to do with the precise definition of the
parameters and perimeter of the Christian religion. In other words, since
some of the new religious movements claim to be unreservedly and totally
Christian, while the orthodox (historical) churches insist that they are not,
then the two camps seem to differ about the precise constitution of
Christianity; in fact, the new religious movements' insistence to be
Christian may well be the real bone of contention.

This, in fact, seems to be what has happened in regard to the older
churches' attitude towards non-Christian religions in predominantly
Christian countries. As Dr Kranenborg has noted, in those countries the
older churches have not generally concerned themselves with other
religions since these do not seem to represent a major threat to Christianity in terms of competition for Christian converts. At least in the third-
world Christian countries, other religions seem not to attract nearly as
many members of the established churches (especially their "financial
members") as the new religious movements have succeeded in doing.
This may perhaps explain why the orthodox Christian churches in those
countries seem to be less disturbed about the presence of other religions
and consequently less hostile to them than they are towards the new
Christian religious movements.

Dr Kranenborg also points out that many of the orthodox Christian
authors who wrote negatively about the new religions of their time knew
in fact little about those movements. They had little first-hand objective

knowledge of the movements' ideologies and therefore reached false and hasty conclusions and even misrepresented the movements.

The challenge for us here is that the Christian church today must do better than those earlier zealous writers; it must try to become better acquainted with and more knowledgeable about the new religions. There are several ways in which the church can do this. First it must be willing to participate in or even initiate discussions with the new religions, whether Christian or not.

Secondly the church should commission or sponsor special studies on aspects of the phenomenon of new religious movements. In this regard the church, represented here by the WCC and LWF, should be challenged by the recent UNESCO-sponsored study published by Sage Publications in London, under the title *New Religious Movements and Rapid Social Change*. Churches and Christian institutions must initiate and support more focused studies and research on the world's new religious movements.

In his introduction, Dr Kranenborg expressed the hope that his choice of the Dutch context would be "representative" of mainline churches' reaction and response to new religious movements in other countries. I think that on the whole his choice is "representative".

Although I do not know the exact situation in other countries, I do know that the Dutch churches' reaction to new religious movements is very similar to that of Nigerian mission churches. I have myself written a study about this; it will be a chapter of a book on Nigeria's new religious movements, shortly to be published by the Edwin Mellen Press in New York. I regret that I have no time to discuss the Nigerian situation here but I have pointed out in that chapter and elsewhere that, while the new religious movements in Nigeria insist that they themselves are Christian through and through, the mission churches continue to deny them that identification, on the basis of the theological and doctrinal differences between them. Listen, for instance, to this description of one Nigerian new religious movement, the Brotherhood of the Cross and Star (BCS), allegedly written by a pastor of one of the mission churches:

> This club or society as it is called is a terrible combination of spiritualism, occult science, mysticism, and allied subject(s) with Christianity. Poor Christianity, as a close study of this cult reveals, is nothing short of a camouflage to the evil machination of this secret society. [1]

Thus, according to the author of this passage, the BCS is everything but a Christian church. It is a club, a secret society, occult science, mysticism, a camouflage. The leader of this particular new religious movement, Olumba Olumba Obu, is of course not unaware of this kind of negative opinion held by the mission churches about his movement. One of his testimonies on the matter runs as follows:

> Have you not heard what people say about Brotherhood? They call Brotherhood of the Cross and Star the church of the evil doers, the church of infidels and that membership is drawn from persons who have never (genuinely) attended any church (or) denomination. [2]

Elsewhere Obu claims that "many people in the world are praying and calling on Jesus to kill the Leader of the Brotherhood fold". [3] He further notes in one of his sermons that "it is generally said that Brotherhood is 'Satan', 'Ghost', 'Devil'". [4]

A further instance of how some of the doctrines of Nigerian new religious movements seem to have been somehow responsible for the hostile attitudes of the older churches is the Cherubim and Seraphim movement which identifies itself with the supposed Seraphim in heaven. In particular, this movement's choice of the Archangel Michael as its "Captain" and Jehovah as its "Founder" is reported to have sparked off a series of press attacks on the society. Archdeacon Ogunbiyi has criticized the explicit comparison of the members with the Seraphim in heaven. [5]

One may wonder why older Nigerian churches seem generally to be antagonistic to the new religious movements in their country. There appears to be a twofold reason. As far as the new religious movements are concerned, they believe that they are being disliked and even sometimes persecuted because older churches are jealous. For example, I asked Obu once why he thought the mission churches were antagonistic towards him and his movement. His answer, which in fact is representative of the answers of other Nigerian new religious movements, was: "Jealousy; that's all I can say. They are jealous because they are losing their members to us." [6] Asked why he thought the mission churches were losing their members, Obu replied:

> Simply because they are not satisfying the needs of their members. Those members come here for help, find the help they need and decide to stay here, on their own accord. We do not press anyone to become a Brotherhood. [7]

This same theme of jealousy as the motive behind the hostility of the mission churches was already stressed in 1951 by Gideon M. Urhobo, the founder of the God's Kingdom Society, another Nigerian religious movement. In his autobiography he wrote about his conflict with the Jehovah's Witnesses:

... When Brown saw that many young men had joined the G.K.S. and (that) the Lord was blessing His Kingdom, he became jealous and took action against me. [8]

The mission churches claim that, as far as their hostility is concerned, they are merely carrying out their God-given responsibility as the defenders of the Christian faith — trying to salvage the "pure" gospel of Jesus Christ from being corrupted by some of the "strange" doctrines of the new religious movements. The mission churches never give thought to the possibility that "the Spirit of truth" (John 14:17; 15:26; 16:13) might have something to say to them through the new religious movements.

Dr Kranenborg's analysis of the generally negative way in which Dutch Christian church historians treated the new religious movements in their time may be sad, especially to us who live in an ecumenical and pluralistic age. However, that sadness may be toned down considerably by the positive lessons we can learn from history — lessons which will hopefully enable us to avoid the reactions or over-reactions of those earlier authors. I think it was George Santayana who said years ago that one who does not know history is bound to repeat the mistakes of history — even the mistakes of church history!

## NOTES

[1] Report presented to the Uyo Inter-Church Study Group by I.B. Ita, June 1963, p.1.

[2] *The Supernatural Teacher*, Book 2, p.29.

[3] *Ibid.*, Book 4, p.39; cf. Book 2, p.76.

[4] Obu, in S.A. Kevin, *The Universal Love*, 1st ed. (n.d.), p.127.

[5] J. Akin Omoyajowo, *Cherubim and Seraphim: the History of an African Independent Church*, New York, NOK Publishers, 1982, p.11; cf. p.17.

[6] Interview with Obu, 11 October, 1980.

[7] *Ibid.*

[8] *Eighteen Year Kingdom Service*, Yaba, Lagos, Sankey Press, 1951, p.21.

# Response of the Churches to New Religious Movements

## A Report from North America

### DIANA L. ECK

"New religious movements" are no longer new in the religious life of North America. It is two decades since the beginning of this upsurge of interest in what have variously been called "sects", "cults", or "new religions". While some groups, such as the Divine Light Mission of the young guru Maharaj-ji, have all but disappeared, others such as the International Society for Krishna Consciousness have persisted with a new quasi-denominational status and have brought to the American religious scene a new texture and complexity. It is clear that some Hindu and Buddhist movements, in one form or another, are here to stay. And that is a new and significant fact for the evolving history of those Eastern traditions, as well as for our own. The sensational or unsavoury activities of Bhagwan Rajneesh or the Rev. Sun Myung Moon may still occasionally capture the attention of the news media, but for the most part new religious movements are not "news".

Of course, the new religious pluralism of North America has to do with changes in immigration patterns as well as with "new religious movements". Canada's multi-cultural society, with large populations of Hindu, Muslim, Sikh, and Buddhist immigrants, may well become a model for multi-culturalism. In the US, the Oriental Exclusion Act, which had blocked Asian immigration to a mere trickle, was repealed in 1965 and a new, though not large, wave of Asian immigration began. Thus the rise of "new religious movements", many of Asian origin, has coincided with a change in the cultural composition of North America. Both facts together have added a new complexity to North American religious life and have made inter-religious relations and dialogue an important issue for even the most ordinary North American community.

### A worldwide issue

How have churches and individual Christians responded to new religious movements? The issue is, of course, not limited to North America.

At the worldwide level, I should note that the issue of new religions has been raised in several ways in the context of the global concerns of the World Council of Churches. In 1978, the *International Review of Mission* of the Commission on World Mission and Evangelism devoted a special issue to the "tentative exploration" of the subject. As Emilio Castro, then Director of the CWME, wrote in his introduction: "We want to open the discussion by providing information, by raising questions for the mission of the church. We do not try to suggest the Christian position or to pass judgment on these groups. What we want to discern clearly is: how does the existence of these new religious movements challenge our own faithfulness to the Gospel?"[1]

The Working Group of the WCC Sub-unit on Dialogue with People of Living Faiths has attempted to keep abreast of the discussion of new religious movements, recognizing that in many parts of the world "dialogue in community", a primary emphasis of the Sub-unit, will surely include people in the community who are members of new religious movements. The *Guidelines on Dialogue*, framed from the Chiang Mai consultation on dialogue in community in 1977, underlines the principle that partners in dialogue should be free to "define themselves". In the atmosphere of alarm that surrounded the recent wave of new religious movements in North America, groups have often been quickly and sweepingly "defined" by others with labels such as "cult". As the *Guidelines* warned:

> Listening carefully to the neighbour's self-understanding enables Christians better to obey the commandment not to bear false witness against their neighbours, whether those neighbours be of long established religious, cultural or ideological traditions or members of new religious groups.[2]

The question of new religious movements is appropriately considered by the World Council of Churches for it is a worldwide issue, raising important questions for those concerned with dialogue the world over — not only in North America and Europe but in East Asia and Africa as well. Throughout the world many new religious movements understand themselves as Christian movements, and the questions that may arise when such groups apply to join national councils of churches are similar, whether the context is the United States or Zaire. And many new religious movements are Hindu, Buddhist, or Sikh in origin, thus making dialogue with people of such movements inextricably and sensitively related to our wider dialogue with people of living faiths. In the last analysis, churches cannot claim an abstract interest in dialogue with Hindus, and yet refuse to have anything to do with Hare Krishna devotees in their own community.

Also at a worldwide level, the recent "Sects or New Religious Movements: a Pastoral Challenge", based on replies to questionnaires sent to regional and national episcopal conferences all over the world, is a major step towards mainline and worldwide church reflection on the issue of new religious movements. [3] The self-reflective "pastoral" approach of the document turns the question of new religious movements away from the specifics of particular movements and towards a critique of the spiritual life and discipleship of Christian communities which have so often failed to engage the commitment and affection of the young. The Vatican document has been of considerable interest to at least one of the new religious movements, the ISKCON or Hare Krishna movement, whose director of inter-religious affairs has already prepared a response to the document. [4]

Finally, at a worldwide level we must note that one of the major initiatives for inter-religious dialogue today is being taken by a new religious movement — the Unification Church through its International Religious Foundation, Inc. Many from all over the world who are being drawn into what I would call "parliamentary" dialogue are doing so in conferences such as the New Ecumenical Research Association series on "God: the Contemporary Discussion" or in the series of three "Assemblies of the World's Religions" that will culminate in 1993 with the centennial of the Chicago World Parliament of Religions. How churches will respond to this dialogue initiative is a worldwide issue, since Christians and their neighbours of other faiths in Ghana, India, Japan, etc. are participants in this dialogue forum. The relation of such religious conferences to the political activities of the Unification Church through its many political subsidiaries is also a question that concerns Christians in Asia, North America, and Latin America.

### The context of North America

A Gallup Poll on Religion in America was taken in the late 1970s. This poll and another more focused poll done in the area of Dayton, Ohio, provide the starting point for George Gallup and David Poling's book, *The Search for America's Faith*. Both the poll and the book are surprisingly unreflective and narrow in terminology and conception. For example, the concern throughout is with "the church", "the churched", and "the unchurched", with such terms as "synagogue" often placed merely in parentheses after "church". It is therefore ironic that the findings of these pollsters indicated that the "church" is not the sole reference point of "America's faith". Of the so-called "churched", 7 percent indicated that they also practised specific techniques of meditation, such as TM, yoga, or Zen. Among young people surveyed in the Dayton, Ohio, area, 31 percent indicated that they had been involved in groups loosely termed "cults". Authors Gallup and Poling remark that 31 percent is "a rather high involvement for a group of which 75 percent state they believe Jesus Christ is the Son of God". [5]

The figures, however accurate or approximate they may be, reveal the interesting fact that many Americans, even those who consider themselves "churched", are nonetheless involved in some aspect of alternative religious life. The commentary on this development provided by Gallup and Poling leaves their own bias and interpretation in little doubt: "The Christian churches of America, liberal, conservative, evangelical, and fundamental, must now perceive a common enemy in the cults or expect serious decline in their current membership and future prospects." [6] Elsewhere, the two speak of the church's ministry to those "demolished by their downhill run with the so-called new religions". [7]

Much about this Gallup Poll is interesting and revealing: its archaic language, scarcely aware of the substantial presence of Jews, much less people of other faiths, on the American religious scene; its arresting statistics on the numbers of Americans involved in "new" traditions or practices; and the pollsters' call to alarm in their interpretation of these figures. At least one American denomination, the Missouri Synod Lutheran Church, has echoed the alarm in advertising its "Response Series" of books on the new religions: "A recent Gallup Poll stated that one out of every eight Americans is engaged in some sort of experimental religion — which may include everything from cults, mysticism, to Eastern religions. No wonder many of your members are deeply troubled by current events!"

As interesting as the poll itself is the way in which it has been subsequently used in this manner as a call to arms. It is difficult to say to what "new" or "experimental" religious movements or techniques respondents referred in the poll. The pollsters do not say. The poll continues to be cited, however, as firm evidence for an alarming, if somewhat unspecified, state of affairs. The 16 May 1986 issue of *Christianity Today* referred again to the 1978 Gallup Poll that "indicated ten million Americans were engaged in some aspect of Eastern mysticism". The article also refers to a poll mentioned in the Christian film, "Gods of the New Age", suggesting that not ten, but sixty million Americans were engaged in

Eastern religious practices and that 23 percent of Americans "believe in reincarnation".[8] The rising new attack on what might be called the "anti-cult" movement is, indeed, not really on "cults" or "movements" at all, but on what is seen as the widespread, subtle, and in their eyes dangerous, insinuation of Eastern ways of thinking into Western Judeo-Christian culture. Their concern is not with those relatively few people who are followers of Rajneesh or Muktananda, but with the millions of ordinary citizens who practise forms of yoga, meditation, relaxation exercices, or bio-feedback, who use terms such as "karma" and "reincarnation", and who speak of "human potential" rather than human fallenness.[9]

## Sorting out the issues

Speaking generally about the context of new religious movements in North America, there are four issues we should underline and distinguish in trying to understand some of the suspicious or hostile response to new religious movements.

1. *The issue of "otherness" — confronting another faith.* While some of the new religious movements are genuinely "new" (such as EST and Scientology), many more of these movements have ancient roots in the Hindu, Buddhist, Sikh, or Muslim traditions and are "new" only to us. Therefore much of the suspicious and hostile response to them has a great deal to do with the simple fact that they are different, that they are foreign. While some are almost entirely American in their constituency, other groups include immigrants to the US or Canada from East Asia, India, the Middle East, or the Caribbean, and are a sign of the emerging cultural and religious diversity of North America. Thus the response of the churches to new neighbours at home is closely related to our hopes for dialogue with people of other faiths around the world. When a Mounds-ville, West Virginia, shopkeeper says: "Those Hare Krishnas set a dummy in the middle of the floor and put flowers on it and feed it, and I'm supposed to believe in that?!" what perplexes him is really not the queer ways of a "new" religious cult, but the distinctive ritual life of Hinduism.[10]

2. *The issue of "heresy" — the distortion of one's own faith.* Some of the new religious movements are rooted in the Christian tradition. Here we might include such movements as the Unification Church, the Church Universal and Triumphant, The Way International, and The Local Church. Some, like the Unification Church of the Reverend Moon, may claim a post-biblical revelation. The response of churches to these movements is not that they are alien or foreign, but that they are a fringe

group, perhaps an heretical fringe, that threatens Christian orthodoxy. Such groups are not "new" in the long history of the Christian tradition, nor is the response to such groups "new". It must be seen in the context of "establishment" and "normative" response to "emergent" and "non-normative" religions, to use the terminology of Robert Ellwood in *Alternative Altars*. In the United States, this goes back to the hostile response to the Shakers, Spiritualists, Theosophists and Swedenborgians in the nineteenth century, and the hostile response to what are now called the "old-line cults" such as the Mormons, the Jehovah's Witnesses, and the Christian Scientists. Some of these "old-line cults" have now moved to the status of "denomination", if not by orthodox acceptance then surely by cultural consensus. Old and new "cults" even make alliances, as seems to be the case in some of the connections between the Mormons and the Unificationists or Moonies.

3. *The issue of illegal or deceptive activities.* The public controversy surrounding "new religions" in North America has to a great extent centred upon legal and political, not theological, matters. First, there is the far-reaching question of what constitutes a "religion", with the final legal fourteen-point definition of a "religion" having been set forth by the ultimate arbiter of such things in the United States — the Internal Revenue Service. The incarceration of the Rev. Moon for tax evasion and the flight of Bhagwan Rajneesh from the US brought again to the public mind the suspicion that many of these "new religions" may be involved in illegal and shady activities. Second, there are the allegations that various "cults" have engaged not only in deceptive or seductive recruitment practices, but in illegal practices loosely called "kidnapping", "brain-washing" or "mind-control". Such allegations have resulted in a number of lawsuits, including several now pending in the state of California against the Scientologists, the Hare Krishnas, and the Church Universal and Triumphant. A third area of legal controversy has been over deprog-ramming. There have been efforts to pass state laws making it possible for parents to be appointed "conservators" of offspring who are no longer minors, in order that they might forcibly remove them from a "cult". Such "anti-cult" laws have for the most part been defeated, so legal suits have also been brought by "cult" members against "deprogrammers", who have been hired by parents to detain their children and "return them to free choice".

4. *The issue of ideology — assault on the dominant culture.* It is important to recognize that in some cases new religious movements challenge not only the religious convictions of the dominant culture, but

its ideological convictions. The WCC *Guidelines on Dialogue* makes the point that "partners in dialogue should be aware of their ideological commitments". Such awareness is often hard to bring to consciousness, however. In North America, egalitarian individualism, private property, and capitalism are held in such sacred esteem that these values easily become confused with and identified with Christianity. That someone should relinquish his or her individual autonomy to a teacher is repugnant on ideological, not theological, grounds. Or that members of a religious movement should sing and dance in the streets, worship Krishna six times a day, or commit their individual earnings and savings to the community in which they live — all this is an ideological challenge.

It is important to hold these four issues in mind when thinking about the response of the churches and of Christians to new religious movements. If one is uneasy about or suspicious of some particular group, is it because (1) it challenges Christians because it is Eastern, "non-Christian", and therefore strange to us? (2) it challenges Christians because it claims to be Christian, but isn't, at least as far as we are concerned? (3) it affronts and challenges people — Christians, Jews, and others — because it seems to be basically fraudulent in its promises or engages in illegal activities? (4) it challenges people — Christians, Jews, and others — because it undermines or controverts some of the ideological values we hold, such as capitalism or individualism?

These issues easily become confused and conflated in the polarization of "pro-cult" and "anti-cult" language so often present in responses to new religious movements. In distinguishing them, we can see that the National Council of Churches in the USA, while it has turned down on theological grounds the application of the Unification Church for membership (point 2), [11] has consistently spoken out on behalf of basic civil and religious liberties for the Unification Church and other new religious movements (point 3). [12] Similarly, there are religiously and politically conservative Americans who would distance themselves from the Unification Church if they were thinking only theologically about its claims (point 2), but who surprisingly lend support to the church because they are ideologically impressed with its strong anti-communist crusade through CAUSA and other subsidiary organizations (point 3).

## Sorting out the responses: the churches and new religious movements

How have Christian churches, at the level of denominational leadership, attempted to address the questions raised by the emergent religious pluralism of North America and the attendant controversy over new religious movements? Having surveyed thirty-six national denominational offices of the Catholic, Orthodox, and Protestant churches in the US and Canada, both in 1981 and in 1986,[13] I can say with some confidence that very few churches have devoted any sustained attention to new religious movements, either in their assemblies, their public statements, their denominational magazines, or their educational materials.

The response to my own study certainly supports the assertion of J. Gordon Melton and Robert L. Moore, whose book, *The Cult Experience: Responding to the New Religious Pluralism*, is one of the most sensitive and important resources for Christians on new religious movements:

> ... the major denominations provide practically no leadership on this matter at the national level. Although some denominations have issued important public statements on religious liberty in the context of alternative religions, they have made little effort to educating denominational constituencies regarding the issues involved.[14]

Writing in the *Journal of Ecumenical Studies* in the summer of 1981, editor Paul Mojzes made a similar point, referring not to the denominational leadership but to the "lay response" to new religious movements. "What is the typical lay response to the new religions? Though admitting almost total ignorance about them, the hair trigger response is totally negative."[15]

In assessing the response of those churches I surveyed, the first and most striking fact to notice was the vast variety of movements that were mentioned as "sects", "cults", or "new religious movements". Some denominational offices responded with articles and information published by their churches on the Mormons, Jehovah's Witnesses, or Christian Scientists. Others mentioned movements such as the Hare Krishna, the Unification Church, the Bahai, or Sokka Gakkai. Among the groups mentioned by the Southern Baptists were the Unitarians, and the Unitarians, in turn, sent statements on the new religious right and the Moral Majority. A sample of the "response" series of booklets sent by the Missouri Synod Lutheran Church was a booklet on Islam. The Presbyterian Church included a copy of its booklet "Para-Church Groups: a Report on Current Religious Movements", which deals with the Campus Crusade for Christ, the Inter-Varsity Fellowship, and the Jews for Jesus. While sociologists of religion who have studied new religious movements have tried to define what it means to speak of a movement as a "cult" or a "sect", it is clear that there is no such consensus in the churches. What to one church is a "cult" to another is simply a "denomination", perhaps their own.

The wide range of what might be called "anti-cult" literature produced in the last ten years has often served only to escalate the confusion by classifying together, often as sequential chapters in a single book, a range of religious movements that have very little in common except the culture in which they have come into being in twentieth-century North America. (See, for example, *The New Cults* [1980] by Walter Martin, Director of the Christian Research Institute in Anaheim, California, and *The Kingdom of the Cults: Prison or Paradise* [1980] by James and Marcia Rudin of the American Jewish Committee; *A Guide to Cults and New Religions* [1983] by Ronald Enroth and other researchers of the Spiritual Counterfeits Project; or more sensational journalism such as *All God's Children* [1977] by Carroll Stoner and Jo Anne Parke, and *The Cults are Coming!* [1978] by Lowell Streiker.)

The extent to which denominations are committed to education and publication on new religious movements varies greatly. The denominations with the most extensive programmes and publications are two very conservative American denominations: the Southern Baptist Convention and the Missouri Synod Lutheran Church. Others, such as the American Lutheran Church, the Presbyterian Church in the USA, and the United Church of Canada have a few programmes and publications. Others have no programmes, publications, or statements on the matter at all, and do not have them precisely because the issue is not seen as a "problem" in the context of their denomination. As the respondent from the Friends General Conference put it in 1981: "There are Quaker families in which a son or daughter has been drawn to or become involved in one of these new movements, but this has not become a problem. To a certain extent liberal Quakers who make up the Friends General Conference would encourage seeking for religious truth through other faiths and new religious movements".

The Missouri Synod Lutheran Church has an entire line of publications, which comprise what is called the "Response Series". It includes such titles as *How to Respond to the Cults, How to Respond to the Science Religions, How to Respond to the Eastern Religions, How to Respond to Islam, How to Respond to the Latter Day Saints,* etc. The "how to" method is aimed at enabling Christians to respond, as is revealed in the description of these publications. For instance, *How to Respond to the Eastern Religions* is advertised as follows: "Transcendental Meditation, Hinduism, Hare Krishna, Buddhism, have all made extraordinary inroads with today's youth. Where will it all end? And what can your members do to let the Good News reach impressionable young people? This book tells how". [16]

The Missouri Synod's work is conducted through its commission organizations, which studies and writes about various movements "from the Lutheran theological perspective". As the executive secretary emphasizes, the commission is an "in-house" service agency: "Its role is to provide resources in information, evaluation and counselling to pastors and congregations of the Synod." The commission now receives over 14,000 requests for information annually. Increasingly, requests for information are coming from other evangelical churches, and according to the executive secretary are always sent with a cover letter that "explains the perspective from which the materials are prepared and declares that no attempt is made to speak for anyone of another persuasion."

While the church has not taken an official stand on deprogramming, the commission on organizations seems generally to accept the plausibility of "brainwashing" charges, to see the need for "some kind of return to free choice and independent thinking on the part of those who have been deceived by a cultic leader", and to offer counselling on the risk of civil disobedience to those parents who might feel it their Christian duty forcibly to "rescue" a son or daughter who has joined a "false or manipulative religious tradition". [17] The executive secretary is quick to point out, however, that not all new religious movements can be called "manipulative or fraudulent" in their recruitment practices.

The Interfaith Witness Department of the Home Mission Board of the Southern Baptist Convention has an assistant director solely responsible for sects and new religious movements. He reported in 1981 that they sent out over 400,000 copies of their published material each year and sponsor about twenty conferences a month on subjects in the area of new religious movements. The extensive publications of the Southern Baptist Convention include a booklet, *The Christian Confronting the Cults*, which contains chapters on Jehovah's Witnesses, the Latter-Day Saints, the Worldwide Church of God, the Unification Church, and the Christian Scientists. While there are a few publications that deal with Eastern religious movements in America, it seems clear that the primary focus of these materials is on the "old-line cults" and the new movements linked to Christian claims. While there is no doubt that the thrust of the programme is towards" effective witness", the programme as a whole seems to have taken a reflective and sensitive approach.

As far as I am aware, the Southern Baptist Convention is the only US denomination with "Guidelines for Effective Interfaith Witness". The guidelines emphasize "not judging, not convicting, but witnessing". Witnessing includes learning to listen, "genuinely to run the risk of opening yourself to another person and to his beliefs". The guidelines caution Christians not to assume a mutual vocabulary, but to take care in finding out what people mean by the terms they use to express their faith; and they caution Christians not to compare the excesses of one tradition with the best ideals of another. "Recognize the ideal in all faiths, and the fact that most believers do not attain the ideals of their faith." [18]

Many of the Southern Baptist resources are bibliographies, pamphlets, or offprints of articles published elsewhere, such as an article on TM which appeared first in the Presbyterian Church publication *A.D.* The "Selected Bibliography on The Latter-Day Saints, Mormons" includes books by both Mormon authors and non-Mormon authors. Another publication, *My God, Your God*, is advertised as follows: "An encounter — with Hare Krishna, Moonist, Mormon, Catholic, Buddhist, and Jew. The book faces religious differences with uncompromising love. It is Christians learning to communicate beliefs and listening." [19] One of the pamphlets produced by the SBC Interfaith Witness Deparment typifies the rather positive tone of the department's work with the challenge: "When was the last time *you* stood on a street corner in the rain to tell a Moonie about Christ?"

Despite the generally acknowledged conservatism of the Southern Baptist tradition, the tone set by its Interfaith Witness Department seems to be positive not polemical, even though the "mission field" for their "interfaith" witness appears to include everyone from "Moonies" to Catholics to Buddhists. Yet there is no hint of the sweeping negativism that, for example, the Episcopal Church of Minneapolis adopted when it launched an anti-cult advertisement campaign in 1980 with an image of Christ captioned, "He died to take away your sins. Not your minds", or a young executive with a bandaged mouth captioned, "There's only one problem with religions that have all the answers. They don't allow questions." [20]

The materials sent by the American Lutheran Church in response to the 1981 survey included a statement made by the General Convention of the church in 1976. The statement is a measured one, acknowledging the "serious and persistent threat" posed by "marginal religious movements", and resolving that the church prepare educational resources for its pastors and congregations and study further the "alleged" tactics of "mind control". It resolved, finally, "that any effort undertaken to deal with this cult phenomenon give special attention to those symptoms of our society and any inadequacies or imbalance in the church's proclamation which may have helped create the seedbed for cult activity". [21] In the same year, a statement entitled "Religious Cults" prepared by Ballard Pritchett of the Office of Research and Analysis also reflects a moderate, balanced response, taking account of the historical, sociological, and psychological context of new religions, which, along with their religious content, might help to place new religious movements in perspective. He concludes: "It is not the church's business, as the church, to level legal charges at other religious groups. Christ's instructions were to allow the tares to grow among the wheat, lest the entire harvest be lost in rooting them out." [22] In 1977, the ALC, in cooperation with the Lutheran Church of America, did indeed publish a seven-part study of movements entitled "Isms and Issues: Religious Movements of our Time". However, according to our respondent, "a suit filed by one of the groups forced this piece off the market".

The United Church of Canada has taken strong leadership in responding and giving guidance to the government of Ontario concerning sects, cults, and new religious movements, opposing "regulations" on their activities and suggesting "a friendly approach, seeking understanding in the way of interfaith dialogue". Both the UCC and the Anglican Church of Canada responded to the Ontario government at the time the Hill Commission in 1979 was investigating what laws, if any, the government should enact to regulate the practices of religious cults. Both denominations strongly opposed legal regulation and advocated, instead, responsible programmes of education. In 1982, the UCC formed a Task Force on Cults and New Religions which put together an educational kit with photocopies of important reports, articles, and interpretative positions.

The Canadian Council of Christians and Jews has also been active in this area and has produced a substantial mimeographed book entitled *Multi-Cultural Expressions: a Directory on the Religions and Philosophical Groups of the New Age in Ontario*. The book is intended to give a fair and brief account of the history, life-style, and spiritual teaching of each movement, based on interviews that pay attention to how each group describes itself. In each case, a short bibliography of the groups' own texts and scriptures is given. This directory is intended to provide basic factual information for people in Ontario, since at the time it was produced in about 1980, much of the public's information was gained through mass media coverage of particular "scandals" or "upheavals", or else through "incautious and sometimes even dubious propaganda projects mounted by some of the groups themselves". The urgency of providing simple practical information was underlined by the Rev. Arthur Gibson in his foreword, where he concludes:

> In this socio-psychological atmosphere, it is unfortunately easy and entirely understandable for citizens, especially concerned parents, to lose perspective and succumb to a witch-hunt mentality. There develops a tendency to forget, in the emergent anxiety over individual cases, the fact that "hard cases make bad laws", and that the fabric of our society will be really undermined if practical religious pluralism is not sturdily defended by all. [23]

## Resource centres for new religious movements

There are a number of centres where resources on new religious movements are available in North America. Eric Pement, who writes on new religions for the Christian magazine *Cornerstone*, has recently published *The 1986 Directory of Cult Research Organizations* which lists thirty secular or non-Christian organizations interested in the study of cults and as many as 250 explicitly Christian organizations pursuing such study. [24] Pement's *Directory* organizes such organizations and centres by specialization, region, and by their Christian or secular orientation.

One of the first study centres was the *Center for the Study of New Religious Movements*, launched by Jacob Needleman in Berkeley in 1977. For a number of years this was a vital centre for the scholarly research, study, and discussion of new religious movements, sponsored by grants from the Rockefeller Fund and the National Endowment for the Humanities. A monthly publication of new acquisitions and references in the area of new religious movements was published under the name, *newtitles*. In addition, the centre produced a number of bibliographies, including *The New Religions: an Annotated Bibliography; A Select Filmography on New Religious Movements; The Christian-Buddhist Encounter: a Select Bibliography; Civil Liberties, "Brainwashing" and "Cults": a Select Bibliography*. These bibliographies include books written from both within and without the movements and are annotated simply and non-prejudicially.

In June 1983, the centre as such closed. The library collection of research materials on new religious movements, however, has continued to be housed at the Library of the Graduate Theological Union in Berkeley, although it has now restricted its continuing collection to follow-up materials on the groups whose life had already been documented in the centre collection. [25]

The Institute for the Study of American Religion, soon to become the Center for the Study of American Religion, is an ambitious ongoing concern run primarily by the energy of J. Gordon Melton. He has recently moved this work from Evanston, Illinois, to the University of California at Santa Barbara where the extensive collection of some 28,000 volumes, 200 periodicals, and twenty filing cabinets of material on new religious movements is now being housed.[26] With Melton's own leadership, this promises to be a major centre for the serious study of new religious movements. In addition to publishing the *Encyclopedia of American Religion*. Melton is directing the compilation of forty volumes of bibliography on new religious movements. Seven volumes, including those on the Bahais, Witchcraft, the Anti-Cult Movement, Gurdjieff, the Jehovah's Witnesses, and the Children of God, are already completed.

Among the specifically Christian or Evangelical Christian centres the best known is the Spiritual Counterfeits Project.[27] The name of this organization reveals the view of new religious movements taken by its researchers and in its publications: that many of these new movements propagate false or counterfeit spirituality. Indeed, the SCP is presently in a serious post-bankruptcy financial crisis following a libel suit brought by one of the groups about which SCP had written, The Local Church of Witness Lee.

SCP emerged from the 1960's Berkeley Christian Coalition. The *SCP Journal* has summed up the aims of the group in four points:
1) to research and biblically to critique current religious groups and individuals;
2) to equip Christians with the knowledge, analysis and discernment that will enable them to understand the significance of today's spiritual explosion;
3) to suggest a comprehensive Christian response;
4) to bring the good news of Jesus Christ and extend a hand of rescue to those in psychological/spiritual bondage.

In addition to its regular *Journal*, the Spiritual Counterfeits Project has had a newsletter, bibliographies, and a large variety of pamphlets and booklets that may be ordered individually or collected in a large three-ring notebook. The SCP also keeps files on approximately 2000 groups and has a library of some 2500 volumes. It provides a telephone information and referral service, which operates three days a week as a "hot-line" for people seeking information on particular groups or seeking referrals for advice and counselling in their own geographical area.

The most extensive description and critique of the Spiritual Counterfeits Project has been written by John A. Saliba — "The Christian

Response to the New Religions: a Critical Look at the Spiritual Counterfeits Project". [28] I would refer interested readers to this piece, and, in brief, would make three points about the approach of the SCP:

*First*, while its publications and bibliographies are said to be educational, they tend to represent but one point of view on the new religious movements, i.e. that of critique from a particular, somewhat fundamentalist, Christian perspective. Its booklets are either written by the in-house research team or are booklets published by groups with a similar perspective, such as the Inter-Varsity Christian Fellowship. No cover letter is sent out, as the Missouri Synod Lutheran Commission does, explaining the perspective from which the material is written. Its bibliographies do not include well-known works by scholars, theologians, or sociologists on the new religions, such as Stillson Judah, Harvey Cox, or Jacob Needleman. Instead, in *An Annotated Bibliography of Literature Related to New Religious Movements*, one finds a one-sided bibliography, with such titles as *The Youthnappers, Transcendental Misconceptions, Thirty Years a Watchtower Slave*, and *Youth, Brainwashing, and the Extremist Cults*.

*Second*, much of the information about new religious movements, both in the SCP publications and in those publications it recommends in its bibliographies, is taken from the testimonies of "cult drop-outs", which would be somewhat like gaining one's perspective on Christianity only from those disillusioned ones who have given up on it and left the church. This approach is not, of course, unique to the SCP. The perspective of the drop-out is important, to be sure; but it should be balanced by the perspective of those who persist in the movement, some of them for nearly twenty years now. It is also significant that the annotated bibliography, while it contains many books *about* TM or the Unification Church, for example, does not contain books by the Maharishi Mahesh Yogi or the Rev. Sun Myung Moon. The dialogical principle of listening to what others have to say about themselves, rather than defining them from an external point of view, is not seen in most of SCP's published work.

*Third*, the research and publications of the SCP can be characterized as Christian apologetic research, but not in the best sense. Many publications seem to begin with the conclusion, i.e. that these various movements are deficient in comparison to Christianity, and then proceed to demonstrate the conclusion by "research" into the movements and their premises. The works tend to slip from apologetic into the genre of "exposé" or even "apocalyptic", taking a stand against the "cults" as the works of darkness and of Satan, and challenging them to respond.

In the past two years, the SCP has undergone the ordeal of a libel suit from one of the movements about which it had written, The Local Church. The organization finally had to declare bankruptcy for financial reorganization and is now in the midst of a fund-raising campaign to recoup its losses and enable it to continue functioning. For the past year SCP has been unable to publish its journal or newsletter, but the hot-line continues to function and researchers are still at work.

Another California-based centre is the Christian Research Institute in Anaheim, California, founded in 1960 by Walter Martin. The CRI is most well known for its specialization in the "old-line cults" and Western Christian movements of the nineteenth and early twentieth century, such as Jehovah's Witnesses and Mormons, but it maintains files on hundreds of religious movements. The CRI, which has a very small staff of researchers, publishes an occasional journal called *Forward* and a quarterly newsletter called *The Insider*. Eric Pement's *Directory* lists many other such organizations, many of them with the anti-cult bias represented by the Spiritual Counterfeits Project and the Christian Research Institute.

In this paper, I have pursued in most detail those churches and Christian institutions that have had the most to say in response to the new religious movements. Not surprisingly, many of these are conservative and evangelical, even fundamentalist, groups. The silence of the "mainline" also speaks loudly in that it communicates the fact that these churches are not as concerned about the various new movements, or do not define such movements as a "problem" for the churches, or do not find education about or dialogue with such movements to be a priority for the churches. Yet, when the "mainline" is silent, the voices that are most audible on this issue are those of the more vocal conservative churches and religious groups.

## A shift in focus: the ethos of the new age

In the past five years there has been a marked shift in some of the most vocal literature and extremist literature of what one might call the "anti-cult" perspective. The "cults" themselves are either dwindling or stabilizing. Some, like the Divine Light Mission of the young guru Maharaj-ji, have virtually disappeared. Others, like the much publicized Rajneesh community in Antelope, Oregon, have had their heyday and are clearly on the wane. Still others, like the small but persistent Hare Krishna movement, are beginning to achieve a quasi-denominational status. One might expect those writers and organizations that have been the most critical opponents of such new religious movements, especially those movements based in Eastern traditions, to be satisfied that the interest in such gurus and groups has peaked and is subsiding. This is not the case, however. The anti-cult concern has shifted from the movements themselves to a far more subtle matter: the ethos and world outlook that has been generated by Eastern religious movements in the West. This ethos and outlook is suggested by the name "New Age", which is increasingly being used to label something which does not have the solidity or boundaries of a movement or "cult", but which seems to have made its way into culture more generally. [29]

The term "New Age" stands, in the mind of those who use it in this particular way, for the gradual acceptance of an "Eastern worldview" in the West. It is not limited to people who have actually joined movements, but it is visible in a vast variety of cultural institutions. In hospitals, for example, doctors are discovering the importance of the breathing and concentration practices associated with yoga to reduce high blood pressure. Nurses are taught therapeutic touch in their nursing schools. Holistic therapies abound. In schools, children may learn relaxation exercises or guided visualizations. In health clubs, women and men practice not only aerobics, but yoga, for physical fitness. People may undertake psychotherapy to discover their own inner resources or "human potential". Even in the churches, ministers might speak of "realizing the Christ within their own consciousness".

Thus, the concern of those who are lauching a crusade against the New Age is not that a few young people are "turning east" by joining marginal religious movements, but that a whole culture is in the process of "turning east". When they look at the new religious movements, especially those that have their roots in the religious traditions of India, they do not, therefore, see the "fringe" groups of Western culture, but the "vanguards" of Eastern culture. Some even speak of a "Hindu conspiracy" to infiltrate the West. These extremist crusader voices are few, but they alert us to some of the deepest fears and imaginings that arise in the encounter with another worldview. And they rightly point beyond particular movements, with their particular insights or their particular failings, to the wider issue of the encounter of worldviews in a world where East is no longer East, West no longer West, where the twain have met, and where the outcome of that meeting is of the utmost consequence for the future of humankind.

NOTES

1 Vol. LXVIII, No. 268, October 1978, p.398.

2 *Guidelines on Dialogue with People of Living Faiths and Ideologies*, Geneva, World Council of Churches, 1979, p.18.

3 "Sects or New Religious Movements: Pastoral Challenge", a progress report, Vatican, 1986.

4 Subhananda Das, "The Catholic Church and the Hare Krishna Movement: an Invitation to Dialogue", *ISKCON Review*, Vol. 2, 1986.

5 Nashville, Abingdon Press, 1980, p.25.

6 *Ibid.*, p.25.

7 *Ibid.*, p.26.

8 Robert J.L. Burrows, "Americans Get Religion in the New Age: Anything is Permissible if Everything is God", *Christianity Today*, 16 May 1986, p.17.

9 See Diana L. Eck, "The Image of 'New Age' Hinduism in America", unpublished paper, manuscript available.

10 Seth H. Lubove, "Hare Krishna Temple Turns Tiny Town into a Tourist Stop", *The Wall Street Journal*, 16 September 1985.

11 See the statement published by the NCCCUSA entitled "A Critique of the Theology of the Unification Church as Set Forth in *Divine Principle*".

12 See the statement published by the NCCCUSA entitled "Religious Liberty for Young People Too", adopted by the Governing Boards of the NCCCUSA in 1974.

13 An essay on the 1981 survey, some of which is duplicated verbatim here, was published in *Current Dialogue*, summer 1983, pp.10-21.

14 New York, The Pilgrim Press, 1982, p.104.

15 Paul Mojzes, "'Am I My Brother's and Sister's Keeper?' The Responsibility of Mainline Churches toward the New Religions", *Journal of Ecumenical Studies*, Vol. XVIII, No. 3, summer 1981, p.475.

16 Advertising materials on Response Series, provided by the commission on organizations, Missouri Synod Lutheran Church.

17 Mimeographed publication of the Commission on Organizations of the Missouri Synod Lutheran Church, entitled, "The New Religions, Brainwashing and Deprogramming".

18 "Guidelines for Effective Interfaith Witness", Interfaith Witness Department, Southern Baptist Convention.

19 From materials supplied by the Interfaith Witness Department, Southern Baptist Convention.

20 The advertisements of the Episcopal Ad Project were printed in the *Boston Globe*, 7 August 1980, in the context of an article entitled "God as Product in Ad Campaign".

21 American Lutheran Church, Resolution on "Marginal Religious Movements — Cults", printed in *Reports and Actions*, 1976.

22 A staff paper entitled "Religious Cults", Minneapolis, The American Lutheran Church, Office of Research and Analysis, August 1976.

23 Robert Avon, *Multi-cultural Expressions: a Directory on the Religious and Philosophical Groups of the New Age in Ontario,* Toronto, The Canadian Council of Christians and Jews, n.d., p.i, from the Foreword by the Rev. Arthur Gibson.

24 Chicago, Cornerstone Press, 1986.

25 The collection of materials is located at The Graduate Theological Union Library, University of California, Berkeley, CA 94709, and is under the management of Diane Choquette.

[26] J. Gordon Melton and the Center for the Study of American Religion will be housed at the University of California at Santa Barbara, Department of Religious Studies, Santa Barbara, CA 93106.

[27] The address of the Spiritual Counterfeits Project is P.O. Box 2418, Berkeley, CA 94702.

[28] *Journal of Ecumenical Studies*, Vol. 18, No. 3, summer 1981, pp.451-473.

[29] For this perspective see Carol Matrisciana, *Gods of the New Age*, Eugene, Oregon, Harvest House, 1985; Dave Hunt, *Peace, Prosperity and the Coming Holocaust*, Eugene, Oregon, Harvest House, 1983. *The SCP Journal* of the Spiritual Counterfeits Project, Vol. 5, No. 1, winter 1981-82, is devoted to the topic empowering the self, a look at the human potential movement, and contains an article by Brooks Alexander on "The Rise of Cosmic Humanism: What is Religion?", Frances Adeney, "Educators Look East", and many others. It was Marilyn Ferguson's book *The Aquarian Conspiracy* (1980) that seems to have sparked much of the "conspiracy" language, and Constance Cumbey's *The Hidden Dangers of the Rainbow* is a recent best-seller in this line of extremist literature.

# Dialogue with
# New Religious Movements?

## KENNETH CRACKNELL

There are no limits to be set to dialogue. This proposition sets out my position exactly, and what follows in this paper is commentary, not qualification. For the necessity for Christians to engage with every kind of person of another faith or ideology has for me a quality of moral absoluteness, which may not be relativized.

But the form in which the question is put to me: "dialogue with new religious movements?" needs re-defining or, rather, to be put within my understanding of what dialogue means. Here I must apologize to those who already know my views on these matters, particularly as they are set out in my recent book, *Towards a New Relationship: Christians and People of Other Faith*,[1] and especially in chapter 6, which deals with the ethics of interfaith encounters, or as I describe it there, "the way we behave in inter-religious dialogue". I have nothing new to add to what may be found there, and yet I cannot take it for granted you all already share my understanding. So, with your permission, I make the following comments in summary of what I have already written.

It is important to notice first of all that much that I wrote there was in exposition of the British Council of Churches' document, *Relations with People of Other Faiths: Guidelines for Dialogue in Britain*.[2] These British *Guidelines* were built around four "principles" themselves derived from the WCC *Guidelines on Dialogue with People of Living Faiths and Ideologies*.[3] I will set out both the BCC and the WCC statements:

*Principle I:* "Dialogue begins when people meet each other" (Guidelines p.4 BCC).
"Dialogue should proceed in terms of people of other faiths, rather than of theoretical impersonal systems" (WCC Guidelines, § 20).
*Principle II:* "Dialogue depends upon mutual understanding and mutual trust" (BCC Guidelines, p.5).

"Dialogue should be recognized as a welcome way of obedience to the commandment of the Decalogue: 'You shall not bear false witness against your neighbour'. Dialogue helps us not to disfigure the image of our neighbours of different faiths and ideologies" (WCC Guidelines, § 17).

*Principle III:* "Dialogue makes it possible to share in service to the community" (BCC Guidelines, p.6).

"Dialogue... is a fundamental part of Christian service within community... It is a joyful affirmation of life against chaos, and a participation with all who are allies of life in seeking the provisional goal of a better human community" (WCC Guidelines, § 18).

*Principle IV:* "Dialogue becomes the medium of authentic witness" (BCC Guidelines, p.7).

"... as Christians enter dialogue with their commitment to Jesus Christ, time and time again the relationship of dialogue gives opportunity for authentic witness. Thus to the member churches of the WCC we feel able with integrity to commend the way of dialogue as one in which Jesus Christ will be confessed in our world today; at the same time we feel able with integrity to assure our partners in dialogue that we come not as manipulators but as genuine fellow-pilgrims to speak with them of what we believe God to have done in Jesus Christ" (WCC Guidelines, § 19).

With the understanding that these four principles are elements in a totality and mutually interdependent (i.e. that they are not to be misconceived as a four-stage programme — "first, you get acquainted, then you clear up points of difficulty, then you work together, and then you give them the gospel") it is convenient if I now turn to expound them one by one, with special relevance to followers of new religious movements.

## Principle I

Here is the first point at which I must demand modification of the title given to me. Just as there is no dialogue with Islam as such, but only with Muslims, no dialogue with Hinduism but only with people whose lives are moulded by the cumulative traditions of India's long and profound religious history, no dialogue with Buddhism but only with individual Buddhists, so Christians meet not new religious movements as such, but men and women who are to varying degrees moulded and shaped by the teachings of new religious movements. Of course it is vastly helpful to have some clear understanding of the teachings that they may be adhering to, but just as, say, any individual Methodist may or may not conform (intellectually) to the norms of evangelical Arminianism or (ethically) to the well-known taboos on the use of alcohol or tobacco, so individual Unificationists may be (intellectually) more or less clear on the Divine

Principle or (ethically) more or less committed to the marriage customs of that church. As I have written elsewhere: "No one person anywhere is the embodiment of or personification of ideas or beliefs that are set out systematically in text books for the convenience of students and other interested outsiders." We are learning not to say to one another: "As a Marxist you must believe in x", or "You Hindus believe in the doctrine of y" or even: "The Holy Qur'an says you Muslims must believe in z". As we meet any given Marxist or Muslim, or Hindu, we discover that he or she may or may not, for whatever reason, believe x or y or z.[4]

I went on then to remark that the label of the faith or ideology that another person professes is only a first clue to discerning his or her rich individuality. "It is sound ethical practice to approach another person with as few presuppositions as possible",[5] and quoted in support of this proposition that great nineteenth-century Anglican divine, Frederick Denison Maurice, who wrote: "A man will not really be intelligible to you if, instead of listening to him and sympathizing with him, you determine to classify him."[6]

Followers of new religious movements are every bit as much entitled to be listened to, and sympathized with, as those who belong within the older religious frameworks. For them, just as much as for Muslims or Hindus, Sikhs or Buddhists, and indeed just as much for Christians, their community of faith determines their life-patterns, sets them ideals and gives them principles by which to live. Their community of faith also sustains them in times of danger and crisis, and comforts and renews them in moments of sorrow and bereavement. But this aspect of their "reality" we shall not discern unless we meet them at a personal level. To study then only their beliefs in terms of "non-Christian religious systems" can only lead to misunderstanding.[7] It was for this reason that those who planned the recent BCC consultation on new religious movements[8] were so insistent that those who were to take part should prepare themselves, not only by reading descriptive material about some twenty NRMs present in the United Kingdom, but by arranging to have personal encounters and conversations with at least two members of such groups.[9]

Two great theological principles are at stake here for Christians. The first is our way of knowing other people. "Man cannot know man except in mutuality; in respect, trust and equality, if not ultimately love... One must be ready not only to receive the other but to give oneself. In human knowledge, at stake is one's humanity, as well as another person's or another community's. At issue is humanity itself."[10] In these words one of the wisest of contemporary students of comparative religion speaks of how any of us may dare speak about other people, and other people's faith. Dialogue at its best is exactly a way of knowing, through profound interpersonal relationships. But this is not only a *sine qua non* for relations with those of older religious traditions. It is in my view essential for our relations with those of NRMs. For even more seriously, not to see the other person, of any other faith or ideological commitment whatsoever, as the bearer of the "image of God" (Gen 1:27) is somehow to make our own selves less than the persons God would have us be. The BCC Guidelines affirm then that the ground of interfaith encounter is nothing less than this common humanity. "What makes dialogue possible between us is our common humanity, created in the image of God. We all face the joys and sorrows of human life, we are citizens of one country, we face the same problems, we all live in God's presence."[11]

## Principle II

At this point I confess to being in a quandary as to how to proceed. In affirming as strongly as I must that knowledge of other people is not derived from books (which give at best an accurate conceptual grasp of "impersonal systems", or the awareness, not unimportant, of other people's investigations), I find myself now only able to proceed by way of personal stories, i.e. stories of my own encounters with followers of new religious movements. I find, too, at this point, that the stories I would like to tell are stories about particular people, whom I count as friends, who happen to be followers of NRMs. But in parading such stories, I would find myself in danger of betraying friendship, and of using profound interpersonal experiences exploitatively. I compromise therefore by omitting circumstantial details as well as personal names and indeed the names of the movements to which my friends belong. The building up of mutual trust and understanding requires no less, and I must not betray that trust and understanding now. Yet I must seek to illustrate how dialogue with followers of new religious movements has as a fundamental element the removing of suspicion and misunderstanding.

So I offer these reflections based on innumerable conversations, "outside Woolworths", in market places, on my own doorstep, and, when my new friends have been willing, in my own study, in my office at the BCC, and in the headquarters of new religious movements themselves.

My first reflection is how few of my friends have ever been listened to seriously by devout and believing Christians. No doubt they are easily brushed off by our secularized and materialist counterparts, and they have come to expect that, but it seems tragic to me that Christian believers should respond so brusquely and discourteously. I remember one winter's night, a young Italian woman coming to my door, selling Christmas cards. "What for?" I asked. "For mission," she replied. "And what do you mean by mission?" "We are caring for old people in — " (she named a neighbouring city). "Well, I think mission is about that, too! Would you like to come in and talk to me about it?" So she did and we sat by my study fire talking about her faith for an hour or more. I recall how many of my own misunderstandings about her movement were dispelled in that conversation, but I recall equally vividly how much she was moved to have had a serious conversation with a Christian minister.

This early experience of mine was reinforced at the time of the so-called Cottrell proposals in 1984, when many leaders of the NRMs in the United Kingdom were in touch with me because of the stand the BCC took at that time. Responding to pressing invitations to visit their communities, I discovered again and again that I was the first Christian minister ever to visit them, despite previous invitations to other church leaders.

Secondly, I would stress the sheer ignorance of what the Christian faith is about that prevails among so many of the members of the NRMs. The story so often told to me is of deeply secularized backgrounds in which there were no resources for satisfying spiritual hungers. The Bible had been for them all a closed book, impenetrable in its mysteries. So one of my friends declared in a first conversation: "You see, I've a faith which is going to unify the world." "So have I," I replied, and I remember his amazement at meeting a Christian with a vision for the whole world. "You're the first one I ever met," he said. I doubt that. I was merely the first who bothered to give him the time to talk.

At this point I must interject a brief comment about the bizarreness of the belief-systems and the dubious moral codes (to Christians) of not a few of the new religious movements. The denial of Jesus as Messiah, for example, is alleged by one of my most frequent correspondents to be sufficient grounds for having nothing to do with new religious movements (he of course refers to them as "cults"). I have no doubt about what may be called by some the "demonic distortions" into which some new religious movements have fallen. But this seems to be all the more reason for seeking to build bridges between even such movements and the Christian community (itself not free from time to time of "demonic distortions"). May I recall once again the comments of the other faith visitors to Nairobi as told to us by Stanley Samartha in his *Courage for Dialogue* (I quote these in full for they have the effect of holding a mirror up for us in order to see how we often appear to our neighbours of other faiths).

> They were not sure why dialogue should be suspect by some Christians and attacked by others. They were disappointed that the question of seeking community in the contemporary world was not taken up with a greater sense of urgency. They felt uneasy to discover that they were part of the statistics that made up the 2.7 billion who were the objects of the proclamation of the Gospel.

Then Dr Samartha went on to point to the paradox involved there:

> The missiologist who described all non-Christian religions as demonic missed the chance of personally meeting these "non-Christian" guests to discover and perhaps to do battle with "demonic" elements in them. At least one of these guests expressed disappointment that no one among those who talked loudest about proclamation actually came to him or others personally to proclaim the love of God in Jesus Christ. [12]

I put on record my own disappointment that the situation remains much the same in my country with those who talk loudest about the demonic elements in new religious movements. But at this point I begin to trespass on the ground I want to cover under principles III and IV.

## Principle III

If dialogue is "a participation with all who are the allies of life in seeking the provisional goals of a better human community", we may well find "allies" within the new religious movements. Some of the provisional findings of the group within the recent BCC consultation that dealt with the "message of the NRMs to the churches" are striking.

The rapporteur of this group, Martin Eggleton, specified the following elements as having been discerned within new religious movements. Under the heading "life-style" he puts what he calls "alternativism" and comments: "There is often a deep sense of vocation and of alternative life-style in NRMs, and alternatives are being explored to the rat-race and to job opportunities"; "wholeness" and he comments: "There is a search for the universality of life through yoga and meditation, a coming to terms with the total relation of cosmos and inner being"; "caring life-style" which he affirms is "exhibited by certain groups which are concerned for the whole family"; and lastly he specifies the widespread concern in NRMs for ecological and other related issues which have to do with "wholeness". [13]

It was clearly the judgment of many in this group (which included many participants from Christian movements at work among students) that our Western churches "have reflected largely the capitalistic, individualistic, status-seeking elements within the society around them". [14] They concluded therefore that despite the perceived dangers in NRMs, the churches "could learn about meaningful commitment to a vision within a community setting", and the sharing of resources together.

It seems to me that these points are all well taken, and begin to lead into the kind of dialogue described by Principle IV; "dialogue becomes the medium of authentic witness", in which our partners in dialogue also have a message to communicate to us.

But of course we have many fellow-Christians who are every bit as concerned with the issues that Eggleton says his group was able to discern within NRMs. One need only to refer to such movements within the framework of orthodox Christianity as the "house churches", the "basic communities" and the monastic orders. We may see in all these the critical attitude towards the world which Thomas Merton spoke of in his last recorded lecture. This was in fact on "Marxism and Monastic Perspectives" and what concerned Merton was the kind of person who took up such attitudes. Such people believe that the "claims of this world" are fraudulent. Merton said that both monk and Marxist want a world open to change and added "the world refusal of the monk is in view of his desire for change". I believe profoundly that we ought to be able to substitute the word "Christian" for "monk" in that last sentence. [15]

This is important in our relations with NRMs, for Hans Wyngaards appears to have it exactly right when he writes that NRMs "are small groups of visionaries, or people who believe themselves to be visionaries, who set out on a course of spiritual renewal and world reform that challenges contemporary society. They challenge established, mainstream churches too." [16] But their denials are often denials that belong also to the Christian tradition and their affirmations, put in different terminology, are as well related to Christian "affirmations of life against chaos". It appears that there are many ways we enter into dialogue with followers of NRMs as "allies of life in seeking the provisional goal of a better human community".

## Principle IV

Some six or so years ago I was travelling through the Netherlands on the Holland-Vienna express. In the same compartment was a young woman who was diligently studying an impressively large dossier. As she turned the pages I saw a photocopy-photograph of the leader of one of the NRMs we are most concerned with. I spoke to her in Dutch, but she responded to me in heavily German-accented English. A long conversation then unfolded, since she was also travelling through the Netherlands to her home in Germany. And so I heard her testimony. As an eighteen-year-old in California she had joined an NRM. Her parents had responded by summoning the assistance of kidnappers and deprogrammers, but in the end she had voluntarily left the movement. I gathered that she had left with much good-will on both sides, but what I find so memorable was her comment. "I owe to them my faith in God, but boy, is their exegesis screwy!" I also gathered that now she was travelling around high school campuses in the Netherlands and West Germany urging her slightly younger contemporaries to "really know what the Bible says".

I tell this story not only for its obvious point, but also to emphasize once again how unaware of the essentials of the Christian message followers of NRMs usually are. As a theologian whose primary concern is with mission, and with the cross-cultural communication of the gospel, I am at a loss to know why those with the special calling to evangelism are not more eager to enter into the kind of dialogue processes which lead to the giving, as well as the receiving, of what the BCC *Guidelines* call "authentic witness". This kind of dialogue I have described fully in *Towards a New Relationship*, where I reflect upon Paul's use of the "school of Tyrannus" for a period of two years. I repeat just these comments. In both the synagogue and the school of Tyrannus, the agenda and the terms of reference of the conversations are set by the other parties to the dialogue. How different from our own habitual modes of operation — we very much tend to invite people to come into our structures (in both the physical and metaphysical sense of the word), where they will be able to listen to monologues of proclamation in an environment where we are totally at home. How much there is to learn about evangelism in general from even this cursory glance at St Paul's missionary methods![17] I am therefore utterly lost for a response when I, or any other fellow-Christian, am reproached for sharing in a meeting organized by Unificationists or Scientologists, or for visiting and accepting the hospitality of Rajneeshies or Hare Krishna devotees. Our very being there is a form of authentic witness, but even more striking, in my experience, is the eagerness with which our speaking about Jesus is received.

That this should be so causes me as a Christian theologian no surprise whatsoever. If the ultimate reality of this world is anything like that which has been affirmed in scriptures and creeds, then the Holy Spirit is at work drawing men and women to the centre, however marginal and peripheral ("eccentric") to the truth human religious movements, whether old or new, may be. On the one hand we may be sure that Gamaliel's criterion is always applicable: "If this plan, or this undertaking is of men it will fail." [18] Our history books are full of instances of failed movements, and there will be many more. On the other hand the history of the church is equally full of movements which were persecuted for being wildly eccentric (certainly in their own times subject to as much opprobrium as, say, some of the African Independent churches in our times) as some of the NRMs which have been on our agenda these past days. From my own country I need instance only the Quakers in the seventeenth century, the Methodists in the eighteenth century and the Salvationists in the nineteenth century. All these movements and many others have in different ways drawn near the centre. So we may take it will many of those we have been discussing. There is a proper expectation that this will be so in the light of our understanding of the Holy Spirit. [19]

Having this great ground for confidence in any kind of dialogue with people of other faith, we are set free to talk with members of NRMs without attacking everything they stand for, and without any over-anxious desire to defend the gospel. [20] We are, in the words of the WCC *Guidelines* "able to assure our partners in dialogue that we come, not as manipulators, but as genuine fellow-pilgrims, to speak with them of what we believe God to have done in Jesus Christ who has gone before us, but whom we seek to meet anew in dialogue" (§ 19). [21]

## Concluding remarks

I began by saying that there are no limits to be set to dialogue. For Christians to draw boundaries and establish frontiers over which neither they themselves nor their fellow-Christians have to pass seems to me morally and theologically wrong. Some urge for example that to talk to members of NRMs "gives them credibility", but I hear this as the sub-ethical language of diplomacy; others speak of rubbing shoulders with heretics, but I hear this as the language of the Inquisition; others fear the contamination of the "demonic", but I know this is to under-rate the expulsive power of the Holy Spirit; others suggest that NRMs need "prophetic denunciation" but such denunciations may well prevent us hearing what God might be wishing to say to us through such movements. Of course, there are times when there is no way in which dialogue is possible, but those limits come from *outside* the Christian community. We cannot talk with people who have no wish to talk to us, but where ever there are those who would enter into dialogue with us, we cannot refuse. There are no limits to be set to dialogue.

NOTES

[1] London, Epworth Press, 1986.

[2] First issued in 1981, revised ed. 1983. These have been widely received and commended for study and action by BCC member churches.

[3] These were commended to WCC member churches at the meeting of the Central Committee in Kingston, Jamaica, in January 1979, "for their consideration and discussion, testing and evaluation, and for their elaboration in each specific situation". To the best of my knowledge the BCC was the first national council of churches to act in the way the Central Committee envisaged. It is worth noting the words of the Central Committee in 1979, "to enter into dialogue requires an opening of the mind and heart to others. It is an undertaking which requires risk, as well as a deep sense of vocation."

[4] *Towards a New Relationship*, p.115. I wonder if other members of this consultation, who were present at the meeting of the working group of the Dialogue Sub-unit in Matrafured, Hungary, in 1980, will remember as vividly as I do the visit to us of a professor at the Institute of Marxist Philosophy at the University of Budapest. He spoke to us of the necessity of dialogue between Marxists and Christians in the future Hungarian state, which he saw as "pluralist" in its future form. I remember telling my English colleague at that meeting, a distinguished political scientist and historian of twentieth-century political movements, what the professor had said, for she had been absent from that session. Her reaction was that such a speech would have been quite impossible: "No real Marxist could possibly say that!"

[5] *Ibid.*, p.115.

[6] *The Religions of the World*, 6th ed., 1886, p.96.

[7] I have on my shelves a series published between 1876 and 1895, but much reprinted after that, with the general title of "Non-Christian Religious Systems". I offer for our reflection the remarks of the Rev. W. St Clair-Tisdall, MA, in his preface to his contribution to the series, *The Religion of the Crescent* (1895). He writes:

"In a very few instances it will be noticed that I have ventured in my notes to have recourse to a dead language in order in some degree to veil a few peculiarities of Muhammadanism which I felt ought not to be treated of in plain English, and to entirely omit or conceal which (as has generally been done hitherto) would be dishonest, and would be inconsistent with my purpose to give, as far as in me lay, a fair and impartial view of the Religion of the Prophet of Arabia. One of the great difficulties which beset any attempt to represent to English people at all correctly any non-Christian religion is that such religions for the most part contain so many things that are *unmentionable*. To omit all the worst points and to exaggerate the merits of all the good ones may procure a writer the credit of being "extremely liberal" in his views, but can hardly be said to be quite a fair way of dealing with either the subject itself or with one's readers" (Italics his).

These are attitudes light years away from those of such Christian interpreters of what it means to be a Muslim as Kenneth Cragg, Wilfred Cantwell Smith, Willem Bijlefeld and Anton Wessels and a host of others. What such people have done with regard to the Islamic tradition must be done for those who live within the frameworks of faith of new religious movements.

[8] This consultation took place on 28 April 1986. It involved participants from virtually all BCC member churches. This consultation's report, still marked *not for publication*, is in the hands of members of the Amsterdam consultation, even though it has not yet been considered by the executive committee of the BCC.

[9] I formed the impresssion that not too many of the participants in the BCC consultation had the opportunity to do this, and were still relying on second-hand information. One member who did (Martin Eggleton, of the Methodist Church Division for Education and Youth), contributed in the devotional sessions two poems, "The Witnesses" and "The Pearl". These will be published in the forthcoming issue of *Discernment: A Christian Journal of Inter-religious Encounter* (BCC, Vol. Im, No. 2, autumn 1986).

[10] Wilfred Cantwell Smith, *Towards a World Theology*, London, 1981, p.77.

[11] BCC *Guidelines*, p.4.

[12] *Courage for Dialogue*, Geneva, 1981, p.57.

[13] See Section C, "What Messages do NRMs Give to the Churches", BCC report, p.7.

[14] Cf. these statements with the findings of the WCC Dialogue Sub-unit's consultation on "Churches Among Ideologies", December 1981, esp. pp.23-4:

"In the societies of Western Europe various ideological elements, sometimes undergirding and sometimes counteracting each other, came together forming a complex cluster of ideological pluralism. Many of these factors, being part of the main currents within society, exercise influence without people being aware of them. Examples include forms of scientism, pragmatic atheism, and consumerism. Nevertheless it is obvious that the economic structures of capitalism, combined with the political structures on Western democracy, provide the framework and shape for the life-styles of most people in Western Europe.

"There are, moreover, increasing ideological and cultural countercurrents that particularly bear impact upon the younger generation. In some countries economic and social tensions, amplified by growing numbers of migrant workers and refugees, tend to lead towards a rebirth of radical ideologies, such as racism and fascism.

"The established churches reproduce among their constituencies most of the ideological tendencies and tensions of society. As most of their members and the church bodies themselves are inclined to follow the predominant social and ideological patterns, the increasing number of grassroot initiatives and "basic" groups and the Christian support for ecological and peace movements reflect the crisis of the Western European civilization, and express the search and hope for a fundamental renewal of this civilization."

[15] See Monica Furlong, *Merton: a Biography*, London, 1980, p.329. I use these remarks of Merton in discussing the new forms of spirituality which are necessary in interfaith relationships, see *Towards a New Relationship*, chapter 7.

[16] In his paper, "Healing Yes, but with Proper Diagnosis", given at the BCC April 1986 consultation, p.1.

[17] *Towards a New Relationship*, p.27.

[18] The full quotation is of course continued with the words, "but if it is of God, you will not be able to overthrow them. You might even be found opposing God!" Acts 5:38-39.

[19] For some clear perceptions of the work of the Holy Spirit in this area, see Harold Turner's article, "Articulating Theology through Relations with New Religious Movements" in the forthcoming issue of *Discernment* (for details see note 9).

[20] I was much indebted, when I first began my work with the BCC to a member of my committee who was of strong Calvinist persuasion. He told me of the saying of Charles Haddon Spurgeon, the great nineteenth-century Baptist preacher, when he was invited to speak "in defence of the gospel". "Defend the Gospel? I would as soon defend a lion."

[21] Dr Harold Turner's new article concludes with six "theses" which he calls also "Tentative Conclusions". I cannot forbear here to quote the fourth, which illuminates so clearly the words of the WCC *Guidelines* just quoted: "That Christ has already claimed members of other faiths, and spanned all gulfs between personal positions, cultures and faiths. He can therefore use other faiths to enlarge our relationship to him."

# Appendices

Appendix

# Summary Statement
# and Recommendations

The World Council of Churches and the Lutheran World Federation held a joint consultation in Amsterdam in response to initiatives in both bodies for the consideration of new religious movements (NRMs). We who have participated in this consultation have come from Europe and North America, as well as from Asia, Africa, and Latin America. We come from local churches, denominational or ecumenical offices, universities, and research and resource centres, and we bring a wide range of experience with new religious movements and with people who are adherents of new religious movements. While our discussion has focused primarily on Europe and North America, which in the past two decades have seen the rise of a great number of new religious movements, we have also benefited from the wider discussion of the many new religions in Japan in the past forty years and the rapid rise of new religious movements in Africa. From the perspective of Asia we were reminded of the appearance of aggressive sectarian forms of Christianity in recent years, which have been perceived as manifestations of new religious movements. From the perspective of Latin America we were reminded of the ideological engagements of some new religious movements.

## I. Introduction

What do we mean by "new religious movements"? As a starting point, we agree that the term "new religious movements" covers a vast range of movements that are very different one from another in their origins and beliefs, their structure and organization, and their self-understanding. Thus, in particular regional and local settings, what is meant by the "new religious movements" needs to be differentiated and nuanced. There are movements which have their origins in the Eastern traditions; there are those that have arisen more as sectarian movements with origins in the Christian tradition; and there are those that have arisen in the encounter of primal traditions or tribal societies with universal religions; and there is also a range of occult and gnostic groups. There is great diversity even within these general groupings. The Eastern new traditions themselves have tremendous diversity, with a wide range of gurus and of practice, some emphasizing yoga, some devotion, some meditation. Similarly, the Christian-based movements are greatly diverse, from the "old new religious movements" such as the Jehovah's Witnesses, the Mormons, and the Christian Scientists to the newer movements such as The Local Church and the Unification Church. Among such Christian-based movements some see themselves as aiming to restore the true church, others as destined to bring about the fulfilment of the Christian mission. In social organization, some new religious movements may be very closely knit communities, others may be seen more loosely as "movements", bound together by adherence to common teachings and practices, but not by daily life and ritual. The same movement may have several circles of commitment, from a wide outer circle of interested people to a committed inner circle of the devout.

In sum, the diversity of what are perceived as "new religious movements" is great, and we must be careful that our response to a particular movement, or its particular excesses, does not colour our understanding of new religious movements as a whole. Indeed, though we use this term for convenience, there is no such thing as "new religious movements", as a whole, for these emergent traditions are as diverse and complex as the established religious traditions. And they raise for the churches and for Christians some of the same questions.

## II. Questions and issues

In thinking about "new religious movements" there are four questions we have considered and discussed in order to clarify the issues: (1) How do we understand the "newness" of new religious movements in the wider context of ongoing religious innovation and change? (2) How do we understand not only the "movements" *per se*, but the worldviews and visions they represent? In what ways do they challenge our own worldview? (3) How do we understand the mission and the methods of mission of new religious movements? (4) In what ways and to what extent do we protect the rights of new religious movements to go about their activities, even though we may radically disagree with their beliefs and worldviews?

### 1. Innovation: what is "new"?
— Religious traditions are not static structures, but dynamic and ever-changing realities. They grow and change through time, and this

growth may be accelerated by political, economic, technological or ideological changes. Religious innovation and the continual emergence of "new religious movements" are evident in the long and varied history of the Christian tradition. It can be seen in the emergence of Christian sectarian and denominational movements, and in the generation of new liberation and feminist movements.

— Contemporary religious traditions also change and new movements arise in the contact and interaction between traditions and across geographical and cultural boundaries. In this sense "new" may mean "new to us". When Buddhism first came from India to China, or Christianity from Europe to some parts of Africa, they were "new religious movements" in this sense. Similarly, the Hindu or Buddhist groups new to the West are described as "new" religious movements.

— "New" may also refer to the dynamic spirit of many movements, emphasizing a revival or renewal of the old established tradition. Such revival may include a renewed emphasis on healing, the reinterpretation and reappropriation of scriptures, or even belief in a new revelation — all of which may at times give a new sense of hope for the future.

— "New" may also refer to alternative religions, movements which are "emergent" or "protest" religions, as opposed to the tradition of the establishment. In Germany, the term "youth religions" has been applied to many new religious movements precisely because it is mainly the young who are attracted.

— "New" in itself is not necessarily good or bad, right or wrong. Sometimes the "new" brings renewal, and sometimes the "new" needs the rigorous critique of the old.

— While some young people may be attracted to certain movements as a rebellion against authority, others may be attracted to more dualistic movements precisely because of the apparent authority and order of the movement. The opportunity for critique and renewal provided by the perspective of the young should be seized by the churches as they engage in mutual dialogue and critique with young people in new religious movements.

## 2. *Movements and worldviews*

— Our encounter as Christians with new religious movements, especially with Eastern religious movements in the West, involves the wider and more significant encounter with other worldviews. Encounter with such religious movements is, indeed, a part of and a stage in the West's encounter with the Hindu, Buddhist, and other Asian traditions and worldviews. Often these Eastern movements themselves undergo change as a result of their encounter with the West.

— A worldview is a whole picture of the cosmos, the "ordered universe". It includes an understanding of Divinity, an understanding of the human being in his/her relation to the Divine, an understanding of the past, present, and future. It is a full picture of life and its meaning.

— Many new religious movements have very fully expressed worldviews, with ready answers to the manifold questions people pose about life and its meaning. "Religion" is not simply a set of activities, practices, and beliefs, but involves a total commitment to a community with a clear sense of its place in the scheme of things. This "clear" sense may at times become totalistic, grandiose, or apocalyptic. Nonetheless, by comparison, many Christians, especially young people, are vulnerable to persuasion because they have not been challenged to think very deeply or clearly about the Christian worldview.

— The many Eastern religious traditions that are new to the West have brought elements of different worldviews to our midst, worldviews that have gained wider cultural currency than the movements themselves. It raises important questions for us as Christians: what does it mean to speak of many "gods" or ways of seeing Divinity, rather than one? What does it mean to speak of the human as potentially divine? Or need of enlightenment or awakening, rather than redemption? What does it mean to speak of history and social commitment in different worldviews? What does it mean to speak of reincarnation rather than resurrection? What does it mean to speak of the natural world as organically whole, inter-related, and interdependent, as is the case in Eastern cosmology, or of creation in the biblical tradition? What does it mean to speak of spiritual "discipline" (yoga) or of discipleship with a guru who is considered to be divine? What does it mean to speak of the "ashram" or the "church" as social community? In many ways, encounter with another worldview may help us to see and articulate our own more clearly.

## 3. Mission and methods of new religious movements

— What is the sense of mission of the new religious movements, and what are their methods of mission? The immediate informed response of people acquainted with a variety of movements is that they are all different, coming from various historical families of faith, with diverse aims, goals, and methods of working. Stereotyping as to the mission and methods of new religious movements can only be misleading.

— What is their mission? It is important to recognize that new religious movements do indeed have a sense of mission and a vision of the world they would like to bring into being. Some think they need to call out the "elect" from among the fallen of the world, that they have the only complete message of salvation. Others assert that other religions may have a partial truth, but that the new movement has an inclusive and perfect understanding in which others may participate. Other groups have an eclectic vision that they think encompasses the truth of other religions in a single worldview.

— What of their political and social mission? The sense of mission may, indeed, not be limited to individual conversions or individual commit-ment, but involves a political/social mission as well. We must take seriously this dimension of the vision of dynamic new religious or quasi-religious groups, as the European experience with the Nazi movement continually reminds us. We should appreciate such politi-cal/social visions where they are enhancing of life and critique them where they are potentially tyrannical or perverse, examining our own Christian missionary vision and activity with the same high standards of honesty and insight.

— What about deceptive or coercive methods? This is especially impor-tant, since allegations about the use of deceptive or coercive methods have been widely circulated. There is no doubt that in some cases such allegations are true or partially true. The churches have on many occasions condemned the use of coercive methods in mission, whether our own or that of others. We should be wise and wary of the zeal of the movements in seeking adherents. At the same time we should reject allegations of deception or coercion that are not substan-tiated.

### 4. Human rights and religious liberty

Article 18 of the Universal Declaration of Human Rights reads: "Everyone has the right to freedom of thought, conscience, and religion; this right includes the freedom to change his religion or belief, and freedom, either alone or in community with others and in public or private, to manifest his religion or belief in teaching, practice, worship and observance."

— Some of the issues raised with regard to new religious movements have to do not only with their theologies or worldviews, or with their sense and methods of mission, but also with the realm of human rights and religious liberty: the right of such groups to exist and to gain adherents by conversion.

— Within this area of freedom, further distinctions could be made: persons should be free to speak their religious convictions, virtually without exception. In the realm of action, however, claims of religious liberty should not normally provide a defence for the violation of criminal law, such as the perpetration of violence upon others, but exceptions to civil law on the basis of religious commitment should be permitted by governments, even if modifications of law may be necessary, unless such actions can be shown to be harmful to others.

— Religious liberty cannot be claimed by some if it is denied to others. (The long history of both religious and civil persecution of new religious movements has been shameful, including the persecution of Anabaptists, Methodists, Mennonites, Quakers and others within past centuries of Christian history.) Vigilance on the matter of religious intolerance and discrimination has been made even more explicit in the 1981 and 1984 adoption of the UN Declaration on the Elimination of All Forms of Religious Intolerance and of Discrimination Based on Religion or Belief.

## III. Recommendations

In considering what should be the response of the churches to new religious movements, we did not begin our discussion in a vacuum. Churches and councils of churches have responded, in a variety of ways, in formal statements and in denominational literature, to new religious movements. Still, there is much that remains to be done, and we submit the following recommendations to the member churches of the WCC and the LWF.

### 1. Education

A. We recommend that theological seminaries and faculties take seriously their responsibility to prepare Christian clergy and laity for ministry in a religiously plural world, recognizing that new religious movements are a part of that pluralism.

B. We recommend that churches review their educational materials in the light of religious pluralism in general, and the rise of new religious movements in particular. We recognize that this may entail the production of new educational materials.

C. We recommend a renewed emphasis on spiritual formation in the context of our own faith. We recognize that taking seriously the new religious movements challenges Christians to a deeper understanding and clearer articulation of their own faith.

D. We recommend that the WCC and the LWF investigate setting up an ecumenical network of information-sharing on new religious movements. This could involve study and research centres, member churches, national and local councils of churches, and individuals with experience in the area of new religious movements.

## 2. *Dialogue*

A. Inter-religious dialogue takes place *in communities*, where people of different religions live as neighbours in a common context. Where people of new religious movements are part of the community, we recommend dialogue with such movements. To build up a foundation of trust and openness, the "dialogue" of daily life may need to precede any attempts at more careful and formal dialogue.

B. We commend the WCC *Guidelines on Dialogue* as a study aid to church people in thinking about the meaning of "dialogue", and the general guidelines that might govern our own participation in dialogue with people of other faiths.

C. There may be particular "guidelines" of special importance to dialogue with people of new religious movements:

— In dialogue, partners should be free to "define themselves" and not be defined by the images or stereotypes of others.

— We enter into dialogue with people, not labels or systems.

— In dialogue one should not compare one's own ideals with the excesses or failings of the other religion.

— Partners in dialogue should be aware of the ideological commitments each may hold, and of the wider political and social vision of their respective traditions.

D. Entering into dialogue does not mean that one supports or ascribes to the ideas or activities of the other. And dialogue does not mean that all will agree. The creative tension of mutual critique is also a part of dialogue.

E. In a climate of fear, mistrust, or misrepresentation, partners in dialogue should be aware of the need for complete honesty if the ground is to be prepared for fruitful dialogue. Church groups should discuss, though not be discouraged by, potential local problems that may arise from dialogue with people of new religious movements: will it imply an endorsement of the group and/or its activities? Will it merely provide an easy forum for the mission of the new religious movement?

F. Because of the great variety of new religious movements, the nature of dialogue and even the possibility of dialogue will depend a great deal on the local situation.

### 3. The ministry and renewal of the church

A. We recommend that churches, especially local churches and regional councils of churches, take seriously the particular tasks of ministry to people affected by new religious movements. This may include an active ministry to those who are or have been members of new religious movements.

B. The church's ministry to people, especially to young people, who are past, present, or potential members of new religious movements is especially important and may have to take place where people are, not necessarily in the church. A flexible ministry — lay ministry, street ministry, teaching ministry or ministry of visitation — is necessary.

C. Churches should take seriously the critique that the rise of so many new and alternative religions presents. What is the spiritual condition of our own churches? How vital is our sense of community and belonging? What visions and hopes do we have for the future?

D. The hunger for a deeper spirituality and for the ordering of life through regular spiritual discipline is evident in the attraction of people to many of the new religious movements. Can the churches recover some of the sources for spiritual guidance and discipline that are a neglected part of our own Christian heritage? Can we respond with the renewal and deepening of our own spiritual life? Can we develop vibrant centres for Christian spirituality?

### 4. Working ecumenically

A. We recommend that, to the extent possible, the LWF and WCC cooperate with the relevant Vatican Secretariats and with long-standing dialogue partners in pursuing further work in this area, including the possibility of international consultations held jointly with representatives of selected new religious movements.

B. We encourage local churches and regional denominational bodies to work ecumenically, with Protestant, Catholic, and Orthodox churches in their area, as they continue their efforts to understand and interact with new religious movements. As a step in this process, we would recommend ecumenical study of the Vatican progress report, *Sects or New Religious Movements: Pastoral Challenge (see Appendix).*

## 5. A specific recommendation

It is recommended that a consultation be organized by representatives of the LWF, WCC and, if possible, the Vatican, with representatives of new religious movements to discuss the issue of human rights in their mutual relations and other activities. The task of the consultation would be to develop some guidelines that express the needs and interests of all parties for the protection of their freedom and integrity both individually and collectively.

For such a consultation an equal number of participants should be invited on behalf of the Christian churches and on behalf of the new religious movements and each party should pay for its own representatives and its share of overhead expenses.

Appendix

# Sects or New Religious Movements

## *Pastoral Challenge*

### Foreword

In response to the concern expressed by Episcopal Conferences throughout the world, a study on the presence of "sects", "new religious movements", "cults" has been undertaken by the Vatican Secretariat for Promoting Christian Unity, the Secretariat for Non-Christians, the Secretariat for Non-Believers and the Pontifical Council for Culture. These departments, along with the Secretariat of State, have shared this concern for quite some time.

As a first step in this study project, a Questionnaire was sent out in February, 1984, to Episcopal Conferences and similar bodies by the Secretariat for Promoting Christian Unity in the name of the aforementioned departments of the Holy See, with the aim of gathering reliable information and indications for pastoral action and exploring further lines of research. To date (October, 1985) many replies have been received from Episcopal Conferences on all continents as well as from regional Episcopal bodies. Some replies included detailed information from particular dioceses and were accompanied by copies of pastoral letters, booklets, articles and studies.

It is clearly not possible to summarize the vast documentation received, and which will need to be constantly updated as a basis for a constructive pastoral response to the challenge presented by the sects, new religious movements and groups. The present report can only attempt to give a first overall picture, *and is based on the replies and documentation received.*

### 1. Introduction

1.1. *What are "sects"? What does one mean by "cults"?* It is important to realize that there exist difficulties in concepts, definitions, and terminology. The terms "sect" and "cult" are somewhat derogatory and seem to imply a rather negative value judgment. One might prefer more neutral terms such as "new religious movements", "new religious groups". The question of the definition of those "new movements" or "groups" as distinct from "church" or "legitimate movements within a church" is a contentious matter.

It will help to distinguish sects that find their origin in the Christian religion, from those which come from another religious or humanitarian source. The matter becomes quite delicate when these groups are of Christian origin. Nevertheless, it is important to make *this distinction*. Indeed, certain sectarian mentalities and attitudes, i.e. attitudes of intolerance and aggressive proselytism, do not necessarily "constitute a sect", nor do they suffice to characterize a sect. One also finds these attitudes in groups of Christian believers within the churches and ecclesial communities. However, those groups can change positively through a deepening of their Christian formation and through the contact with other fellow Christians. In this way they can grow into an increasingly ecclesial mind and attitude.

The criterion for distinguishing between *sects* of Christian origin, on the one hand, and *churches and ecclesial communities*, on the other hand, might be found in the "sources" of the teaching of these groups. For instance, sects could be those groups which, apart from the Bible, have other "revealed" books or "prophetic messages"; or groups which exclude from the Bible certain proto-canonical books, or radically change their content. In answer to Question 1 of the Questionnaire, one of the replies states: "For practical reasons a cult or sect is sometimes defined as 'any religious group with a distinctive world-view of its own derived from, but not identical with, the teachings of a major world religion'. As we are speaking here of special groups which usually pose a threat to people's freedom and to society in general, cults and sects have also been characterized as possessing a number of distinctive features. These often are that they are authoritarian in structure, that they exercise forms of brain-washing and mind control, that they cultivate group pressure and instil feelings of guilt and fear, etc. The basic work on these characteristic marks was published by an American, Dave Breese, *Know the Marks of Cults* (Victor Books, Wheaton Ill., 1985)."

Whatever the difficulties with regard to distinguishing between sects of Christian origin and churches, ecclesial communities or Christian movements, the responses to the Questionnaire reveal at times a serious lack of understanding and knowledge of other Christian churches and ecclesial communities. Some include among "sects" churches and ecclesial communities which are not in full communion with the Roman Catholic

Church. Also adherents of major world religions (Hinduism, Buddhism, etc.) may find themselves classified as belonging to a sect.

1.2. However, and apart from the difficulties mentioned, almost all the local churches do see the *emergence* and rapid *proliferation* of all kinds of "new" religious or pseudo-religious movements, groups and practices. The phenomenon is considered by almost all the respondents as a *serious matter*, by some as an alarming matter; in only a very few countries there does not seem to exist any problem (e.g. in predominantly Islamic countries).

In some cases the phenomenon appears within the mainline churches themselves (*sectarian attitudes*). In other cases it occurs outside the churches (independent or free churches; messianic or prophetic movements), or against the churches (sects, cults), often establishing for themselves church-like patterns. However, not all are religious in their real content or ultimate purpose.

1.3. The phenomenon develops fast, and often quite successfully, and poses *pastoral problems*. The most immediate pastoral problem is that of knowing how to deal with a member of a Catholic family who has become involved in a sect. The parish priest or local pastoral worker or adviser usually has to deal first and foremost with the relatives and friends of such a person. Often the person involved can be approached only indirectly. In those cases when the person can be approached directly in order to give him or her guidance, or to advise an ex-member on how to re-integrate into society and the Church, psychological skill and expertise is required.

1.4. *The groups that are most affected.* The most *vulnerable* groups in the Church, esp. the youth, seem to be the most affected. When they are "footloose", unemployed, not active in parish life or voluntary parish work, or come from an unstable family background or belong to ethnic minority groups, or live in places which are rather far from the Church's reach, etc..., they are a more likely target for the new movements and sects. Some sects seem to attract mainly people in the middle-age group. Others thrive on membership from well-to-do and highly educated families. In this context, mention must be made of university campuses which are often favourable breeding grounds for sects or places of recruitment. Moreover, difficult relations with the clergy or an irregular marriage situation can lead one to break with the Church and join a new group.

Very few people seem to join a sect for evil reasons. Perhaps the greatest opportunity of the sects is to attract good people and good motivation in those people. In fact, they usually succeed best when society or Church have failed to touch this good motivation.

1.5. *The reasons for the success* among Catholics are indeed manifold and can be identified on several levels. They are primarily related to the needs and aspirations which are seemingly not being met in the mainline Churches. They are also related to the recruitment and training techniques of the sects. They can be external either to the mainline Churches or to the new groups: economic advantages, political interest or pressure, mere curiosity, etc.

An assessment of these reasons can be adequately done only from *within the very particular context* in which they emerge. However, the results of a general assessment (and this is what this report is about) can, and in this case do, reveal a whole range of "particular" reasons which as a matter of fact turn out to be almost universal. A growing interdependence in today's world might provide us with an explanation for this.

The phenomenon seems to be symptomatic of the *depersonalizing structures* of contemporary society, largely produced in the West and widely exported to the rest of the world, which create multiple crisis situations on the individual as well as on the social level. These crisis situations reveal various needs, aspirations and questions which, in turn, call for psychological and spiritual responses. The sects claim to have, and to give, these responses. They do this on both the affective needs in a way that deadens the cognitive faculties.

These basic needs and aspirations can be described as so many expressions of the human search for wholeness and harmony, participation and realization, on all the levels of human existence and experience; so many attempts to meet the human quest for truth and meaning, for those constitutive values which at certain times in collective as well as individual history seem to be hidden, broken, or lost, especially in the case of people who are upset by rapid change, acute stress, fear, etc.

1.6. The responses to the Questionnaire show that the phenomenon is to be seen not so much as a threat to the Church (although many respondents do consider the aggressive proselytism of some sects a major problem), but rather as a pastoral challenge. Some respondents emphasize that, while at all times preserving our own integrity and honesty, we should remember that each religious group has the right to profess its own faith and to live according to its own conscience. They stress that in dealing with individual groups we have the duty to proceed according to the principles of religious dialogue which have been laid down by the Second Vatican Council and in later Church documents. Moreover, it is imperative to remember the respect due to each individual, and that our *attitude* to sincere believers should be one of openness and understanding, not of condemnation.

The responses to the Questionnaire show a great need for information, education of believers, and a renewed pastoral approach.

## . 2. Reasons for the spread of these movements and groups

Crisis situations or general vulnerability can reveal and/or produce needs and aspirations which become basic motivations for turning to the sects. They appear on the cognitive as well as on the affective level, and are *relational* in character, i.e. centered upon "self" in relation with "others" (social), with the past, present and future (cultural, existential), with the transcendent (religious). These levels and dimensions are *inter-related*. These needs and aspirations can be grouped under nine major headings, although in individual cases, they often overlap. For each group of "aspirations" we indicate what the sects are seen to offer. The main reasons for their success can be seen from that point of view, but one must also take into account the recruitment practices and indoctrinational techniques of many sects (cf. below 2.2.).

### 2.1. NEEDS AND ASPIRATIONS: WHAT THE SECTS APPEAR TO OFFER

#### 2.1.1. The quest for belonging (sense of community)

The fabric of many communities has been destroyed; traditional life-styles have been disrupted; homes are broken up; people feel uprooted and lonely. Thus the need to belong.

Terms used in the responses: belonging, love, community, communication, warmth, concern, care, support, friendship, affection, fraternity, help, solidarity, encounter, dialogue, consolation, acceptance, understanding, sharing, closeness, mutuality, togetherness, fellowship, reconciliation, tolerance, roots, security, refuge, protection, safety, shelter, home.

*The sects appear to offer:* human warmth, care and support in small and close-knit communities; sharing of purpose and fellowship; attention for the individual, protection and security, especially in crisis situations; re-socialisation of marginalized individuals (for instance, the divorced or immigrants); the sect often does the thinking for the individual.

#### 2.1.2. The search for answers

In complex and confused situations, people naturally search for answers and solutions.

*The sects appear to offer:* simple and ready-made answers to complicated questions and situations; simplified and partial versions of traditional truths and values; a pragmatic theology, a theology of success, a syncretistic theology proposed as "new revelation"; "new truth", to people who often have little of the "old" truth, clearcut directives; a claim to moral superiority; proofs from "supernatural" elements; glossolalia, trance, medium-ship, prophecies, possession, etc.

### 2.1.3. The search for wholeness (holism)

Many people feel that they are out of touch with themselves, with others, with their culture and environment. They experience brokenness. They have been hurt by parents or teachers, by the Church or society. They feel left out. They want a religious view that can harmonize everything and everybody; worship which leaves room for body and soul, for participation, spontaneity, creativity. They want healing, including bodily healing (African respondents particularly insist on this point).

Terms used in the responses: healing, wholeness, integration, integrity, harmony, peace, reconciliation, spontaneity, creativity, participation.

*The sects appear to offer:* a gratifying religious experience, being saved, conversion; room for feelings and emotions, for spontaneity (e.g. in religious celebrations); bodily and spiritual healing, help with drug or drink problems; relevance to the life situation.

### 2.1.4. The search for cultural identity

This aspect is very closely linked with the previous one. In many Third World countries, the society finds itself greatly dissociated from the traditional cultural, social and religious values; and traditional believers share this feeling.

The main terms used in the responses are: inculturation/incarnation, alienation, modernization.

*The sects appear to offer:* plenty of room for traditional cultural/religious heritage, creativity, spontaneity, participation, a style of prayer and preaching closer to the cultural traits and aspirations of the people.

### 2.1.5. The need to be recognized, to be special

People feel a need to rise out of anonymity, to build an identity, to feel that they are in some way special and not just a number or a faceless member of a crowd. Large parishes and congregations, administration-oriented concern and clericalism, leave little room for approaching every person individually and in the person's life situation.

Terms used in the responses: self-esteem, affirmation, chances, relevance, participation.

*The sects appear to offer:* concern for the individual; equal opportunities for ministry and leadership, for participation, for witnessing, for expression; awakening to one's own potential, the chance to be part of an élite group.

### 2.1.6. The search for transcendence

This expresses a deeply spiritual need, a God-inspired motivation to seek something beyond the obvious, the immediate, the familiar, the controllable, and the material, to find an answer to the ultimate questions of life, and to believe in something which can change one's life in a significant way. It reveals a sense of mystery, of the mysterious; a concern about what-is-to-come; an interest in messianism and prophecy. Often the people concerned are either not aware of what the Church can offer, or are put off by what they consider to be a one-sided emphasis on morality or by the institutional aspects of the Church. One respondent speaks of "privatised seekers": "Research suggests that a surprisingly large proportion of the population will, if questioned, admit to having had some kind of religious or spiritual experience, say that this has changed their lives in some significant way, and most pertinently add that they have never told anyone about the experience... Many young people say that they have been afraid of being laughed at or thought peculiar were they to broach the subject of spiritual or religious experience and that they have frequently known difficulty in getting teachers or clergy to discuss, let alone answer, their most important and ultimate questions".

*Terms used* in the responses: transcendence, sacred, mystery, mystical, meditation, celebration, worship, truth, faith, spirituality, meaning, goals, values, symbols, prayer, freedom, awakening, conviction.

*The sects appear to offer:* the Bible and Bible education; a sense of salvation; gifts of the Spirit; meditation; spiritual achievement. Some groups offer, not only permission to express and explore ultimate questions in a "safe" social context, but also a language and concepts with which to do so, as well as the presentation of a clear, relatively unambiguous set of answers.

### 2.1.7. The need of spiritual guidance

There may be a lack of parental support in the seeker's family, or lack of leadership, patience and personal commitment on the part of church leaders or educators.

Terms used: guidance, devotion, commitment, affirmation, leadership, guru.

*The sects appear to offer:* guidance and orientation through strong, charismatic leadership. The person of the master, leader, guru, plays an important role in binding the disciples. At times, there is not only submission, but emotional surrender, and even an almost hysterical devotion to a strong spiritual leader (messiah, prophet, guru).

### 2.1.8. The need of vision

The world of today is an interdependent world of hostility and conflict, violence and fear of destruction. People feel worried about the future, often despairing, helpless, hopeless, and powerless. They look for signs of hope, for a way out. Some have a desire, however vague, to make the world better.

Terms used: vision, awakening, commitment, newness, a new order, a way out, alternatives, goals, hope.

*The sects appear to offer:* a "new vision" of oneself, of humanity, of history, of the cosmos. They promise the beginning of a new age, a new era.

### 2.1.9. The need of participation and involvement

This aspect is closely linked with the previous one. Many seekers not only feel the need of a vision in the present world-society and towards the future; they also want to participate in decision-making, in planning, in realizing.

The main terms used are: participation, active witness, building, elite, social involvement.

*The sects appear to offer:* a concrete mission for a better world, a call for total dedication, participation on most levels.

By way of summary one can say that the sects seem to live by what they believe, with powerful (often magnetic) conviction, devotion and commitment; going out of their way to meet people where they are, warmly, personally, and directly, pulling the individual out of anonymity, promoting participation, spontaneity, responsibility, commitment..., and practising an intensive follow-up through multiple contacts, home visits, and continuing support and guidance. They help to re-interpret one's experience, to re-assess one's values, and to approach ultimate issues in an all-embracing system. They usually make convincing use of the word: preaching, literature, mass media (for Christian groups strong emphasis on the Bible); and often also of the ministry of healing. In one word, they present themselves as the only answer, *the* "good news" in a chaotic world.

However, although all this mostly accounts for the success of the sects, other reasons also exist, such as the recruitment and training techniques and indoctrination procedures used by certain sects.

### 2.2. RECRUITMENT AND TRAINING TECHNIQUES, INDOCTRINATION PROCEDURES

Some recruitment, training techniques, and indoctrination procedures, practised by a number of sects and cults, which often are highly sophisticated, partly account for their success. Those most often atttracted by such measures are those who, firstly, do not know that the approach is often staged, and, secondly, who are unaware of the nature of the contrived conversion and training methods (the social and psychological manipulation) to which they are subjected. The sects often impose their own norms of thinking, feeling, and behaving. This is in contrast to the Church's approach which implies full-capacity informed consent.

Young and elderly alike who are at loose ends are easy prey for those techniques and methods which are often a combination of affection and deception (cf. the "love-bombing", the "personality test" or the "surrender"). These techniques proceed from a positive approach but gradually achieve a type of mind control through the use of abusive behavior modification techniques.

*The following elements are to be listed:*
— subtle process of introduction of the convert and his gradual discovery of the real hosts;
— overpowering techniques: "love-bombing", offering "a free meal at an international center for friends", "flirting fishing" technique (prostitution as a method of recruitment);
— ready-made answers and decisions are being almost forced upon the recruits;
— flattery;
— distribution of money, medicine;
— requirement of unconditional surrender to the initiator, leader;
— isolation: control of the rational thinking process, elimination of outside information and influence (family, friends, newspapers, magazines, television, radio, medical treatment, etc.) which might break the spell of involvement and the process of absorption of feelings and attitudes and patterns of behavior;

— processing recruits away from their past lives, focussing on past deviant behavior such as drug use, sexual misdeeds, playing upon psychological hang-ups, poor social relationships, etc.;

— consciousness-altering methods leading to cognitive disturbances (intellectual bombardment), use of thought-stopping clichés; closed system of logic; restriction of reflective thinking;

— keeping the recruits constantly busy and never alone, continual exhortation and training in order to arrive at an exalted spiritual status, altered consciousness, automatic submission to directives: stifling resistance and negativity; response to fear in a way that greater fear is often aroused;

— strong focus on the leader; some groups may even downgrade the role of Christ in favor of the founder (in the case of some "Christian sects").

## 3. Pastoral challenges and approaches

A breakdown of traditional social structures, cultural patterns, and traditional sets of values, caused by industrialization, urbanization, migration, rapid development of communication systems, all-rational technocratic systems etc., leaves many individuals confused, uprooted, insecure, and therefore vulnerable. In these situations there is naturally a search for a solution, and often the simpler the better. There is also the temptation to accept the solution as the only and final answer.

From an analysis of the responses some symptoms of the pathology of many societies today can be listed. Many people suffer from them. They feel anxious about themselves (identity crisis), the future (unemployment, the threat of nuclear war). Questions about the nature of truth and how it is to be found, political uncertainty and helplessness, economic and ideological domination, the meaning of life, oneself and others, events, situation, things, the "hereafter".

They suffer a loss of direction, lack of orientation, lack of participation in decision-making, lack of real answers to *their* real questions. They experience fear because of various forms of violence, conflict, hostility: fear of ecological disaster, war and nuclear holocaust, social conflicts, manipulation.

They feel frustrated, rootless, homeless, unprotected; hopeless and helpless and consequently unmotivated; lonely at home, in school, at work, on the campus, in the city; lost in anonymity, isolation, marginalization, alienation, i.e. feeling that they do not belong, that they are misunderstood, betrayed, oppressed, deceived, estranged, irrelevant, not listened to, unaccepted, not taken seriously.

They are disillusioned with technological society, the military, big business, labor, exploitation, educational systems, church laws and practices, government policies.

They might have learned to want to see themselves as conscientious "doers", not worthless drifters or self-seeking opportunists, but often do not know what to do or how to do it.

They are at a loss at various "in-between" times (between school and university, between school and work, between marriage and divorce, between village and city).

They become empty, indifferent, or aggressive, or they may become "seekers".

In summary one could say that all these symptoms represent so many forms of alienation (from oneself, from others, from one's roots, culture, etc.). One could say that the needs and aspirations expressed in the responses to the Questionnaire are so many forms of a search for "presence" (to oneself, to others, to God). Those who feel lost want to be found. In other words, there is a vacuum crying out to be filled, which is indeed the context in which we can understand not only the criticisms towards the Church which many responses contain, but foremost the pastoral concerns and proposed approaches. The replies to the Questionnaire point out many deficiencies and inadequacies in the actual behavior of the Church which can facilitate the success of the sects. However, without further insisting on them, we will mainly emphasize the positive pastoral approaches which are suggested or called for. If these are acted upon, the challenge of the sects may prove to have been a useful stimulus for spiritual and ecclesial renewal.

## 3.1. SENSE OF COMMUNITY

Almost all the responses appeal for a rethinking (at least in many local situations) of the traditional "parish community system"; a search for community patterns which will be more fraternal, more "to the measure of man", more adapted to people's life situation; more "basic ecclesial communities": caring communities of lively faith, love (warmth, acceptance, understanding, reconciliation, fellowship), and hope; celebrating communities; praying communities; missionary communities; out-going and witnessing; communities open to and supporting people who have special problems: the divorced and "re-married", the marginalized.

### 3.2. FORMATION AND ON-GOING FORMATION

The responses put strong emphasis on the need for evangelization, catechesis, education and on-going education in the faith — biblical, theological, ecumenical — of the faithful, at the level of the local communities, and of the clergy and those involved in formation. (One reply advocates "reflective courses" for teachers, youth leaders, clergy and religious). This on-going process should be both *informative*, with information about our own Catholic tradition (beliefs, practices, spirituality, meditation, contemplation, etc.), about other traditions and about the new religious groups, etc., and *formative*, with guidance in personal and communal faith, a deeper sense of the Transcendent, of the eschatological, of religious commitment, of community spirit, etc. The Church should not only be a sign of hope for people, but should also give them the reasons for that hope; it should help to ask questions, as well as to answer them. In this process there is an overall emphasis on the centrality of Holy Scripture. Greater and better use should be made of the mass-media of communication.

### 3.3. PERSONAL AND HOLISTIC APPROACH

People must be helped to know themselves as unique, loved by a personal God, and with a personal history from birth through death to resurrection. "Old truth" should continually become for them "new truth" through a genuine sense of renewal, but with criteria and a framework of thinking that will not be shaken by every "newness" that comes their way. Special attention should be paid to the experiential dimension, i.e. discovering Christ personally through prayer and dedication (e.g. the Charismatic and "born again" movements). Many Christians live as if they had never been born at all! Special attention must be given to the healing ministry through prayers, reconciliation, fellowship and care. Our pastoral concern should not be one-dimensional, it should extend, not only to the spiritual, but also to the physical, psychological, social, cultural, economic and political dimensions.

### 3.4. CULTURAL IDENTITY

The question of inculturation is a fundamental one. It is particularly stressed by the responses from Africa which reveal a feeling of estrangement to Western forms of worship and ministry which are often quite irrelevant to people's cultural environment and life situation. One respondent declared: "Africans want to be Christians. We have given them accommodation, but no home... They want a simpler Christianity, integrated into all aspects of daily life, into the sufferings, joys, work, aspirations, fears and needs of the African... The young recognize in the Independent Churches a genuine vein of the African tradition of doing things religious."

### 3.5. PRAYER AND WORSHIP

Some suggest a rethinking of the classic Saturday evening/Sunday morning liturgical patterns, which often remain foreign to the daily life situation. The word of God should be rediscovered as an important community-building element. "Reception" should receive as much attention as "conservation". There should be room for joyful creativity, a belief in Christian inspiration and capacity of "invention", and a greater sense of communal celebration. Here again, inculturation is a must (with due respect for the nature of the liturgy and for the demands of universality).

Many respondents insist on the biblical dimension of *preaching*; on the need to speak the people's language; the need for careful preparation of preaching and liturgy (as far as possible done by a team, including lay participation). Preaching is not mere theorizing, intellectualizing and moralizing but presupposes the witness of the preacher's life. Preaching, worship and community prayer should not necessarily be confined to traditional places of worship.

### 3.6. PARTICIPATION AND LEADERSHIP

Most respondents are aware of the growing shortage of ordained ministers and of religious men and women. This calls for stronger promotion of diversified ministry and the on-going formation of lay leadership. More attention should perhaps be given to the role that can be played in an approach to the sects — or, at least, to those attracted by the sects — by lay people who, within the Church and in collaboration with their Pastors, exercise true leadership, both spiritually and pastorally. Priests should not be identified mainly as administrators, office-workers and judges, but rather as brothers, guides, consolers and men of prayer. There is too often a distance that needs to be bridged between the faithful and the bishop, even between the bishop and his priests. The ministry of bishop and priest is a ministry of unity and communion which must become visible to the faithful.

## 4. Conclusion

In conclusion, what is to be our attitude, our approach to the sects? Clearly, it is not possible to give one simple answer. The sects themselves are too diverse; the situations — religious, cultural, social — too different. The answer will not be the same when we consider the sects in relation to the "unchurched", the unbaptized, the unbeliever, and when we are dealing with their impact on baptized Christians, and especially on Catholics or ex-Catholics. Our respondents are naturally concerned mainly with this last group.

Clearly, too, we cannot be naively irenical. We have sufficiently analysed the action of the sects to see that the attitudes and methods of some of them can be destructive to personalities, disruptive of families and society, and their tenets far removed from the teachings of Christ and his Church. In many countries we suspect, and in some cases know, that powerful ideological forces as well as economic and political interests are at work through the sects which are totally foreign to a genuine concern for the "human" and are using the "human" for inhumane purposes.

It is necessary to inform the faithful, especially the young, to put them on their guard, and even to enlist professional help for counselling, legal protection, etc. At times we may have to recognize, and even support, appropriate measures on the part of the state acting in its own sphere.

We may know, too, from experience that there is generally little or no possibility of dialogue with the sects; and that not only are they themselves closed to dialogue, but they can also be a serious obstacle to ecumenical education and effort wherever they are active.

And yet, if we are to be true to our own beliefs and principles: respect for the human person, respect for religious freedom, faith in the action of the Spirit working in unfathomable ways for the accomplishment of God's loving will for all humankind, for each individual man, woman and child, we cannot simply be satisfied with condemning and combatting the sects, with seeing them perhaps outlawed or expelled, and individuals "deprogrammed" against their will. The "challenge" of the new religious movements is to stimulate our own renewal for a greater pastoral efficacy.

It is surely also to develop within ourselves, and in our communities, the mind of Christ in their regard; trying to understand "where they are", and, where possible, reaching out to them in Christian love.

We have to pursue these goals, being faithful to the true teaching of Christ, with love for all men and women. We must not allow any preoccupation with the sects to diminish our zeal for true ecumenism among all Christians.

## 5. Invitation from the 1985 Synod

5.1. The Extraordinary Synod of 1985 called to celebrate, assess and promote the Second Vatican Council, gave certain orientations concerning the renewal of the Church today. These orientations which address themselves to the general needs of the Church are also a reply to needs and aspirations which some people seek in the sects (3.1). They underline the pastoral challenges and the need for pastoral planning.

5.2. The final report of the Synod notes that the world situation is changing and that the signs of the times must be analyzed continually (I D7). The return to the sacred is acknowledged and the fact that some people seek to satisfy their need for the sacred through the sects (II A1). The Church is often seen simply as an institution, perhaps because it gives too much importance to structures and not enough to drawing people to God in Christ.

5.3. As a global solution to the present problems, the Synod's invitation is to an integral understanding of the Council, to an interior assimilation of it and putting it into practice. The Church must be understood and lived as a mystery (II A, cfr. 3.1.6.) and as a communion (II B, cfr. 4.1, 4.6). The Church must commit itself to becoming more fully the sign and instrument of communion with God and of communion and reconciliation among men (I A2; cfr. 4.1, 3.1.6). All Christians are called to holiness, that is, to conversion of heart and participation in the trinitarian life of God (II A4; cfr. 3.1.1, 3.1.5). The Christian community needs people who live a realistic and worldly holiness. Since the Church is a communion, it must embody participation and co-responsibility at all levels (II C6; cfr. 4.6, 3.1.9). Christians must accept all truly human values (II D3) as well as those specifically religious (II D5) so as to bring about inculturation, which is "the intimate transformation of authentic cultural values through their integration in Christianity and in the various human cultures" (II D4; cfr. 3.7.4, 4.4). "The Catholic Church refuses nothing of what is true and holy in non-Christian religions. Indeed, Catholics must recognize, preserve and promote all the good spiritual and moral, as well as socio-cultural, values that they find in their midst" (II D5). "The Church must prophetically denounce every form of poverty and oppression, and everywhere defend and promote the fundamental and inalienable rights of the human person" (II D6, cfr. 3.2).

5.4. The Synod gives some practical orientations. It stresses spiritual formation (II A5; cfr. 3.1.7, 4.2), commitment to integral and systematic evangelization and catechesis to be accompanied by witness which interprets it (II Ba2; cfr. 3.1.8, 3.1.3), precisely because the salvific mission of the Church is integral (II D6; cfr. 4.3) securing interior and spiritual participation in the liturgy (II B6; 3.1.9, 4.5); encouraging spiritual and theological dialogue among Christians (II C7), and dialogue "which may open and communicate interiority"; fostering concrete forms of the spiritual journey such as consecrated life, spiritual movements, popular devotion (II A4; cfr. 3.1.7), and giving greater importance to the Word of God (II Bal), realizing that the gospel reaches people through witness to it (II Ba2).

## 6. Questions for further study and research

N.B. Where possible, the study and research should be undertaken in ecumenical cooperation.

### 6.1. THEOLOGICAL STUDIES

a) The different types of sect in the light of *Lumen gentium*, 16, *Unitatis redintegratio* and *Nostra aetate*.
b) The "religious" content of "esoteric" and "human potential" sects.
c) Christian mysticism in relation to the search for religious experience in the sects.
d) The use of the Bible in the sects.

### 6.2. INTERDISCIPLINARY STUDIES

(historical - sociological - theological - anthropological)
a) The sects and the early Christian communities.
b) The ministry of healing in the early Church and in the sects.
c) The role of prophetic and charismatic figures (during their life-time and after their death).
d) The sects and "popular religiosity".

### 6.3. PSYCHOLOGICAL AND PASTORAL STUDIES

(It is in this field that most work seems to have been done already):
a) Recruitment techniques and their effects.
b) After-effects of sect membership and "de-programming".
c) Religious needs and experiences of adolescents and young adults and their interaction with sexual development, in relation to the sects.
d) Authority pattern in the sects, in relation to the lack of and need for authority in contemporary society.
e) The possibility or impossibility of "dialogue" with sects.

### 6.4. SECTS AND THE FAMILY

a) Reactions in the family to sect membership of children or other family members.

b) Family break-up or irregular family status in relation to the attraction of the sects.

c) Sect membership and the solidity of the family; family pressures on children of sect members.

d) Family patterns and conjugal morality in the sects.

6.5. WOMEN IN THE SECTS

a) Opportunities for self-expression and responsibility (cf. sects founded by women).

b) Inferior position of women in different types of sect: Christian fundamentalist groups, Oriental sects, African sects, etc.

6.6. *Acculturation and inculturation* of sects, and their evolution in different cultural and religious contexts: in traditionally Christian cultures, in recently evangelized cultures, in totally secularized societies or those undergoing a rapid process of secularization (with its diverse impact on Western and "non-Western" cultures). Migration and the sects.

6.7. A comparative historical and sociological study of *youth movements* in Europe before the second world war and youth membership in contemporary cults and sects.

6.8. *Religious freedom* in relation to the sects: ethical, legal and theological aspects. Effects of government action and other social pressures. Interaction between political, economic and religious factors.

6.9. The images of sects in *public opinion*; and the effect of public opinion on sects.

## 7. Appendix. The Questionnaire

*Question 1:* To what extent and in what way is the problem of the sects present in your country or region? For instance: what type of sects (of Christian origin or not)? How many adherents? To what extent are they attracting Catholics?

*Question 2:* What are the principal pastoral problems posed by this phenomenon? What groups of Catholics are most affected? Young people? Families?

*Question 3:* What action has the Church in your country been able to take concerning this problem? Listing the sects, studying them, drawing up a directory, drawing up a plan for pastoral action?

*Question 4:* What seem to be the reasons for the success of sects among Catholics in your country or region? (Special socio-cultural or political conditions? Unsatisfied religious or psychological needs?...).

*Question 5:* What attitude does the Gospel require us to take regarding this situation?

*Question 6:* What significant documents or books on the question of sects have been published in your country or region (either by Catholics or by members of other Churches or ecclesial communities which are facing the same problem)?

*Question 7:* Are there people with special competence in this matter who could take part, at a later stage, in carrying this consultation further? *

---

* The replies to Question 7 provided many names of competent persons and specialized Institutes which should prove useful in further stages of work to be undertaken in relation to the sects. It seemed premature to make any choice among these for this summary report.

# Appendix

# List of Participants

AAGAARD, Prof. Johannes M.
Dialogcenter
Katrinebjergvej 46
8200 Aarhus N.
Denmark

BARKER, Dr Eileen
London School of Economics
Houghton Street
London, WC2A 2AE
United Kingdom

BERTHRONG, Dr John
United Church of Canada
85 St Clair Ave. East
Toronto, Ont. M4T 1M8
Canada

BORDELON, Mr Marvin
Conference Director
11905 Oden Court
Rockville, MD 20582
USA

COWAN, Rev. James A.J.
Box 538
Lumsden, Sask.
Canada SOG 310

CRACKNELL, Rev. Kenneth R.
Lecturer in Interfaith Relations
Wesley House
Cambridge
United Kingdom

DROOGERS, Dr André
Institute for the Study of Religion
Free University
P.O. Box 7161
1007 MC Amsterdam
Netherlands

DUARTE, Pastor Carlos
Bv. Orono 645
2000 Rosario, Santa Fe
Argentina

ECK, Dr Diana
Professor of Comparative Religion
and Indian Studies
Harvard University
Cambridge, MA 02138
USA

HAAN, Mr Wim
Bezinningscentrum
Free University, P.O. Box 7161
1007 MC Amsterdam
Netherlands

HAACK, Pastor Friedrich W.
Bunzlauerstrasse 228
8000 Munich 50
Federal Republic of Germany

HAUTH, Pastor Rüdiger
Volksmissionarisches Amt
der Evangelischen Kirche von Westfalen
Röhrchenstrasse 10, Witten
Federal Republic of Germany

HEINO, Pastor Harri O.
Research Institute
of the Lutheran Church of Finland
PL 239
33101 Tampere
Finland

HOCKMAN, Rev. Prof. Remi
Pontificia Universita S. Tommaso
Largo Angelicum 1
00184 Rome
Italy

HUMMEL, Dr Reinhart
Evangelische Zentralstelle
für Weltanschauungsfragen
Hölderlinplatz 2A
7000 Stuttgart 1
Federal Republic of Germany

KANAI, Prof. Shinji
University of Tokyo
2-3-2, Higashi Nihonbashi
Chuo-ku, Tokyo 103
Japan

KELLEY, Dr Dean M.
National Council of the Churches of Christ
475 Riverside Drive, Room 572
New York, NY 10115
USA

KRANENBORG, Dr Reender
Free University
Institute for the Study of Religion
P.O. Box 7161
1007 MC Amsterdam
Netherlands

LANDE, Pastor Aasulv
Swedish Institute of Missionary Research
Götgatan 3
752 22 Uppsala
Sweden

LITTELL, Rev. Dr Franklin H.
P.O. Box 172
Merion, PA 19066
USA

MAMAY, Ms Inge
Kaltenbachblick 7
6968 Walldürn-Glashofen
Federal Republic of Germany

MAYER, Dr Jean-François
P.O. Box 83
1700 Fribourg
Switzerland

MBON, Dr Friday M.
Department of Religious Studies
University of Calabar
Calabar, Cross River State
Nigeria

MELANCHTHON, Rev. G.D.
United Theological College
PB 4613
Benson Town, Bangalore 560 046
India

MSHANA, Bishop Eliewaha E.
Evangelical Lutheran Church, Pare Diocese
P.O. Box 22
Same
Tanzania

MULDER, Dr D.C.
Jacob Marisstraat 108
1058 JB Amsterdam
Netherlands

MÜLLER, Rev. Joachim
Schmiedgasse 4
9403 Goldach
Switzerland

O'CONNOR, Father Thomas P.
Dialogcenter
Katrinebjergvej 46
8200 Aarhus N.
Denmark

SLAGTAND, Ms Marjory I.L.
Develstein 710
1102 AK Amsterdam
Netherlands

SMULDERS, Ms Petra
Free University
P.O. Box 7161
1007 MC Amsterdam
Netherlands

TAVES, Dr Ann
School of Theology at Claremont
1325 N. College Avenue
Claremont, CA 91711
USA

THELLE, Dr Notto R.
University of Oslo
Nordengveien 29
07755 Oslo 7
Norway

THOMSON, Dr Jack
Centre for New Religious Movements
Selly Oak Colleges
Birmingham B29 6LQ
United Kingdom

TURNER, Dr Harold W.
Centre for New Religious Movements
Selly Oak Colleges
Birmingham B29 6LQ
United Kingdom

WIKSTRÖM, Rev. Lester
Commission on International
and Ecumenical Affairs
Box 438
Uppsala 751 06
Sweden

WINTER, Ms Ruth K.
P.O. Box 359
Coronach, Sask.
Canada SOH OZO

**WCC and LWF staff**

BROCKWAY, Rev. Allan R.
Sub-Unit on Dialogue, WCC

NOETZLIN, Ms Margaret
Department of Studies, LWF

RAJASHEKAR, Dr Paul
Department of Studies, LWF

VAN ELDEREN, Mr Marlin
Editor, ONE WORLD
WCC

# Appendix

# Contributors

Prof. Johannes **Aagaard** is at the Institute for Mission and Ecumenical Theology, Aarhus University, Aarhus, Denmark, and is director of the Dialogcenter, Aarhus.

Dr Eileen **Barker** is dean of undergraduate studies, London School of Economics and Political Science, London, UK.

Rev. Kenneth **Cracknell** was, at the time of the meeting, with the British Council of Churches. He is now lecturer in interfaith relations at Wesley House, Cambridge, UK.

Dr Diana **Eck** is professor of comparative religion and Indian studies at Harvard University, Cambridge, Mass., USA.

Pastor Rüdiger **Hauth** is secretary for sects and ideologies with the Volksmissionarisches Amt der Evangelischen Kirche von Westfalen, Witten, Federal Republic of Germany.

Dr Reinhart **Hummel** is director of the Evangelische Zentralstelle für Weltanschauungsfragen, Stuttgart, Federal Republic of Germany.

Prof. Shinji **Kanai** is at the Faculty of Letters, University of Tokyo, Japan.

Dr Dean M. **Kelley** is director for religious liberty at the National Council of the Churches of Christ in the USA, New York, USA.

Dr Reender **Kranenborg** is with the Institute for the Study of Religion, Free University, Amsterdam, The Netherlands.

Dr Jean-François **Mayer** is specialist/consultant on questions of new religious movements, Fribourg, Switzerland.

Dr Friday M. **Mbon** is at the Department of Religious Studies, University of Calabar, Nigeria.

Dr J. Paul **Rajashekar** is secretary for church and people of other faiths, LWF, Geneva.

Dr Harold W. **Turner** is senior research fellow at the Centre for New Religious Movements, Selly Oak Colleges, Birmingham, UK.